Foundation Web Design with Dreamweaver 8

Craig Grannell

friendsof

DESIGNER TO DESIGNER™

an Apress® company

Foundation Web Design with Dreamweaver 8

ISBN-13 (pbk): 978-1-59059-567-1

ISBN-10 (pbk): 1-59059-567-X

Printed and bound in the United States of America 9 8 7 6 5 4 3 2 1

Trademarked names may appear in this book. Rather than use a trademark symbol with every occurrence of a trademarked name, we use the names only in an editorial fashion and to the benefit of the trademark owner, with no intention of infringement of the trademark.

Distributed to the book trade worldwide by Springer-Verlag New York, Inc., 233 Spring Street, 6th Floor, New York, NY 10013. Phone 1-800-SPRINGER, fax 201-348-4505, email orders-ny@springer-sbm.com, or visit www.springeronline.com.

For information on translations, please contact Apress directly at 2560 Ninth Street, Suite 219, Berkeley, CA 94710. Phone 510-549-5930, fax 510-549-5939, email info@apress.com, or visit www.apress.com.

The information in this book is distributed on an "as is" basis, without warranty. Although every precaution has been taken in the preparation of this work, neither the author(s) nor Apress shall have any liability to any person or entity with respect to any loss or damage caused or alleged to be caused directly or indirectly by the information contained in this work.

The source code for this book is freely available to readers at www.friendsofed.com in the Downloads section.

Credits

Lead Editor	**Assistant Production Director**
Chris Mills	Kari Brooks-Copony
Technical Reviewer	**Production Editor**
Jason Nadon	Kelly Winquist
Editorial Board	**Compositor**
Steve Anglin, Dan Appleman,	Dina Quan
Ewan Buckingham, Gary Cornell,	
Jason Gilmore, Jonathan Hassell,	**Proofreader**
James Huddleston, Chris Mills,	Linda Seifert
Matthew Moodie, Dominic Shakeshaft,	
Jim Sumser, Matt Wade	**Indexer**
	Brenda Miller
Project Manager	**Cover Image Designer**
Elizabeth Seymour	Corné van Dooren
Copy Edit Manager	**Interior and Cover Designer**
Nicole LeClerc	Kurt Krames
Copy Editor	**Cover Image Photography**
Andy Carroll	Craig Grannell
Manufacturing Director	
Tom Debolski	

CONTENTS AT A GLANCE

CONTENTS

Chapter 7: Creating Navigation for Your Website 155

ABOUT THE AUTHOR

Craig Grannell is a well-known web designer who's been shouting about web standards at whoever will listen for the past few years, and who's been fiddling around with Dreamweaver since the very first version was released.

Originally trained in the fine arts, Craig eventually became totally immersed in the world of digital media. Along the way, his creative projects encompassed everything from video and installation-based audio work, to strange live performances, sometimes with the aid of a computer, televisions, videos, and a P.A. system, and sometimes with a small bag of water above his head. His creative, playful work, which usually contained a dark, satirical edge, struck a chord with those who saw it, leading to successful appearances at a number of leading European media arts festivals.

However, Craig soon realized he'd actually have to make a proper living. Luckily, in the mid-1990s, the Web caught his attention, initially as a means to promote his art via an online portfolio, but then as a creative medium in itself, and he's been working with it ever since. It was during this time that he founded Snub Communications (www.snubcommunications.com), a design and writing agency whose clients have since included the likes of 2000 AD, IDG UK, and Swim Records.

Along with writing the book you're holding right now, Craig recently authored *Web Designer's Reference: An Integrated Approach to Web Design with XHTML and CSS* (friends of ED, 2005), and he coauthored previous releases in the Foundation Dreamweaver series. He's also written numerous articles for *Computer Arts*, *MacFormat*, *Practical Web Design*, *.net*, the dearly departed *Cre@te Online*, and many other publications besides.

Craig lives in a small town in northeast Hampshire, UK, with his wife, Kay, sometimes dreaming of global superstardom by way of his eclectic audio project, the delights of which you can sample at www.projectnoise.co.uk.

ABOUT THE TECHNICAL REVIEWER

Jason Nadon started using Dreamweaver around the release of version 2.0. He manages the Ann Arbor Macromedia User group and is an active member of the Macromedia community.

Jason has been in the information technology field for nine years, building web applications and solutions with Macromedia tools for the past six. He holds several industry certifications and is currently employed by Thomson Creative Solutions as a Web Services Administrator.

ABOUT THE COVER IMAGE DESIGNER

 **Corné van Dooren** designed the front cover image for this book. Having been given a brief by friends of ED to create a new design for the Foundation series, he was inspired to create this new setup combining technology and organic forms.

With a colorful background as an avid cartoonist, Corné discovered the infinite world of multimedia at the age of 17—a journey of discovery that hasn't stopped since. His mantra has always been "The only limit to multimedia is the imagination," a mantra that is keeping him moving forward constantly.

After enjoying success after success over the past years—working for many international clients, as well as being featured in multimedia magazines, testing software, and working on many other friends of ED books—Corné decided it was time to take another step in his career by launching his own company, *Project 79*, in March 2005.

You can see more of his work and contact him through www.cornevandooren.com or www.project79.com.

If you like his work, be sure to check out his chapter in *New Masters of Photoshop: Volume 2*, also by friends of ED (ISBN: 1590593154).

INTRODUCTION

Dreamweaver is the leading web design application for good reason: since its original release in 1997, it's evolved from a relatively simple HTML editor into a highly sophisticated design and development tool that no serious web designer can do without. Whether you're a relative newcomer or a long-time design professional, Dreamweaver is an ideal solution; along with offering advanced web standards-based design tools, it enables you to create dynamic websites. Graphic designers feel at home using Design view, whereas coders can work in Code view to create documents that implement all manner of web technologies. Those who like a little of each can combine the two views.

Dreamweaver MX 2004 massively improved the application's ability to deal with web standards, centering its workflow around **Cascading Style Sheets (CSS)**, a technology that enables designers to create low-bandwidth, accessible, flexible, cutting-edge layouts. Dreamweaver 8 takes this a stage further, cementing workflow firmly in the area of web standards and providing a number of massively useful visual tools for working with CSS-based layouts.

If you're a little concerned about all this, don't be. CSS makes it much easier for designers to create and tweak page layouts—often site-wide—just by editing a few rules in a single CSS document. Dreamweaver 8 makes this cutting-edge technology accessible to all designers, no matter what their level of expertise.

All in all, Dreamweaver 8 is the perfect application for web designers, no matter what type of site they want to create. Because it's a fantastic visual design tool with support for powerful server-side technologies, it enables you to create great-looking dynamic websites efficiently and effectively. Now you *can* have it all, and the Foundation Dreamweaver series from friends of ED shows you how.

The aim of this book

This book provides you with a thorough foundation in the use of all the essential design-oriented features of Dreamweaver 8—and even some of the lesser-known elements. You'll learn how to work with Dreamweaver 8 to create typography, work with images, create the basics of page layouts, and then combine all of these things to create cutting-edge website designs. With the book's modular nature, you will be able to "mix and match," combining elements from various chapters to create your own work.

Although this entry in the Foundation Dreamweaver series is primarily design-oriented, it doesn't just concentrate on graphic design. Within, you'll learn everything you need to create great-looking, fast and efficient static websites: in addition to layout tasks, we'll explore how to get feedback from a website and how to work with Dreamweaver 8's excellent template facilities, thereby speeding up workflow and site maintenance. Furthermore, general site concept and management techniques will be outlined, giving you the full picture about how to create and maintain a site.

By the time you reach the end of the book, you will be ready to deploy your skills developing modern, standards-compliant sites to meet a variety of needs.

What you'll need

You'll need a copy of Dreamweaver 8 installed, and you'll also need to know your way around your preferred operating system—either Windows (XP or 2000) or Mac OS X 10.3 or higher—and be comfortable creating folders, naming files, and so on. Which platform you use is up to you. In the book, I'll be working with the Mac version of the application, but it works in exactly the same way as the Windows version, and keyboard shortcuts will be provided for both systems (and in the very few areas where there are differences, I'll be sure to point them out). You also need an Internet connection if you want to download the source files for this book.

Remember that if you need additional help while working your way through the book, the friends of ED forums (www.friendsofed.com/forums) are there for free technical support. Help is close at hand!

> *You'll notice that I don't make any recommendations regarding what platform to use, and this is for good reason. Both PCs and Macs are equally capable of creating the kind of websites we'll be working on in this book, hence my decision to be platform-neutral throughout. Dreamweaver's authors have made my job easier by continuing to unify the application's interface across both platforms, so the tutorials and information in this book will be equally useful to you whether you use a Mac or PC.*

Conventions

In order to ensure this book is as clear and easy to follow as possible, only a few layout styles have been used:

- Important words or phrases appear in **bold type**.
- Words and phrases that appear onscreen (including Menu ➤ Commands) are presented in one font, and code, filenames, and hyperlinks, such as www.friendsofed.com are presented in another.
- One or more lines of code are set separately:

  Blocks of code appear in this style

- Steps in the exercises are laid out like this:
  1. Open up Dreamweaver 8.
  2. Save your file as index.html.
  3. And so on . . .

> *When code is too long to fit on one line, you'll see a code-continuation character (➡)*
> *to show that the next line of code is on the same line in Dreamweaver. If you come*
> *across such a symbol, don't go pressing the Enter key just yet.*

Download files

All source files for the completed versions of the exercises in this book are available for download
at www.friendsofed.com. Feel free to experiment with them, and if things go wrong with your
version, take advantage of Dreamweaver's ability to compare your file with the completed one—it
often helps. Dreamweaver 8 also offers an option to print your code (File ➤ Print Code)—print out
your version and the downloaded one, clearly mark any differences, and change your version
accordingly.

> *Please note that all photographic images contained within all of the*
> *tutorials shown in this book remain the copyright of Craig Grannell*
> *(who can be contacted via www.snubcommunications.com) and should*
> *not be reused without written permission.*

friends of ED

For news, books, sample chapters, downloads, author interviews, and more, point your browser to
www.friendsofed.com. Be sure to sign up for our monthly newsletter to get all the latest on
upcoming books.

You can also visit our support forums at www.friendsofed.com/forums for help with any of the
tutorials in this book, or just to chat with like-minded designers and developers. You'll find a variety
of designers talking about all manner of tips, tricks, and techniques, and they may be able to
provide you with help, ideas, insights, and inspirations.

Even if you don't have a problem, email feedback@friendsofed.com to let us know what you think
of this book—we'd love to hear from you! Whether it's to request future books, ask about friends
of ED, or tell us about sites you've created after reading this book, drop us a line!

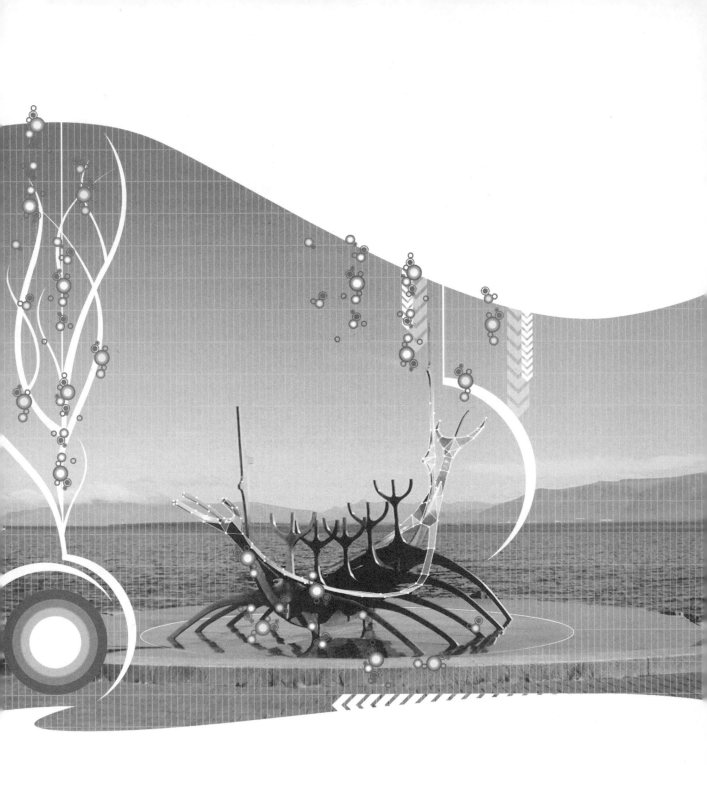

Chapter 1

A NEW KIND OF WEB DESIGN

In this chapter . . .

- Introducing the Internet and web design
- Why you should design a website
- Organizing and planning web page content
- Introducing web standards

About the Internet

The Internet's rise has been nothing short of meteoric. We may take it for granted today, using it for all manner of tasks, but just over ten years ago few people had even heard of the Internet, let alone used it. For businesses and individuals, the Internet is now often the communication medium of choice, enabling them to interact with the world. But the Internet's origins were more ominous and rather different from the ever-growing, sprawling free-for-all that exists today.

Back in the 1960s, the American military was experimenting with methods by which the U.S. authorities might be able to communicate in the aftermath of a nuclear attack. The suggested solution was to replace point-to-point communication networks like the telephone with a system that was more robust. They decided to create a network and to send packets of data from one node of the network to the other in a sort of relay race. This meant that information could find its way from place to place even if certain sections of the network were destroyed. Despite the project eventually being shelved by the Pentagon, the concept itself lived on, eventually influencing a network that connected several American universities.

During the following decade, this fledgling network went international and began opening itself up to the general public. The term **Internet** was coined in the 1980s, and the Transmission Control Protocol/Internet Protocol (TCP/IP) was invented—the networking protocol that makes possible communication between computers running on different systems. For the first time, corporations began using the Internet as a means of communication, both amongst themselves and also with customers who were clued in to this exciting medium.

Despite the technology's healthy level of expansion, the general public remained largely unaware of the Internet until well into the 1990s, when a combination of inexpensive hardware, the advent of highly usable web browsers such as Mosaic, shown below, and improved communications technology saw an explosion of growth that continues to this day. Initially, only the largest brands dipped their toes into these new waters, but soon thousands of companies were online, enabling customers all over the globe to access information, and later even to shop online.

Home users soon got in on the act, too, once it became clear that the basics of web design weren't rocket science, and that everyone could do it—all they needed was a text editor, an FTP client, and some web space. Therefore, unlike most media, the Web is truly a tool for everyone, and in many countries the Internet has become the medium of choice, supplementing—if not supplanting—print and video.

So, from its obscure roots as a concept for military communications, the Internet evolved into an essential tool for millions of people, enabling them to communicate with each other, research and gather information, telecommute, shop, play games, and become involved in countless other activities on a worldwide basis. But websites don't appear by magic—someone has to create them . . .

A brief history of web design

Mosaic was the Web's first "killer app," the one that finally enabled non-computer-literate people to simply point and click to browse. It appeared on both Windows and Macintosh computers and opened up the Web to a whole new audience—one that had wildly different expectations than the primarily technically oriented souls who'd been using the system until that time. Now, people weaned on magazines and advertising demanded similarly visually appealing, usable content from the Web, but the process was long and—for the designers at least—difficult.

Browsers have always been the sticking point with regards to what's possible in web design, and early browsers were particularly limited in what they could display. Early sites tended to be strictly static affairs, perhaps with the occasional graphic to break things up. The Web was also a very boring place: Flash and online videos were some way off, and connection speeds were extraordinarily slow compared to what the majority of users are using today.

The mid-1990s was when things started to gain speed. A group of web gurus founded the World Wide Web Consortium (W3C—see www.w3.org/Consortium), providing technical specifications for web infrastructure. Over 35 such specifications were released in its first five years of existence. In 1995, Netscape 2 exploded onto the scene, introducing the world to frames, LiveScript (soon to be renamed JavaScript), and plug-ins like RealPlayer. Multimedia content was becoming a reality online, although postage-stamp-sized video was pretty much all anyone could cope with, due to the fledgling compression formats and slow connection speeds of the day. It was around this time that Microsoft noticed what was going on, swiftly following up its half-hearted Internet Explorer with versions 2 and 3. The latter version was free, and it matched Netscape's latest release for features, and offered rudimentary style sheet implementation. Sites gradually started using many of the new features, although some were over-used: frames became ubiquitous, despite the massive problems they caused search engines and users alike; gaudy text became the norm, as did some fairly hideous fonts. However, many designers got around the limitations and avoided the fads, and this period saw some of the first really great designs on the Web.

In its quest for world domination, Microsoft next bought WebTV Networks, and then practically welded Internet Explorer to Windows, which usurped Netscape as the default Mac OS browser. Microsoft and Netscape traded blows, each company's browser offering its own **Cascading Style Sheet** (CSS) standard and **Document Object Model** (DOM), causing a headache for designers, who had to effectively produce a version of each site they were working on for each browser, due to the major differences in anything other than the most basic features.

At the same time, web design applications finally came of age, including the increasingly impressive Dreamweaver, opening up web design to the masses, who no longer had to have encyclopedic knowledge of HTML to create a site. Also, the Web Standards Project (WaSP—see `www.webstandards.org`) started campaigning for browser manufacturers to support web standards, claiming that it would otherwise soon be impossible to create sites that would be accessible on a variety of platforms.

Around the turn of the century, Netscape pretty much imploded, conceding defeat to the increasingly dominant Internet Explorer and releasing half-hearted, buggy browsers that made few friends. However, both Netscape and Microsoft, along with the increasingly popular Opera, finally introduced relatively thorough standards support, and design on the Web continued to improve, often aping minimal magazine style. Notably, Macromedia's Flash Player plug-in was now installed by default, and estimates suggested that more than 80 percent of users could view Flash content. Many designers dropped HTML in favor of Flash. Some created beautiful, subtly animated, and highly usable Flash content; others saw fit to inflict eye candy on everyone. (Flash intros, complete with "skip intro" buttons, became so common that they eventually spawned a parody site, which can still be accessed at `skipintro.nl/skipintro`.) Unfortunately, the bubble soon burst: the meteoric rise in popularity of the Internet had birthed hundreds of web design companies, many of whom charged a fortune for their services. The infamous "dot bomb" crash put paid to that, removing a shockingly large number of companies from the scene, and giving a rather harsh slap of reality to the entire industry.

Every cloud has a silver lining, though, and the last few years have perhaps been the best for web design. In many ways, the medium has grown up. Most professional designers now know which tools to use for which job, leading to stunning sites that combine standards-compliant mark-up for content with CSS for styling, and occasional subtle use of Flash for animation, video, and interactive elements. Special emphasis is placed on **usability** and **accessibility**, ensuring sites are usable and accessible by all, and designers now understand that this needn't come at the expense of visual design. And most designers are finally aware that content is king.

> *Accessibility* is a much-used word in the web design world these days. It refers to the practice of ensuring that a site is accessible to everyone, including, for instance, those people using screen readers. Various techniques are available to help make a site more accessible, and some of these will be explored in this book.

The onset of broadband made online audio and video feasible for the first time. Browser manufacturers began to play ball with regards to standards, and the relatively new Firefox (created from the ashes of Netscape) has even managed to bite into Internet Explorer's supposedly unassailable market share. While there are still bugs and omissions here and there, you can now author a web-standards-compliant site and know you'll only have to tweak a few things to get it working in a huge number of devices. The Web Standards Project's attention had also turned to developers of web design applications, and Macromedia was one of the first companies to wholeheartedly embrace standards, basing Dreamweaver's workflow around CSS (something that continues apace with Dreamweaver 8).

What the future will bring, no one knows. However, this book aims to ensure that you're armed with a strong understanding of the medium and of Dreamweaver, so you'll be ready to tackle whatever the Web evolves into next.

Creating a website

Surprisingly few designers ask themselves why they are creating a website, but it's a question that should be asked at the beginning of every project. Before delving into your digital box of tricks, it pays to plan and prepare. The worst websites online—those that are unfocused, unusable, or just plain bad—are often the product of poor planning. In most cases, such problems can be overcome by taking the time to work out what's best for your site and why you're creating it in the first place.

Most of the questions you need to ask are generic and can be applied to the majority of projects you're likely to work on:

- What is the purpose of the website?
- Who will visit the site?
- How will this target audience affect your approach?
- Is there a client involved, and if so, what are its needs?
- What content will the site contain?
- From where will the content be sourced?
- How will the site be structured?
- What will the site look like?
- When is the deadline?

These aren't the only questions you should ask yourself, but they're a good start. Also bear in mind that there are rarely any wrong answers, but whatever you discover may help consolidate ideas. Let's take a look at some of the questions in more depth.

What is the purpose of the website?

A successful site's purpose is often reflected in its design. For instance, Play.com's aim is to sell as much product as possible to as wide a range of customers as possible. Therefore, the structure and navigation of the site—if you'll pardon the expression—is idiot-proof. The navigation is intuitive, and searches that take you deep into the site are easily available. The visual design is somewhat bland and inoffensive, so while it won't excite anyone, it won't annoy them either.

Typically, successful content-oriented sites have a similar approach: Wired.com and BBC News (http://news.bbc.co.uk/) have thousands of pages, and yet all information can easily be found. However, while both sites partially adhere to their corporate branding, neither would be considered "exciting" design.

At the other end of the spectrum, you'll find the likes of Yugop.com, shown next. This is an experimental Flash-based website, yet the interface still makes perfect sense, enabling you to rapidly access the content. This is, in many ways, proof that even if your content is outside the mainstream, you needn't forego usability. However, because this site's main aim is to showcase content, the navigation is very succinct, and the majority of the available space is given over to presenting the various animation projects.

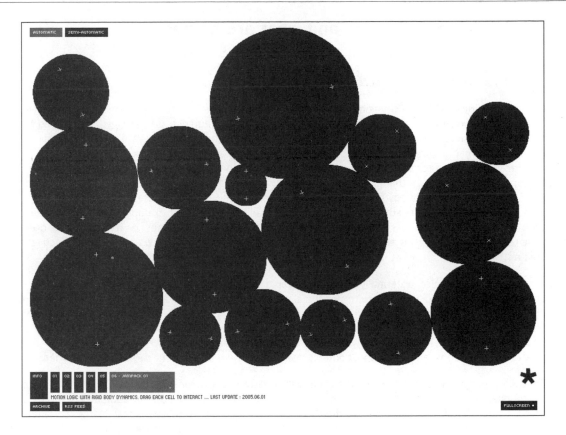

Ultimately, you will need to decide what the focus of your site is, and ensure that it's prominent and that all the content is easy to access.

Who will visit the site?

The worst designers are those who only design for themselves. This almost always results in self-indulgent and inappropriate results. If you're working for a client, find out about the expectations of its audience and design accordingly. You needn't compromise every step of the way, but you need to ensure that a site's visitors will be in-tune with whatever it's trying to get across and won't be put off by how the site appears. If appealing to a very wide audience—everyone from the clued-up techie to the new-to-technology granny— keep things simple and toned down. Ensure that your site is simple to use and navigate, and that it's obvious where each type of information is to be found. If appealing to a very specific audience, find out what they want. For instance, a site for children's book illustration should be appealing to parents and small children, and is unlikely to require harsh colors, bold angles and hours of video and animation footage. Similarly, a gaming site is going to need high-impact graphics, access to screen shots and gaming footage, but probably not a pastel color scheme and introductory page about the organization itself (gamers tend to want to get right to the content).

Is there a client involved, and what are its needs?

Most designers create work for others, but even when you're creating work for yourself, the ultimate client remains the audience. Often, projects become a delicate balancing act, harmonizing your ideas, those of your client, and the expectations of the audience.

Chances are, ideas will keep changing along the way, often because of external factors. You might have a preference for certain colors or layouts, but if most of your audience disagrees, you may need to rethink. Be flexible: just because clients are not artists, you shouldn't disregard their opinions. Of course, the dynamic nature of the Web can make such changes relatively quick and cost-effective to put into practice, especially when using the techniques we'll be covering in this book. By comparison, if a print brochure needs changing, the whole thing must be reprinted, or a supplement bolted on. Such a print job won't be any cheaper the second time around if changes are made. However, for a web site, this isn't the case—the existing content can easily be edited. For example, correcting a major typo on the introductory page of a printed catalogue might cost thousands, or have to be ignored (due to cost), but correcting the same thing on a website may only take a few minutes and effectively cost nothing.

Turnaround time is also potentially much more rapid online. If the site is your own, you can make changes almost immediately. If you're not the client, you'll need to get approval from whoever is in charge, but the changes are still likely to happen fairly rapidly. Perhaps the best advice I can offer about working with clients is to communicate constantly. Never assume you know what a client wants, or that a client knows exactly what you mean, unless things are explicit. Write everything down, get written specifications, and draw up a contract saying exactly what the client can expect and when.

Set milestones in the project, which the client will have to sign-off for (and maybe pay a percentage of the overall costs for), such as after the visual design, site design, and content addition and upload. Make it clear that if the client changes the specifications at any point, there may be charges for alterations if they're substantial. And keep communicating throughout; the worst web sites usually come about because those involved didn't talk to each other about their needs and those of the end users.

What content will the site contain?

Content is king, and you need to think about what content the site will contain before you even consider the visual design. For instance, there's little point in creating a small, graphics-heavy template if it turns out your client has no images and plenty of text for the website.

You need to ensure the client understands what content is required and in what format it should be sent to you. When working for or with a company, find out who has the responsibility for supplying you information, and set dates when it should be sent (dates well before your final deadline)—if a client doesn't send you content on time, you shouldn't be expected to turn around the site's design by the previously agreed deadlines. Also, ensure that you specify specific file types and settings (such as resolution)—there's little worse in the world of web design than having to rapidly produce a website after receiving a CD full of images that you cannot open or use.

Keep in mind that copyright exists on the Web the same as everywhere else, despite what some people might think. Do not just grab a load of images or text from other websites unless you have written permission from the copyright owner (who is not necessarily the site's creator) to do so. Failure to do this could mean anything from a harsh email to a lawsuit.

How will the site be structured?

Most sites have some sort of "home" or "news" or "introduction" page, an "about" page describing the site, a "contact" page indicating how users can get in touch, and any number of pages containing the majority of the site's content (typically products or services for a commercial site). Overly complicated structures tend to wreck websites, so keep everything as simple and logical as possible, grouping categories and pages in a consistent and coherent manner.

Wherever possible, make all top-level category pages accessible from a central location (such as a navigation bar) and keep subpages to a minimum. In some cases, this can be achieved by the clever use of layout.

As mentioned earlier, the site should be straightforward to use, which means stripping back the navigation area to the bare essentials, and making good use of succinct copy. Icons should be avoided—after all, the word "contact" is unambiguous, but a picture of an envelope could mean "mail," "email," or several other things.

When is the deadline?

This is an important question for any project. A wonderful masterpiece of design, with a beautiful, highly animated interface is of no use to a client if you've only had time to create the home page. If deadlines are too tight for what's been asked of you, talk to the client about it. If the client is you, give yourself a good talking to, and try to be more realistic about deadlines in the future.

One thing that should always be avoided is "under construction" pages. They look shoddy and unprofessional at best. If an area of a site is not going to be ready for the launch date, remove the links to it (which is relatively simple when using the technologies outlined in this book). Even better, if the site is new, delay its launch and put up a small holding page containing contact information and a small message saying when the completed site will be online. (It should go without saying that you must stick firmly to whatever deadline you've published for all the world to see.)

In any case, you should be able to make reasonable deadline estimates based on previous jobs. If in doubt, try to deal with the content (sourcing, structure, and formatting) first, and then with the design. You can spend an age messing around with visual design, but if there's no content, any such fiddling is academic.

Gathering and organizing content

Gathering content is one thing, but keeping it organized is something else entirely. There are plenty of people who claim they work better in a jumbled mess, but this doesn't really work with computers, even when taking into account the "find file" functions built into Windows and the Mac OS. After all, you may not remember the filename of something you're searching for, especially when working with images from digital cameras, which may have such "useful" filenames as 02032045023450.jpg. Logical organization and naming of all your files means you should be able to find what you need at any point during a project.

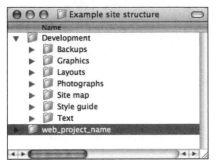

Before getting any content, set up a folder structure on your hard drive to store everything in. The structure shown here isn't in any way set in stone, but it is a general guide that you can adapt to each project as you see fit.

As you can see, the project folder has two folders within it, the second of which is the local copy of the website. (Rather than just calling this "web," it should include the project name; it soon becomes difficult to find a specific web folder when you have dozens of folders called "web" on your hard drive.)

The other folder is called Development, and it houses all the files you might need to complete a website, including original text (perhaps in the form of Word, text, or RTF documents), graphics (such as logos), layouts, photographs, and the site map (for reference purposes). In the photographs folder you can keep full-quality copies of your photos, so if you need to resize one at a later date, you can do so from the original, without having to search various other locations to find the relevant images.

> *Underscores are used instead of spaces in the folder set aside for the website files (web_project_name) because some scripting languages require this. While such scripts aren't used in this book, it's a good habit to get into the naming convention shown. Note that for "source" files (photographs, text, and so on), this doesn't matter—they can be placed within folders that have spaces in their names.*

Finally, note the backups folder. Web design can be a tricky business, so it's a good idea to take backups of your local web folder on a regular basis. If you suddenly find that something stops working, you can revert to (or at least make a comparison with) your most recently working version.

Creating a site map

A site map is essentially a diagram that provides a structural overview of a website. You can use applications such as Adobe Illustrator, Macromedia Freehand, Microsoft PowerPoint, and others to make them, or you can use good old squared paper and a pencil. Most site maps are structured in a similar fashion to the diagram here:

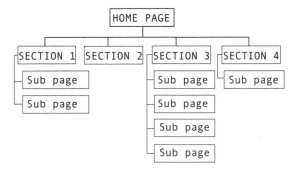

The home page is the initial page users will access, so it is at the top of the tree. Main sections are then listed horizontally underneath. Perhaps, in tandem with the home page, these will form the basis for the site's navigation bar (or at least the most prominent parts of it). Underneath each section are listed the pages found within. For larger sites, these may actually be subsections, with more pages being listed under them.

> *As is often the case within this book, I'm providing ideas rather than concrete guidelines. This most definitely isn't the only way of creating a site map; whatever method you end up using, ensure that you understand it well, and that it's easy to explain to a potential client.*

Introducing web standards

Before we start with Dreamweaver, let's look briefly at the two web standards we'll be using most often in this book. While Dreamweaver's interface largely enables you to avoid hand coding, you'll be better off if you understand some of the concepts behind web standards such as XHTML and CSS, not only for when you have to tweak the code Dreamweaver produces, but also when you're using some of the application's dialog boxes, which may be rather cryptic if you don't understand the terminology.

XHTML

No, a rogue "x" hasn't snuck in front of the preceding heading—**Extensible Hypertext Markup Language** (XHTML) is HTML reformulated in XML, providing greater interpolation with numerous devices. Because XHTML is a more recent standard than HTML, it's recommended that you use XHTML wherever possible—indeed, Dreamweaver 8 defaults to XHTML when you create a new web page via File ➤ New. Note that despite the change in name, the file extension remains the same (.html, or .htm if you like using archaic 8.3 DOS conventions).

CSS

Cascading Style Sheets (CSS) is the W3C standard for defining the visual presentation for web pages.

HTML was designed as a structural markup language, but the demands of users and designers encouraged browser manufacturers to support and develop presentation-oriented tags. These tags "polluted" HTML, pushing the language to focus more on decorative style than logical structure. Its increasing complexity made life hard for web designers, and source code began to balloon for even basic presentation-oriented tasks. Along with creating needlessly large HTML files, things like font tags created web pages that weren't consistent across browsers and platforms, and styles had to be applied to individual elements—a time-consuming process.

By comparison, CSS enables you to separate design and presentation from content—XHTML deals with the basic structure of a page, and a separate CSS document is used for the site-wide application of visual presentation (including element margins and padding, backgrounds, borders, and so on).

Although many designers are aware of CSS, relatively few use it for anything more than styling fonts. However, Dreamweaver 8 makes it relatively easy to create CSS-based web page layouts, as you'll see during the course of this book. That said, Dreamweaver doesn't do quite everything for you, and something you need to know is which CSS selector type to use in each case when creating a CSS rule (these are outlined in Chapter 4).

Summary

In this chapter, you've learned about how the Internet came to be, and also many important things you need to do before working with Dreamweaver. You've also read overviews on XHTML and CSS—technologies that will prove essential as you work your way through the book.

In the next chapter, we'll take a look at Dreamweaver itself, so you can learn how to create a new document and you can familiarize yourself with the application's interface.

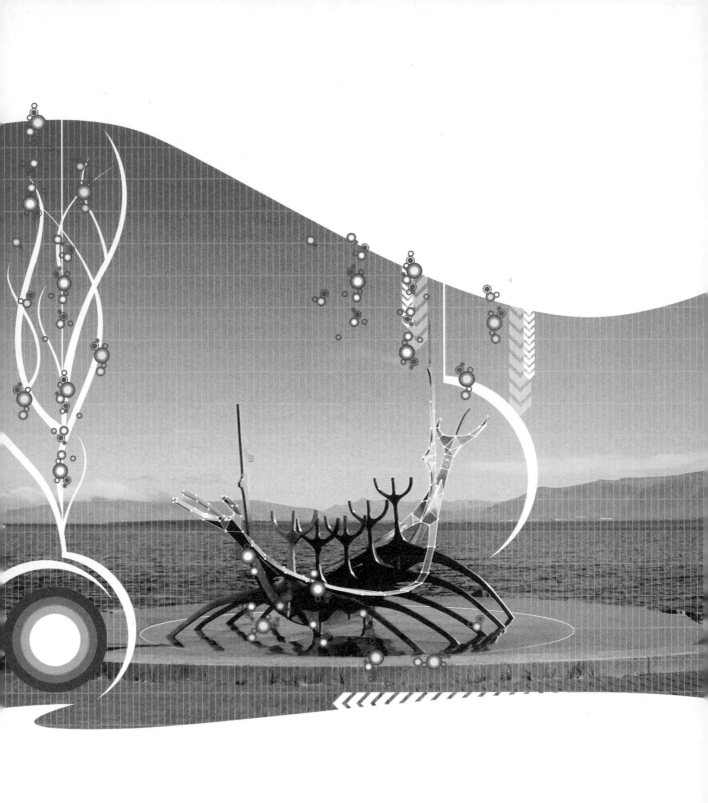

Chapter 2

GETTING STARTED WITH DREAMWEAVER

In this chapter...

- The Start Page
- Creating a document
- The Dreamweaver interface
- Tweaking Dreamweaver preferences
- Setting up preview browsers

What is Dreamweaver?

Dreamweaver is a software application that enables you to create web pages. Version 1 was released nearly a decade ago, in 1997, and since then Dreamweaver has become the leading application in the field. This is largely due to three essential factors:

- Dreamweaver's interface enables people at all levels to understand the application, regardless of their preferred methods of working.
- Dreamweaver is powerful enough to enable you to create almost any type of website.
- Dreamweaver has always been one of the first applications in its field to embrace and integrate new technologies.

Dreamweaver 8 includes many new features; for instance, it builds on Dreamweaver MX 2004's CSS-based workflow by streamlining working with that technology and by greatly enhancing Design view to show outlines of CSS boxes. The program caters to graphic designers by providing guides and zoom tools, enabling more precise layout, and hand coders will be happy to discover the new Code View toolbar, which provides quick access to commonly used commands.

Of course, Dreamweaver 8 still excels at integrating with other Macromedia products—Fireworks, Flash, and FreeHand—and it enables you to customize your workspace (and save different workspace layouts).

Don't worry if you're new to Dreamweaver, because we'll be starting from the very beginning. And if you're already familiar with the application, you'll still learn plenty, because the application has evolved from previous versions and we'll be using the newest techniques rather than legacy methods.

Creating a new document—the Start Page

The first thing that pops up when you open Dreamweaver 8 is the Start Page.

Your first instinct might be to check the Don't show again check box, especially if you're a seasoned pro, but it's worth leaving it alone for a while. Not only does it provide single-click access to various file types via the Create New column, but it also provides easy access to built-in sample sets, and the Dreamweaver Exchange.

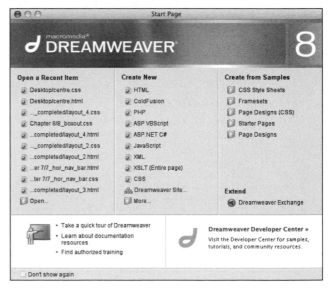

*The **Dreamweaver Exchange**, found at www.macromedia.com/cfusion/exchange/index.cfm, is a useful repository for free or affordable components that can make it easier for you to add functionality to your web pages. Elements for download are usually built by members of the design community, and there's no doubting that it's an essential resource for any Dreamweaver user. However, beware of downloads that only function accurately in specific browsers or on specific platforms—any such components should generally be avoided. After all, good websites work in all browsers—imagine a scenario where a potential client cannot use your site, or part of your site, because it only works in one browser, and they use a different one. You will almost certainly lose that business, because a client may find it easier to find a competitor rather than go to the hassle of switching web browsers. Using web standards, as we will throughout this book, means such a scenario shouldn't happen.*

The Start Page also provides rapid access to items you've recently worked on, via the Open a Recent Item column. While many applications (including Dreamweaver) contain similar functionality via File ➤ Open Recent, the Start Page makes this process just that little bit faster, and those few saved seconds for each opened file soon add up.

Should you click Don't show again and later change your mind, the Start Page can be reactivated by going to Edit ➤ Preferences (Dreamweaver ➤ Preferences on Mac), selecting General, and then checking Show start page, found in the Document options area.

Choosing a document to work with

Click the More option in the Start Page's Create New column, and the New Document dialog box appears. (This can also be accessed via File ➤ New.) There are two tabs at the top—General and Templates. The first provides access to built-in examples and blank documents, while the latter enables you to access any templates you've created (see Chapter 10 for more on Dreamweaver templates).

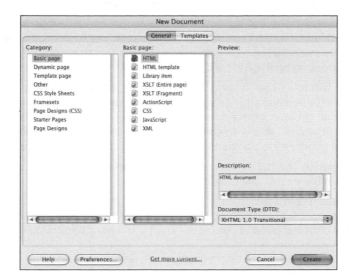

For now, stick with the General tab and select Basic page from the Category list. You'll see that the second column's name is the same as the category you selected and that a list of documents is displayed. Choose a document, and a description is provided in the Description field. (Because the Basic page category provides access to blank documents, the Preview area remains blank, but if a document has content, it will be shown there.)

At the bottom right of the dialog box is a new feature of Dreamweaver 8—a Document Type (DTD) menu. All standards-compliant web pages require a document type, which tells a browser what type of code is being used, enabling the browser to render it accordingly. Previous versions of Dreamweaver merely had a check box that determined whether you wanted to make your HTML document XHTML compliant, but Dreamweaver 8 provides seven choices: None, two versions of HTML 4.01, two versions of XHTML 1.0, and one option each for XHTML 1.1 and XHTML Mobile 1.0. For the vast majority of web pages, XHTML 1.0 Transitional (the default option) should be fine—it's a slightly more flexible document type definition (DTD) than XHTML 1.0 Strict and XHTML 1.1, but it still enables you to create modern, standards-compliant web pages.

Click the Create button and a new page is created.

The Dreamweaver interface

Although Dreamweaver's interface may look complex at first, you'll find that after a little practice it soon becomes familiar and intuitive. The interfaces for the Mac and Windows versions are more or less identical (the only real difference is that the Windows version allows "docking" for windows and panels other than those in the main panels section, meaning you can collapse the Properties panel and dock further panels underneath—on the Mac version, the Properties panel cannot be collapsed).

The interface is essentially made up of five elements, each of which will be explained in more detail later in this chapter:

- **Menus:** These are at the top of the screen. They provide access to the bulk of Dreamweaver's features, and also list keyboard shortcuts.

- **Insert bar:** By default, this is at the top of the screen just below the menus, and it contains icon-based shortcuts to common web page items and functions. A drop-down menu provides access to various technology-specific items.

- **Document window:** This is where you spend most of your time when working with Dreamweaver. Depending on your settings, it shows your work in Design view, Code view, or a combination of the two, often referred to as **Split** view or **Code and Design** view. The top of the document window has a toolbar that houses various icons and icon-based drop-down menus, most of which enable you to customize the aforementioned views.

- **Properties panel:** This is a dynamic panel, which enables you to change settings related to the currently selected item in any view.

- **Other panels:** These supplementary panels have a number of functions relating to Design view, Code view, storage of information, file management, CSS, and much more. The relevant ones will be explored in detail later in the book, although a brief overview of some of them is included in this chapter.

Although Dreamweaver 8 streamlines the interface somewhat, there's still repetition between the various interface elements. This is useful, because different designers approach projects in different ways, depending on applications they've used previously, or the jobs they've taken on to date. Some are more comfortable with visual design, while others prefer digging into the source code of their projects.

Therefore, Dreamweaver 8 enables designers to get used to coding, and coders to learn how to work with a WYSIWYG (what you see is what you get) interface. Within this book, various methods will be explored to achieve different tasks, but you should remember that these methods are just one way of achieving those goals. As with all software, you will benefit from spending time experimenting with the interface prior to working on any projects. For instance, you may initially spend lots of time using the menus, then begin to use the Insert bar more, and then learn to favor a combination of keyboard shortcuts and panel selections once you become more familiar with the application.

What's new?

Unsurprisingly, Dreamweaver 8 includes a number of enhancements over earlier versions of the application, and several of the changes are interface-oriented:

- The Mac version finally includes document tabs, to make it easier to switch between open files. (The Windows version introduced this feature in Dreamweaver MX 2004.)
- CSS workflow has been streamlined, and the CSS Styles panel now includes the Rule Tracker, Property Grid, and a new Composite view.
- CSS-based sites are now easier to work with in Design view: the rendering has been significantly improved, and CSS layout elements can now be outlined.
- The Design view now enables you to zoom in and out, and also to set guides to aid in creating pixel-perfect design.
- Code view now has its own toolbar and a number of editing improvements.
- Panel sets can now be created and saved.

The way the interface works is largely the same as in previous versions—the combination of pop-up menus and collapsible panels should be familiar to most users of professional-grade software. However, if you've not used Dreamweaver before, do take time to get used to the interface—not only where things are stored, but also how the various elements work.

Menus

Let's first look at the menus, which are located at the top of the screen.

Some options will be familiar and others less so. You'll return to some items again and again, but you may never use others. One thing's for certain, though—there are most definitely a lot of menu items, and Dreamweaver's creators have tried to make them as user friendly as possible by logically categorizing them.

- **File:** As with most other applications, this menu deals with opening, saving, printing, importing, exporting, and converting files. This menu also houses the Preview in Browser and Check Page submenus, enabling you to test your pages in a number of defined browsers and to validate your pages, respectively.

> *The* File *menu also has a* Design Notes *item that enables you to leave notes for other members of a project team when working in a collaborative environment. This book concentrates on working with Dreamweaver on your own, so we will only be covering design notes briefly—see "Adding Design Notes" in Chapter 4.*

- **Edit:** This menu includes the usual Cut, Copy, and Paste commands, selection options (to select all, select the parent tag, or select the child tag), Find and Replace commands, various options relating to code formatting and hints, and access to the Tag Library Editor (Tag Libraries). On Windows, it also provides access to the application's preferences (which are found in the Dreamweaver menu in the Mac version).

- **View:** This menu deals with the main interface, enabling you to zoom the page; toggle between Design view, Code view, and Split view; toggle toolbars, the head content icons, and visual aids; switch the visual preview between various media types; and deal with guides, grids, and rulers.

- **Insert:** If you need to insert new items into your documents, including template objects, this is the menu to use. As the name may suggest, many items accessible in this menu are also accessible via the Insert bar.

- **Modify:** This menu enables you to edit items that already exist on your page, or the properties of the page itself.

- **Text:** This menu provides options for modifying and styling text-based elements.

- **Commands:** This menu includes various source-formatting and HTML-cleaning options, along with items to create and replay automated tasks.

- **Site:** This menu contains options relating to file and site management.

- **Window:** This menu enables you to toggle panels on and off, to save and load workspace layouts, and to access open documents.

> *Remember that Dreamweaver enables you to swap between open documents by using tabs, and you can also use your operating system's standard keyboard shortcuts: Ctrl+Tab for Windows and Cmd+~ for Mac.*

- **Help:** This menu provides access to Dreamweaver's internal documentation and resource files, and also to tutorials, Dreamweaver Exchange, related Macromedia websites, and online registration.

Depending on what type of sites you want to create, you may find yourself regularly using all of these menus, or perhaps very few of them. In most cases, there's a quicker and easier method of doing things than rummaging through menus, but if you end up looking for something, the menu titles should make it easy to find.

Insert bar

Usually located above the document window, the Insert bar can be toggled on and off via Window ➤ Insert.

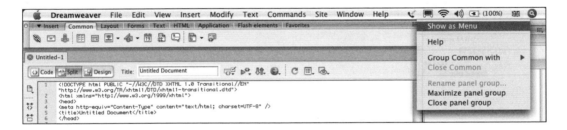

The Insert bar offers eight categories of icons. If you find the menu-based selection not to your taste, the Insert bar can also be formatted as a tab-based panel by choosing Show as Tabs from its drop-down menu.

To turn it back again, select Show as Menu from the panel's context menu.

Choosing a different option from the Insert bar's drop-down menu changes the icons that are displayed. Clicking an icon does one of two things: for standard icons, it adds the associated element to your web page; for icons with a downward-pointing black triangle, it displays a menu of related icons. For instance, the following image shows the options that can be accessed via the Head drop-down menu, which allows you to change the header information in an HTML document.

Although we're not going to cover each individual Insert bar menu option, the following is a brief outline of what each set contains:

- **Common:** This set is used to insert common web page elements, such as links, images, and other media, template regions, tables, and comments. It also provides access to the Tag Chooser and the utterly essential Add Div Tag command.

- **Layout:** This set is used to add and edit tables, layers, frames, and tabular content. It also provides another way of accessing the Add Div Tag command.

- **Forms:** This set is used to add form elements.

- **Text:** This set is used to format text on your web pages.

- **HTML:** This set provides access to HTML elements, such as horizontal rules, head element content (such as meta tags), table and frame elements, and script elements.

- **Application:** This set is used to insert elements for dynamic websites. We won't be going into this stuff, as it's beyond the scope of this book. For information on developing dynamic websites with Dreamweaver 8, check out *Foundation PHP for Dreamweaver 8* by David Powers (ISBN: 1590595696) and *Foundation ASP for Dreamweaver 8* by Omar Elbaga and Rob Turnbull (ISBN: 1590595688), both published by friends of ED.

- **Flash elements:** This set is used to store any prebuilt Flash elements that you may want to include within your designs. The default item included with Dreamweaver is an image viewer, which can be used as the basis of a web photo album.

■ **Favorites:** This final set is customizable and can be used to store your most commonly used elements. Once set up, this proves to be a massive time-saver. (The following brief exercise shows how to customize this set.)

| Favorites | Control-click to customize your favorite objects. |

Although many of the icons on the Insert *bar are fairly obvious, some are a little cryptic. To help out, tooltips appear with an explanation of what the icon represents if you hold the mouse pointer over an icon for a couple of seconds.*

Customizing favorite objects

1. To customize the Favorites set, right-click (Ctrl-click on the Mac) the Insert bar and choose Customize Favorites. In the Customize Favorite Objects dialog box, select objects from the list on the left and use the >> button to add them to your Favorite objects list. Note that the Available objects list is context-sensitive, and the list can be made more specific by making a selection from the drop-down menu.

Customize Favorite Objects

Available objects:

Text

- Acronym
- Line Break (Shift + Enter)
- Non-Breaking Space
- Left Quote
- Right Quote
- Em Dash
- Pound
- Euro
- Yen
- Copyright

Favorite objects:

Hyperlink
Left Quote
Right Quote

Pound
Euro

OK
Cancel
Help

>>

Add separator

2. You can edit the Favorite objects list by using the buttons next to the list's title and the Add separator button underneath (which, as you'd expect, adds a separator). The wastebasket button deletes the currently selected item, while the up and down arrows move a selected item up and down the list. When you're done, click OK. The Favorites set should now include whichever objects you selected in the previous step.

| Favorites | " " £ € |

The document window

This window is where you see your work take form. Dreamweaver offers several ways to display in-progress web pages, so let's take a look at them.

You'll need a file to view, so on the friends of ED website (www.friendsofed.com), navigate to the download files for this book, and find the folder called Chapter 2. Open the document_window.html file in Dreamweaver.

Design view

At the top of the document window, click the Design button and you should see something like the following simple page that contains an image and a single line of text:

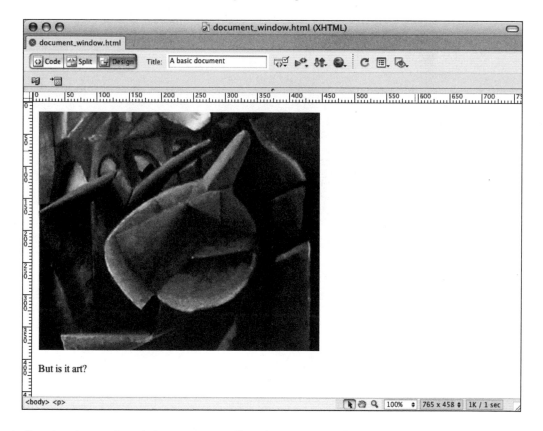

As I've already mentioned, Dreamweaver offers three ways to view your work. Design view provides you with a visual representation of your work, approximating how it will appear in web browsers.

Resizing windows

Document windows can be maximized, minimized, and resized by using your operating system's standard window controls, or by dragging the bottom-right corner of the window. Dreamweaver also provides a menu at the bottom right of the document window's status bar to approximate how your page will look in various monitor resolutions.

Choosing one of these size menu options immediately snaps the document window to the selected size. Using this menu helps you to avoid creating designs that require horizontal scrolling, which is annoying to users with smaller monitors.

> On Windows, you may have to go to Windows ➤ Cascade in order to use this function. Alternatively, for individual windows that you want to resize, use the Restore Down/Maximize button to ensure that the window isn't maximized; otherwise the options in the Windows menu will be grayed out.

It's also possible to add your own sizes to this menu, by accessing the Status Bar category of Dreamweaver's preferences, as shown next. Just click under the existing Width, Height, and Description fields, and add your own values. The width and height measurements are not an indication of monitor resolution, but are instead the available display area (when default toolbars are taken into account) within the web browser's window when the browser is maximized. The description contains the resolution.

Preferences			
Category	Status Bar		
General			
Accessibility	Window sizes:		
Code Coloring	**Width**	**Height**	**Description**
Code Format	536	196	(640 x 480, Default)
Code Hints	600	300	(640 x 480, Maximized)
Code Rewriting	760	420	(800 x 600, Maximized)
Copy/Paste	795	470	(832 x 624, Maximized)
CSS Styles	955	600	(1024 x 768, Maximized)
File Compare	544	378	(WebTV)
File Types / Editors	592	200	(592 x 200, Custom)
Fonts			
Highlighting			
Invisible Elements			
Layers			
Layout Mode			
New Document			
Preview in Browser			
Site			
Status Bar			
Validator			

Connection speed: 56.0 ⇕ Kilobits per second

(Help) (Cancel) (OK)

Estimating download times

Next to the resize menu at the bottom of the document window is another read-out, which shows the **page size**, measured in kilobytes (K), along with an estimation of how long the page will take to download. This estimate is based on whatever speed you set within the Status Bar preferences.

As a rule, it's best to keep this set to the common 56Kbps speed—while you may have broadband, many web users don't. One goal of good web design is to keep loading times as short as possible, but without compromising aesthetics and functionality.

Zooming in and out in Design view

New to Dreamweaver is the ability to zoom your design out so you can see how the whole thing looks, or in for pixel-perfect precision. Values from 6 percent to 6,400 percent are available. You can also use the Fit Selection command to make the entirety of the currently selected item visible, Fit All to see the entire design, or Fit Width to ensure the site's width fits within the display area.

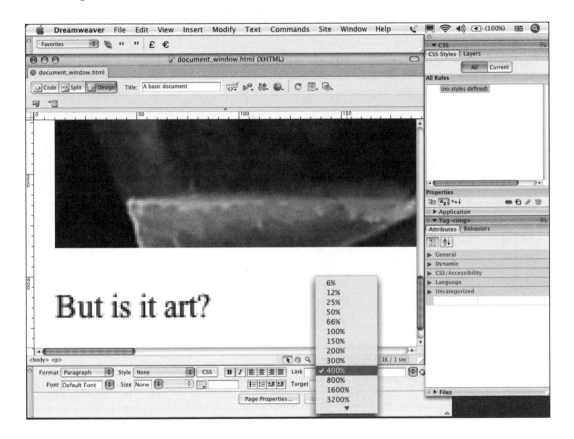

Code view

The bedrock of the Web, regardless of the content of your web page, is code—mainly HTML. Choose Design view, and then click on the Code button. In place of the image and line of text, you'll see the HTML that the browser interprets to display your page.

If you've not used HTML before, don't worry if it seems a little confusing—in Dreamweaver, you can generally avoid typing most HTML by hand, and even when you do, there are ways of speeding up the process.

Split (Design and Code) view

The final view is **Split view**, or Design and Code view. This is a mixture of the two views mentioned previously. By default, it shows Code view above Design view. The bar between the two can be moved, to change the proportion of available space each view uses.

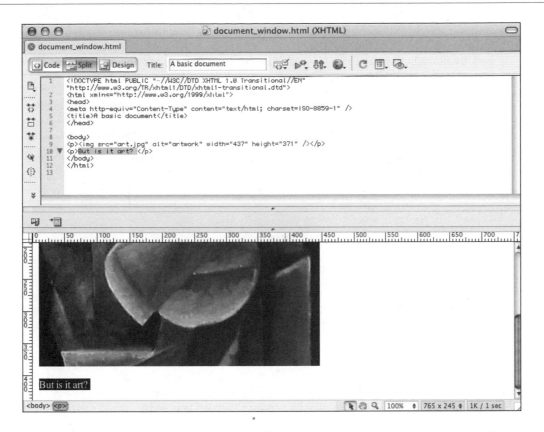

As you can see, this can be very practical. Highlighting something in one view highlights it in the other—for instance, if you select the paragraph of text in Design view, the relevant HTML is highlighted in Code view. This enables you to tweak and streamline your code, and if you are new to HTML, Split view can help you learn faster, because you can work in the Design view area and see how your actions affect the code.

Document window menus

Dreamweaver's document window includes a number of icon-based drop-down menus that provide quick access to highly useful features and options. These are, from left to right, the browser check menu, the Validate markup menu, the File management menu, the Preview/Debug in browser menu, the Refresh Design View button, the View options menu, and the Visual Aids menu.

- **Browser check:** This menu provides options for checking your site against a number of target browsers, flagging errors when it finds them. Generally, when working with web standards (as we'll be doing in this book), you shouldn't be targeting any one browser in particular, but this feature can nonetheless prove handy for immediately flagging code that will fail in any browser. To decide which browsers to check against, select Settings from the drop-down menu, and use the check boxes and drop-down menus to select browsers and version numbers.

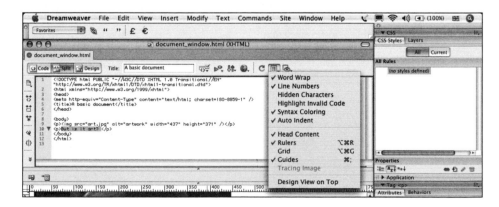

- **Validate markup:** Use this menu to validate the current document, the whole site, or selected documents in the site. Validation checks that your code is valid with regards to the type of document you're working on. Generally, you won't find errors if you work in Dreamweaver's Design view.

- **File management:** This menu provides quick access to some of the commands available via the Files panel.

- **Preview/Debug in browser:** This menu enables you to rapidly access defined browsers to preview your site. (The "Setting up preview browsers" section later in this chapter explains how to configure this menu.)

- **View options:** This menu enables you to change how various things in the views are displayed. You can change how code is formatted—for instance, you can set soft wrapping (meaning you don't have to scroll horizontally to read long lines of code) and toggle syntax coloring and auto indent on and off. You can flag hidden characters and invalid code, and you can turn line numbers on and off. For visual designers, there are options to toggle the display of the Head Content toolbar (which provides rapid access to otherwise invisible content), and you can turn on and off rulers, the grid, and any guides you've added to the page.

■ **Visual Aids:** This is essential for anyone working in Design view. You can use it to toggle the display of all manner of aids that make it far easier to see your page's structure. For instance, it can be used to highlight CSS blocks, table borders, image map areas, and more. We'll see how many of these aids function later in the book.

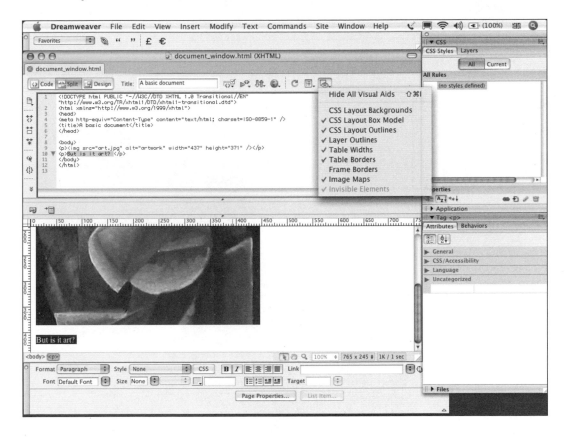

The Properties panel

The Properties panel is a very important interface element, located underneath the document window. It can be toggled on and off by going to Window ➤ Properties.

The previous image shows the panel in its default state, which provides the user with various options for formatting text. Across the top half of the panel, you can see pop-up menus for applying formatting and styles, and there are various icons for making text bold or italic and for justifying it. This interface element is also the main one used to add links.

If you've already experimented with the Style pop-up menu and are wondering where the Manage Styles option has gone, most CSS workflow options have been shifted to the CSS panel.

The Properties panel is context-sensitive, providing the options you need for a specific element and no more. This is useful for saving space on screen and for working more efficiently. For instance, when you click on an image, the Properties panel changes, displaying attributes related to working with images (such as Src for defining its source, and Alt for adding alternative text). Click on some text, and the Properties panel changes back to how it looked in the previous image.

If you're only seeing a half-size Properties panel, click the arrow at its bottom right to expand the panel to full size. I suggest leaving the panel at full size at all times.

Other panels

A quick look at the Window menu will show you just how many panels Dreamweaver has. These sit at one side of your screen—to the right on the Mac or Windows if you select the **Designer** workspace layout when first opening the application, and to the left on Windows if you select **Coder** workspace layout. (On the Mac, the equivalent of the Coder workspace layout—Application—still places the other panels at the right of the screen.) Note that your layout selection can be changed at any time by going to Window ➤ Workspace Layout, and you can drag and drop screen elements to new locations if you want to.

If you're using an old monitor with a maximum resolution of 800 × 600, now would be the time to upgrade. At the very least, I recommend a resolution of 1,024 × 768 when working with Dreamweaver, and even higher, if possible.

Dreamweaver intelligently stacks panels and panel groups, giving priority to ones that are opened, so you can get at the controls. Clicking on the triangles opens and collapses the panels or panel groups. Note that on Windows, closed panels are differentiated by their titles appearing in plain text (open panels are bold). On the Mac, closed panels have a light grey background, and open ones have a blue background.

We're not going to go into any depth about the various panels on offer here—they'll be explored where relevant later in the book.

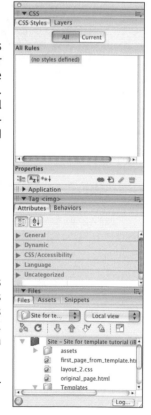

Panel groups

As previously mentioned, panels are organized into groups, which is apparent if you note the spacing in the Window menu. The first two items are for the Insert bar and Properties panel. The next three are design-oriented, providing access to the all-important CSS Styles panel and also to the Layers and Behaviors panels. The next four options, Databases, Bindings, Server Behaviors, and Components are for application creation. The following three—File, Assets, and Snippets provide access to file and code-snippet management tools. Next, there is a set of seven inspector or reference-oriented items. The remaining items in the menu deal with workspace layouts and accessing your documents.

> *By using each panel's menu, accessible at its top-right corner, you can change its grouping via the* Group [panel name] with *option. You can also rename, maximize, and close a panel group, or just close an individual panel. However, while it is easy to rearrange panels, Dreamweaver's default setup should be fine for most designers.*

Web page editing preferences

Dreamweaver is a complex but flexible application, so it should come as no surprise that there are a lot of preferences that can be tweaked (by going to Edit ➤ Preferences, or Dreamweaver ➤ Preferences on Mac). Categories are selected by highlighting options in the Category list, whereupon associated options appear on the right.

Most of Dreamweaver's default settings are fine, and I'll mention when anything needs changing. Note that Dreamweaver's dictionary settings can be changed in the General category by selecting a different Spelling dictionary setting, limited by what you have installed. One other default that may prove useful to change is Always show tabs—check this option if you want the tabs to appear even if you only have one document open.

In the Accessibility category, check all the boxes. This will prompt dialog boxes for you to set important attribute values when you add certain things to your web pages. (*Accessibility*, as mentioned in the previous chapter, is a word that encompasses the practice of making a website accessible to all, including those who use alternative means of accessing the Internet. For a thorough guide, read *Web Accessibility: Web Standards and Regulatory Compliance* by Jim Thatcher et al. (ISBN: 1590596382).)

> *Note that Dreamweaver's accessibility preferences do not automatically make your page accessible, as some users seem to think—they merely assist you in making a page more accessible by prompting for attribute values that might otherwise not be included in your web pages.*

In the Code Format category, ensure that Automatic Wrapping is turned off (this is the default setting). This won't actually make a great deal of difference to you right now, but it helps behind the scenes. Turning Automatic Wrapping on forces hard line wrapping in your HTML, which can often make it trickier to edit files at a later date (even when using Dreamweaver's visually oriented Design view).

> *This hard line wrapping is not the same as the wrapping mentioned in the "Document window menus" section, earlier in this chapter. The* Word Wrap *option mentioned there turns on soft wrapping, meaning that code wraps to the window width, reflowing as the window is resized, but the code is actually unchanged in the file itself—line numbers remain the same. Hard wrapping inserts line breaks in your code after a predefined number of characters, which can make pages awkward to edit later, especially when working directly with code.*

In the CSS Styles category, check all of the Use shorthand for check boxes, and set Use shorthand to According to settings above. This produces leaner CSS code, which is faster to download and simpler to edit. For instance, if you weren't to use shorthand and were to define separate margin values for each edge of a box, you'd end up with four separate property/value pairs in your style sheet. By using shorthand, these pairs are combined into one property/value pair.

This category of the preferences also determines what happens when you click a rule in the CSS Styles panel—you can set the edit process to happen in the CSS Style Definition dialog box, the Properties panel, or directly in Code view.

The New Document category enables you to easily set defaults for new documents that you create. The defaults are generally fine, but Unicode UTF-8 (Unicode 4.0 UTF-8 on Mac) is perhaps a better Default encoding option than the Western (ISO Latin 1) encoding option that Dreamweaver has as its default.

Preferences

Category	New Document

General
Accessibility
Code Coloring
Code Format
Code Hints
Code Rewriting
Copy/Paste
CSS Styles
File Compare
File Types / Editors
Fonts
Highlighting
Invisible Elements
Layers
Layout Mode
New Document
Preview in Browser
Site
Status Bar
Validator

Default document: HTML
Default extension: .html
Default Document Type (DTD): XHTML 1.0 Transitional
Default encoding: Unicode 4.0 UTF-8
☑ Use when opening existing files that don't specify an encoding
Unicode Normalization Form: None
☐ Include Unicode Signature (BOM)
☑ Show New Document dialog box on CMD+N

Help   Cancel   OK

Setting up preview browsers

One of the most important of the Dreamweaver preferences is the Preview in Browser category. A lot of designers get sucked into Design view, relying on it to present an accurate view of how a site will look online. While this aspect of Dreamweaver has improved in leaps and bounds in the last few revisions of the application, it's far from perfect. Additionally, each web browser has its own quirks, so you should always ensure you test your pages in a number of different browsers.

On Windows, the standards-compliant Firefox is a good browser to use as your primary browser, with the widespread Internet Explorer as your secondary browser. Opera is also worth installing and testing your sites in. On the Mac, you should probably use Firefox as your main browser, with the Mac-only Safari making a good second choice. Mac users should also test in Opera. (Wherever possible, Windows users should test sites on a Mac and vice versa, although you cannot do this via Dreamweaver.)

Dreamweaver makes rapid preview testing very simple. Access the Preview in Browser category in the Preferences dialog box, and you'll see a field that contains one or more browser names. By clicking the plus icon above the list, you can navigate to and add any web browsers installed on your computer to this list. The list of browsers can later be edited—including the browser names—by selecting them and clicking the Edit button, or you can delete a browser from the list by selecting it and clicking the minus sign. In addition, it's possible to assign one browser as your Primary browser and one as your Secondary browser by selecting a browser from the list and checking the relevant check box. A preview in the primary browser can then be created by pressing F12 (Opt+F12 on Mac), and a preview in the secondary browser by pressing Ctrl+F12 (Cmd+F12 on Mac). These preview options can also be accessed (along with the entire browser list you've defined) via the document window's Preview/Debug in browser menu and also via File ➤ Preview in Browser, both of which also contain the Edit Browser List option to get back to the Preferences dialog box.

Keyboard shortcuts

A final and most welcome customization option in Dreamweaver is the ability to amend keyboard shortcuts, adding and deleting presets as per your wishes. By going to Edit ➤ Keyboard Shortcuts (Dreamweaver ➤ Keyboard Shortcuts on Mac) you can bring up the Keyboard Shortcuts dialog box.

Here you can use the collapsible lists and the fields to add, edit, or delete shortcuts. Note that the Current set menu provides several predefined sets (including shortcuts for Dreamweaver MX 2004, BBEdit, and HomeSite), while the four icons at the top right of the dialog box enable you to duplicate the current set, rename the set, export the set as HTML, or delete the set. The export option is actually quite handy—export the set, open it in a browser, and then print it for a handy shortcut reference guide.

Summary

You should now be comfortable working with Dreamweaver's interface, tweaking its preferences, and creating new documents. However, documents need a home, so in the next chapter we'll be looking at how to set up a site in Dreamweaver.

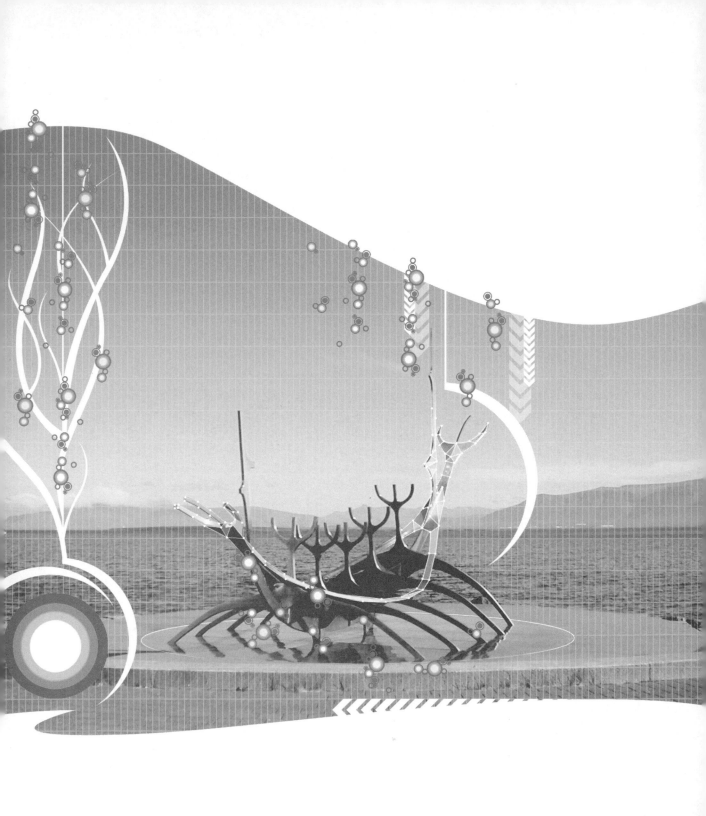

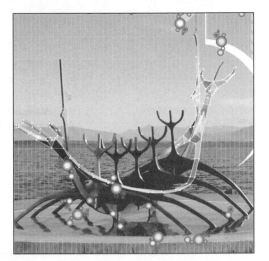

Chapter 3

SETTING UP A WEBSITE

In this chapter . . .

- Defining a site in Dreamweaver
- Working with the Files panel
- Uploading and downloading to your web space

Defining a site in Dreamweaver

In Chapter 1, I explained how to set up a folder structure on your hard drive, ready for your website and development files. Now we'll look at how to set up a website in Dreamweaver.

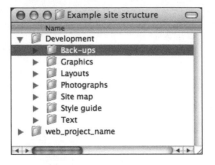

As well as being a capable design tool, Dreamweaver has plenty going for it in terms of site maintenance. In fact, even if you were to hand code your sites in a text editor, Dreamweaver would still come in very handy for those occasions when you have to rename a file or move a web page to a different location in the site's structure.

First, however, you have to set up a site, which you can do by following the steps in the following exercise.

How to set up your website

1. Either go to Site ➤ New site, or if you're on the Start Page, click Dreamweaver Site (in the Create New column). This brings up the Site Definition dialog box. Ensure Basic is selected at the top of the dialog box—this provides a walkthrough wizard to lead you through the steps of setting up a site. Then type your website's name in the first field (don't leave this as-is, or you'll end up with a site called "Untitled Site [X]"). If you have somewhere to host your website, add your site's URL to the second field. Click Next to continue.

Site Definition for Snub Communications

Basic | Advanced

Site Definition

Editing Files   Testing Files   Sharing Files

A site, in Dreamweaver, is a collection of files and folders that corresponds to a website on a server.

What would you like to name your site?

Snub Communications

Example: mySite

What is the HTTP Address (URL) of your site?

http://www.snubcommunications.com

Example: http://www.myHost.com/mySite

If you want to work directly on the server using FTP or RDS, you should underline{create an FTP or RDS server connection}. Working directly on the server does not allow you to perform sitewide operations like link checking or site reports.

Help   < Back   **Next >**   Cancel

In the screenshots, I'm using the details for my own website, Snub Communications— you will need to enter details (names, URLs, etc.) for your own site in the relevant fields!

2. Now you'll see a question asking whether you want to work with a server technology. Most of this book doesn't explore such things, so check No, I do not want to use a server technology, and click Next.

3. You'll next see a screen that asks how you want to work with your files during development. While you can work directly with a live site stored on your web hosting space, that means you can't check changes before they are made live for the whole world to see. Therefore, check the first option, which enables you to work with copies on your local machine and then upload them when you're ready. In the dialog box's field should be a path where the application recommends you store your files (in [user]\My Documents on Windows and [home]/Sites on Mac). These default settings are fine, but should you want to change where Dreamweaver stores this site, you can do so by clicking the folder icon and choosing a new location on your hard drive. Click Next.

Site Definition for Snub Communications

Basic   Advanced

Site Definition

Editing Files, Part 3   Testing Files   Sharing Files

How do you want to work with your files during development?

⦿ Edit local copies on my machine, then upload to server when ready (recommended)

◯ Edit directly on server using local network

Where on your computer do you want to store your files?

iBook HD:Users:craiggrannell:Sites:Snub Communications:

Help   < Back   Next >   Cancel

4. You will now be asked How do you connect to your remote server? Several options are available: None, FTP, Local/Network, WebDAV, and RDS. If you have access to your web hosting space over a network, choose Local/Network, and click the folder icon to then choose the folder your remote (live) files are to be stored in. Most people, however, are likely to use FTP. Your web hosting company will provide you with details to connect via FTP, including the FTP address of your web space (if you have a domain name, you can often just use that), the folder to store your files in, and your FTP username and password. If you are in doubt about any of these details, contact your ISP or hosting company for advice.

When you have the relevant details, type your web space FTP address in the top field, the folder where you store your files in the second field, your username in the field entitled What is your FTP login? and your password in the field entitled What is your FTP password? If your machine is secure and this version of Dreamweaver is only accessible by you and trusted parties, check the Save check box to save your password, so that you don't have to type it in every time you want to connect to the Web.

Once you've added all your details, click Test Connection. If Dreamweaver can successfully connect to your website, a dialog box will say so, as shown here, and you can continue by clicking OK and then Next.

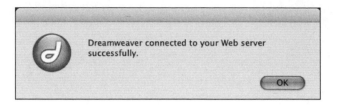

If Dreamweaver cannot connect, you'll see a dialog box like the one below. In such a case, recheck your settings and try again.

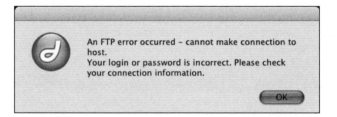

5. The following screen asks whether files should be checked in and out, to stop those working in groups from editing documents at the same time. If you're working alone, check the No option; if you're part of a collaborative team, all working from the same local files, check the Yes option. Once you've made your decision, click Next to continue.

Site Definition for Snub Communications

Basic | Advanced

Site Definition

Editing Files   Testing Files   **Sharing Files, Part 2**

Do you want to enable checking in and checking out files, to ensure that you and your co-workers cannot edit the same file at the same time?

○ Yes, enable check in and check out.

● No, do not enable check in and check out.

Help   < Back   Next >   Cancel

6. The final screen is a summary, showing the details you've configured. If everything's fine, click Done. If you want to make changes, you can either click the < Back buttons until you access the relevant page, or just click Done and then go to Site ➤ Manage Sites to bring up the Manage Sites dialog box, from which you can select your site and then use the Advanced tab to make specific changes. (You can also use this dialog box to duplicate or remove a selected site or export or import a site—handy when moving between computers.)

Manage Sites

Snub Communications

New...
Edit...
Duplicate
Remove
Export...
Import...

Help   Done

The Advanced tab

In order to easily edit site details, you need to use the Advanced tab of the Site Definition dialog box. Although it may look quite complex, the vast majority of users don't need to use most of the options within. Open up the site you just created by selecting it and clicking Edit in the Manage Sites dialog box (Site ➤ Manage Sites). Then select the Advanced tab.

The following image shows the Local Info category. This contains information about the copy of the website that's stored on your hard drive. This information was specified in steps 1–3 of the previous exercise.

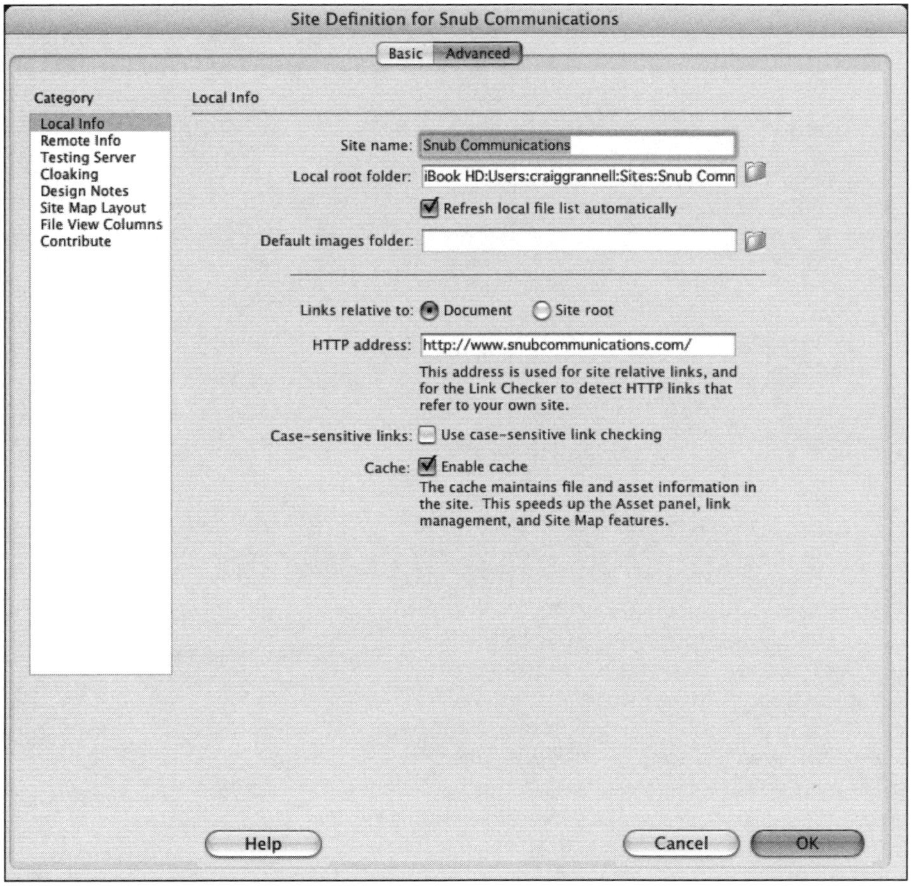

The Remote Info category contains the information defined in step 4 of the exercise. Note that if you have trouble connecting to your web host, you could try checking Use passive FTP and then clicking the Test button. At the foot of this window is the check in/out option defined in step 5 of the exercise, along with an option enabling you to automatically upload files to a server when they are saved. This is perhaps best left unchecked, because you really should test locally before uploading files.

Site Definition for Snub Communications

Basic | Advanced

Category
- Local Info
- Remote Info
- Testing Server
- Cloaking
- Design Notes
- Site Map Layout
- File View Columns
- Contribute

Remote Info

Access: FTP

FTP host: www.snubcommunications.com

Host directory: /public_html/

Login: snubcomweb   Test

Password: •••••• ☑ Save

☐ Use passive FTP

☐ Use firewall   Firewall Settings...

☐ Use Secure FTP (SFTP)

Server Compatibility...

☑ Maintain synchronization information
☐ Automatically upload files to server on save

Check in/out: ☐ Enable file check in and check out

Help   Cancel   OK

The remaining categories enable you to fine-tune your settings further, but they are rarely touched by the majority of designers and aren't required for working through this book.

Editing and uploading files

Although you can use a separate FTP application to upload and download your web pages, Dreamweaver's built-in client is sufficient for basic file management.

The preferences for tweaking Dreamweaver's FTP client are found in the Site category of the application's preferences (accessed via Edit ➤ Preferences on Windows, and Dreamweaver ➤ Preferences on Mac). For some reason, Dreamweaver's default is to put local files on the right side of two-pane file windows, unlike pretty much every FTP application out there, so I set Always show to Left. Other than that, the settings are fine.

The Files panel is the one you use to manage your files, and it's placed by default within the panel group that's typically found at the right of the screen. The panel in its collapsed state is fine for the odd task here and there, but it's awkward for more lengthy edits and for uploading. For such things, it's better to use the expanded version of the panel, which is accessed by clicking the Expand/Collapse button (which is the button furthest to the right, signified by an expanding window icon).

Note that in collapsed mode, the Files panel still enables you to access both local and remote files by way of its view drop-down menu, at the top right. However, for most file management, it's far better to use the panel in expanded mode.

When you expand the Files panel, it becomes a more familiar two-pane interface, as shown in the following image; you can click the Expand/Collapse button to shrink it down again. (I've added a completed website to the local files, in this example, to show you how to work with this panel.)

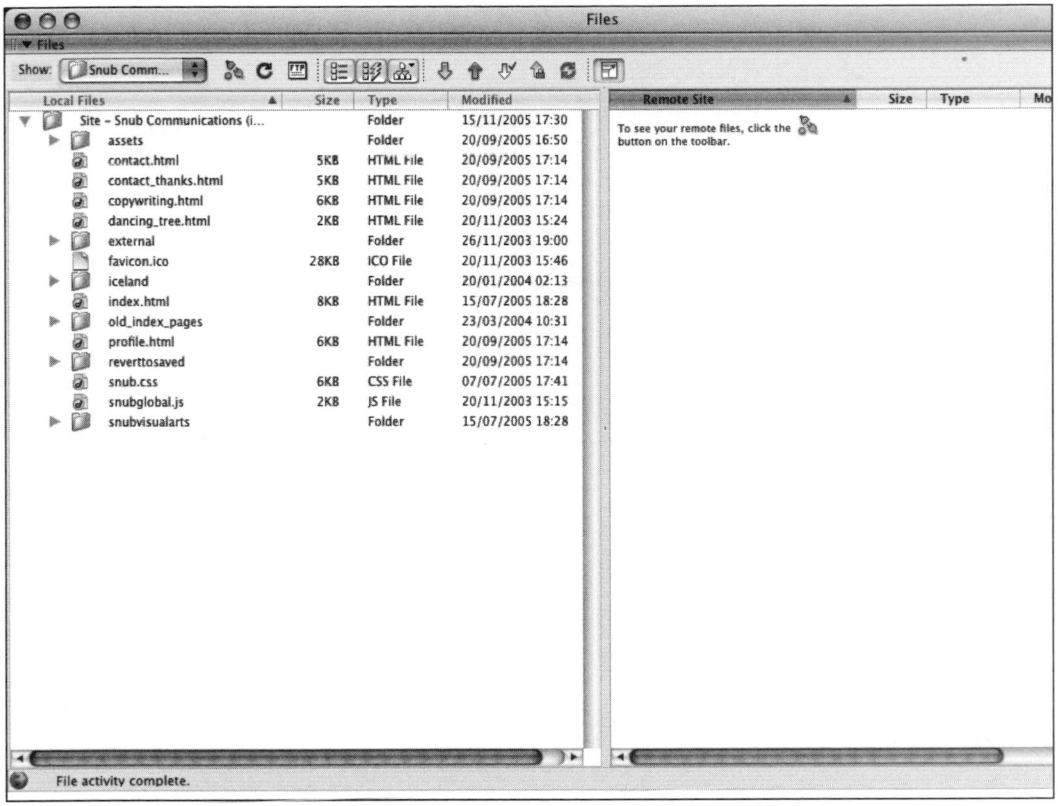

The toolbar across the top of the panel provides you with a number of options. The drop-down menu enables you to access your hard drive or any defined sites. Next to that is the Connects to remote host button, which you use to access the remote web server defined earlier in this chapter. Along from that is the Refresh button (a circular arrow), a button for opening the FTP log (a square icon with FTP written on it), icons to enable you to access your site files, testing server, and site map (which Dreamweaver automatically creates, based on the links it finds in your web pages). The next group includes Get (a green downward-pointing arrow) and Put (a blue upward-pointing arrow) buttons for downloading and uploading, respectively, check in and out buttons for when you're working collaboratively, and a Synchronize button (a double circular arrow), which enables you to synch your local and remote sites in a number of different ways (you can synch a selection or the entire site, and you can synch in either direction, uploading newer files to your server, downloading newer files from your remote server, or both).

When you click the aforementioned Connects to remote host button, you'll see the remote files on your server appear in the right pane (assuming you defined the preferences as I mentioned earlier). To upload files from your local site on your hard drive to your FTP space on your web server, select them and click the Put button. To download files from your web server to your hard drive, select them and click the Get button.

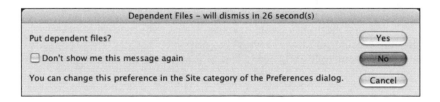

When you first attempt to upload files, Dreamweaver asks whether you want to also upload **dependent files**. Dependent files are files required by the files you're uploading. For instance, if a web page has a number of images and a style sheet attached to it, the images and style sheet would be dependent files. I'm a fan of knowing exactly what I'm uploading, rather than relying on an application to upload dependent files related to a file I'm uploading, so I recommend checking Don't show me this message again and then clicking No. That way, the only things that'll be uploaded are files I've specifically selected.

Once you confirm that you want the files to be uploaded or downloaded, Dreamweaver works away in the background until the changes are completed—Dreamweaver's ability to work in the background is a new feature of the application.

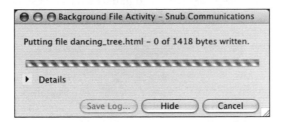

The Files panel isn't just for uploading and downloading—it also enables you to perform edits on files. Its contextual menu (accessed by right-clicking or Ctrl-clicking) enables you to create new files and folders, or to perform numerous actions on a selected item. You can open the selected item in Dreamweaver or a different application if you choose Open With ➤ Browse. The Edit submenu allows you to cut, copy, or paste the file, to delete it, duplicate it, or rename it (saving you from having to use Windows Explorer or Finder to do so). The contextual menu also includes the Preview in Browser command, a Check Links submenu, and an option to reveal the selected item in your operating system's file browser.

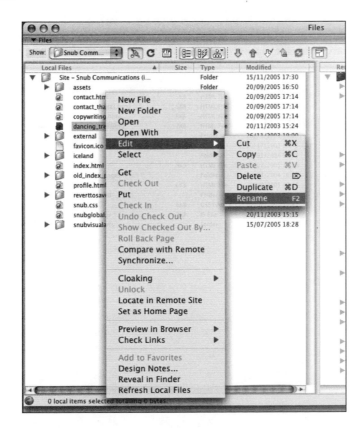

One of the Files panel's best features is its ability to update links. For instance, if you drag a web page into a folder, its place in the website's hierarchy is altered, which means the links on your site may become broken. Dreamweaver realizes this, figures out what pages are affected, and then displays the Update Files dialog box, asking whether you want to update links in these files. Unless you fancy having a site full of broken links after you move a file, click Update!

```
                    Update Files

Update links in the following files?          Update
/iceland/profile.html
/copywriting.html                           Don't Update
/index.html
/contact.html
/contact_thanks.html



                                               Help
```

Summary

In this chapter, you learned how to set up a site and how to work with files in Dreamweaver's Files panel. It's a good idea to experiment with the various options, and with uploading and downloading files, to get comfortable with file management—you'll be doing a lot of this when you start working on a live site.

Speaking of which, the next chapter covers the background you'll need to create web pages—the essential components of web pages and sites, including all the "behind the scenes" elements that are so important when creating successful pages.

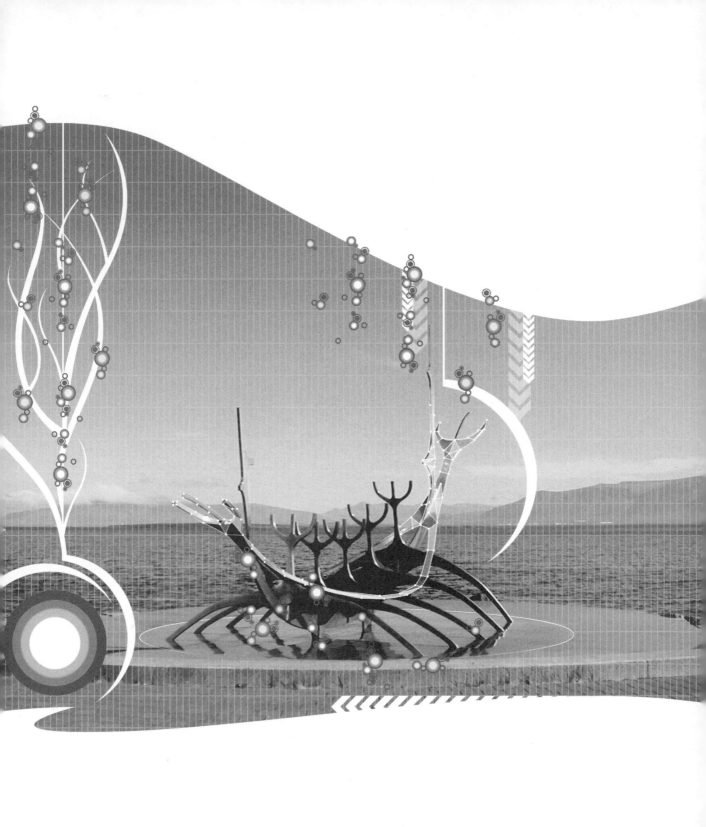

Chapter 4

WEB PAGE ESSENTIALS

In this chapter . . .

- Using different document types
- Defining a default character set
- Setting web page titles
- Adding meta tags and other head elements
- Attaching external documents
- Creating CSS styles
- Adding web page backgrounds
- Adding web page comments

This chapter will teach you everything you need to do with a web page prior to working on the layout and content, including creating the initial documents, attaching external documents to your web pages, dealing with the header (or, in web terms, **head** section of the web page), and so on. Although this isn't dramatic stuff, it's *essential* for any quality web page, as the chapter's title states, even if exciting things aren't happening visually.

Once we're done looking at these largely invisible elements, we'll take a look at Dreamweaver's CSS panel, and at how to create CSS rules—something that is essential for creating good, modern websites. Once you're familiar with Dreamweaver's CSS dialog boxes, we'll use this knowledge to deal with web page defaults, including padding, margins, fonts, and background images. Note that some of the techniques we'll discuss are somewhat modular: for example, the methods used to attach backgrounds to a web page can also be used to attach a background to any web page element (such as divs, tables, headings, or paragraphs)—such is the power of CSS. But before we get into any CSS shenanigans, we'll look at how web pages are formed, and what Dreamweaver offers as its default setup.

Anatomy of a web page

There are essentially two sections of a web page document that a designer has direct control over: the <head> section and the <body> section.

The page's <head> section tends to contain information about the document that is invisible to the person viewing the page, with the exception of the page's title, which is usually displayed at the top of the web browser window. Other elements define things like keywords and descriptions for search-engine results pages, or attach documents to the web page, such as CSS files and scripting documents (such as JavaScript).

The <body> section houses the document's content—in other words, it contains the things displayed in a web browser's display area.

Dreamweaver defaults

Select File ➤ New, and the New Document dialog box appears. Select the Basic page category, and HTML in the second column, and you'll see a Document Type (DTD) drop-down menu at the bottom right of the dialog box. This menu provides you with several choices for the DOCTYPE.

What a DOCTYPE declaration does is tell a web browser what type of HTML code is being used, enabling the browser to interpret the code and lay out the page accordingly. XHTML 1.0 Transitional is Dreamweaver's default option, and this should be suitable for all your projects.

Once you've selected the document type, click Create, and Dreamweaver will create a new document. Click Split at the top of the document window to access Split view, and you should see the following code:

```
<!DOCTYPE html PUBLIC "-//W3C//DTD XHTML 1.0 Transitional//EN" ➡
"http://www.w3.org/TR/xhtml1/DTD/xhtml1-transitional.dtd">
<html xmlns="http://www.w3.org/1999/xhtml">
<head>
<meta http-equiv="content-type" content="text/html; ➡
charset=utf-8" />
<title>Untitled Document</title>
</head>

<body>
</body>
</html>
```

Everything prior to the <html> tag is the DOCTYPE declaration. Next is the <html> start tag, which includes a **namespace** (xmlns="http://www.w3.org/1999/xhtml") that reduces the ambiguity of defined elements in the web page, ensuring browsers interpret elements as XHTML unless otherwise overridden elsewhere in the document.

Next comes the <head> section, which initially includes a <meta> tag and a <title> element.

Defining the document's character set

The <meta> tag defines the content type used in the document. By default, Dreamweaver sets this to ISO-8859-1, sometimes referred to as Latin-1. As I mentioned in Chapter 2, it's possible to change this by accessing the New Document category within Dreamweaver's preferences and selecting a new Default Encoding option. I recommend choosing Unicode UTF-8 (Unicode 4.0 UTF-8 on Mac) because it enables a web page to display a wide range of extended characters without them having to be encoded.

Changing the page's title

By default, each new Dreamweaver web page is called "Untitled Document". Unless you change this, that's what will appear at the top of the web browser window when the page is loaded. Seeing as there are literally tens of thousands of "untitled documents" on the web, I can only assume that many web designers are so keen to get on with designing that they forget to name each of their documents—make sure it's the first thing you do when you create a new document.

Naming a page is simple: after you've opened a new or existing HTML document, type your text into the Title field at the top of the document window and press Enter. If you have Split or Code view open, you should then see the content of the `<title>` element update itself accordingly.

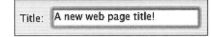

If you're wondering what title you should give your web page, bear in mind that it's usually the most prominent thing returned in search-engine results pages, and it's also relied on by many search engines for indexing. Keep titles clear, concise, and utterly to the point. Use too many words and the title will be clipped; use too few (or try to get "arty" with characters) and you may end up with something that stumps search engines and potential visitors.

Generally speaking, for the home page at least, include the name of the site or organization, followed by an indication of the site's reason for existence (and location, if relevant). For instance: Company - name - service - location, country.

Some designers use the same title throughout their site, but this is a bad idea—web page titles are used as visual indicators by visitors trawling bookmarks or their browser's history. This is why I generally tend to use titles as a form of "breadcrumb navigation," showing where a page sits within the website's hierarchy, so I'd have titles like this:

> Company name - Services - Service name

> Company name - Contact details - Map and directions

> Company name - Products - Product section - Product name

> *Note that you should be mindful of character limits when creating web page titles. Search engines and browser title bars both crop lengthy titles. (For instance, Google only lists the first 65 characters, after which it places ellipsis points.)*

Editing the head section

Because head content is invisible in Design view, and it is full of fairly arcane tags, Dreamweaver offers another way for you to edit existing elements and add new ones. Go to View ➤ Head Content and a toolbar appears with icons that represent existing head area content. If you're using Design view, these appear directly under the Code/Split/Design buttons; if you're using Split view, these appear between the Code and Design views.

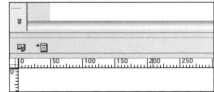

If you click one of these icons, the Properties panel enables you to edit its details.

| | Meta | Attribute | HTTP-equiv | Value | Content-Type |
| | | Content | text/html; charset=UTF-8 | | |

Adding keywords and a description

To add keywords and a description to your web page, select HTML from the Insert bar menu, and click the Head menu. This provides you with a number of useful options that enable you to add head content.

Selecting the Keywords and Description options enables you to add content that may assist search engines in indexing your website. In each case, simply select the option, type your content in the dialog box that appears, and then click OK.

The content for keywords is supposed to be a list of words or short phrases (usually separated by commas) that users might type into a search engine to find your site. Because of abuse (such as websites including thousands of keywords in order to show up in just about any search results), this tag is often ignored by search engines these days. Generally, they now use page content and the number of links to a page to determine its relevance to someone's search term. However, it's still worth adding keywords for those search engines that still use them.

Thirty or fewer words or short terms are sufficient as keywords. You should also use as many unique terms as possible. Generic terms are unlikely to enable anyone to find your website, because hundreds of thousands of other websites may use such keywords.

The contents of the description element are often returned by search engines in the results page, along with the web page's title. As with the title, keep the description succinct, so that it is less likely to get truncated in the results page. Most search engines display a maximum of 200 characters, so 25 well-chosen words are all you can afford.

> To edit the content of the keywords and description, just ensure head content is visible (select View ➤ Head if it's not), click the relevant icon in the toolbar, and then edit the content in the Properties panel.

Adding other meta elements

Although the <meta> elements covered so far are the only ones generally deemed essential, there are a few more that can prove useful when creating websites. These can be added by selecting the Meta option from the Head menu in the Insert bar's HTML section.

When the Meta option is selected, the Meta dialog box appears. The Attribute menu defaults to Name, but can also be set to http-equiv—select one of these and then add the appropriate content to the Value and Content fields. Table 4-1 shows some examples of <meta> elements you can add:

Table 4-1. Examples of <meta> elements

Attribute	Value	Content	What it does
Name	revisit-after	A number of days, e.g., 30 days	Tells a search engine to revisit the site every 30 days, because that's how often the site is likely to be updated.
Name	Robots	Possible values are all, index, noindex, follow, nofollow	Determines whether automated search engine robots are allowed to access a page and follow its links or not. The all value enables robots to do both. Use of index and nofollow would allow the page to be indexed, but the links not to be followed. The use of noindex and follow would stop the page from being indexed but allow links to be followed. And so on. Note that when multiple values are used, they should be separated by a comma.
Name	Author	The name and URL of the author	Declares the author's name and details, but it is of little use other than that.
http-equiv	imagetoolbar	False	Disables Internet Explorer's image toolbar.
http-equiv	Pragma	no-cache	Stops a browser from locally caching a document, regardless of the browser's settings.

Some <meta> elements should be used with care. While the Internet Explorer image toolbar is annoying, disabling it is interfering with the browser's default behavior without the user's consent, despite there being an option to turn off this feature should the user not like it. Also, the pragma *setting should only be used on pages that are regularly updated (such as news pages) and not for every page on your site—otherwise you may find users having to download each page on your site every time they access it, thereby making the site appear sluggish.*

Attaching JavaScript documents

Although JavaScript can be embedded directly in the head section of a web page, it makes far more sense to use an external document. By doing so, you can create and manage one or more scripts that are housed in a single file but that can be attached to as many pages on your site as you wish. JavaScript won't feature heavily in this book, but we will be making occasional use of it, in order to provide some additional functionality to our web pages. Therefore, you need to know how to create a blank JavaScript document, and how to attach a JavaScript document to a web page.

Creating a new JavaScript document is simply a case of going to File ➤ New, selecting the Basic page category, selecting JavaScript from the list shown, and then clicking the Create button. JavaScript files should be saved with the .js file extension. (Dreamweaver adds this by default when you attempt to save such a document.)

To attach a JavaScript document to a web page, click the Head Content toolbar (found above Design view; select View ➤ Head Content if this toolbar isn't visible), then click the Script button in the HTML section of the Insert bar, and click the folder icon next to the Source field to browse to and select your file. In Code view, the <script> element will appear before the </head> tag.

Attaching CSS files

A blank CSS document is created like any other document—go to File ➤ New, select Basic page and CSS, and then click Create.

The dialog box required to attach a style sheet is accessed by clicking the Attach Style Sheet button, found at the bottom of the CSS Styles panel (although you can also choose Attach Style Sheet from the panel's options menu).

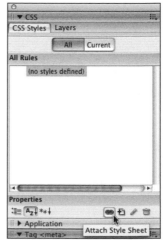

When the button is clicked, the Attach External Style Sheet dialog box appears.

The Browse button enables you to navigate to and select your CSS file.

Underneath are two Add as options: Link and Import. The first of those specifies a relationship between the document you're working on and the document it's being linked to. The problem in using Link for a general style sheet that contains CSS styles for displaying pages is that the link method is understood by even obsolete browsers that cannot render CSS. By comparison, the import method is only understood by more modern browsers. Choosing Import essentially "hides" the CSS from obsolete browsers, meaning they can access the content, but won't display garbled layouts from trying to deal with CSS that wasn't in common use when the browser was created. Therefore, choose Import.

The Media field is new to Dreamweaver 8, and it enables you to target a style sheet at specific media types—a specific type can be selected by using the drop-down menu, or you can manually type a comma-separated list of types. For screen-based styles, Screen is the option to choose.

Once your options have been defined, click OK to attach your style sheet.

Generally speaking, any version 5 (or later) browser from Microsoft or Opera will be able to deal with most CSS in this book satisfactorily. (When this isn't the case, I'll show some cunning CSS hacks for dealing with browser bugs.) Furthermore, version 6 (and above) of Netscape, version 1.0 of Mozilla, and all final releases of Firefox and Safari can deal with CSS well enough. When I refer to "obsolete" browsers, I'm talking about the likes of Netscape 4 and Internet Explorer 4—browsers that are still very occasionally used, but that are no longer in common use. While it's important to ensure that all web users can access the content of your site, the visual design isn't essential—after all, there's little point in compromising the entire site for a minute portion of the users. That's why I recommend hiding the CSS from obsolete browsers.

Understanding CSS

Understanding how to work with CSS in Dreamweaver is fundamental to creating good, modern websites. In this section, I'll first provide an overview of CSS rules and selector types, and then I'll show how to create a new style, how to edit an existing style, and how to apply a style to elements on a web page. Terminology and methods outlined here will be referred to again and again, later in the book, so please ensure that you understand everything in this section before tackling later chapters in the book.

When working with Dreamweaver, it's unlikely that you'll have to write many (or even any) CSS rules yourself. However, when you add a CSS rule to your style sheet, Dreamweaver needs to know what element to apply it to and what type of CSS rule you want to create. Therefore, it's essential that you understand the difference between a tag selector, a class selector, an ID selector, and so on. These types are outlined in the following sections.

The rules of CSS

Style sheets consist of a number of rules that define how various web page elements should be displayed. Although sometimes bewildering to newcomers, CSS rules are simple to understand. Each rule consists of a **selector** and a **declaration**. The selector begins a CSS rule and specifies which part of the HTML document the rule will be applied to. The declaration consists of a number of property/value pairs that set specific properties and determine how the relevant element will look. In the following example, p is the selector and everything thereafter is the declaration:

```
p {
color: #000000;
font-weight: bold;
}
```

As you probably know, <p> is the HTML tag for a paragraph, hence the use of p for the selector used to create a CSS rule to style paragraphs. Therefore, if we attach this rule to a web page, the declaration will be applied to any HTML marked up as a paragraph, thereby setting the color of said paragraphs to #000000 (which is black in hex) and making them bold.

By hex, I'm referring to hexadecimal notation, a numbering system that has 16, rather than 10, as its base. Digits range from 0 to F, with 0 to 9 representing the same values as normal numbers, and the letters A to F representing 10 to 15. Letters can be in upper- or lowercase when working in hex. Although it's possible to use other systems to set color values in web design (there are 17 recognized keywords, and you can also use bracketed RGB values), the vast majority of web designers use hex, so it's what is used throughout this book.

When writing CSS rules, the declaration is placed within curly brackets {}, and this is how rules look in Dreamweaver's Code view. Properties and values are separated by a colon (:), and property/value pairs are terminated by a semicolon (;). Technically, you don't have to include the final semicolon in a CSS rule, but most designers consider it good practice to do so, and Dreamweaver does this by default. This makes sense—you may add property/value pairs to a rule at a later date, and if the semicolon is already there, you don't have to remember to add it.

Tag selectors

In the previous example, we used the most basic style of selector, known in Dreamweaver as a **tag selector** (sometimes also referred to as an **element selector**). This defines the visual appearance of the relevant HTML element. In the sections that follow, we'll examine some other types of CSS selectors: class, ID, grouped, and contextual selectors.

Class selectors

Class selectors are used to modify an element or a group of elements. For instance, you may create a class whose property/value settings set the color to red. This class could then be applied to several paragraphs on the same page, or just to a small section of text within a paragraph.

A class selector in Code view may look something like this:

```
.red {
color: red;
}
```

ID selectors

ID selectors can be used only once on each Web page. In Dreamweaver, these are added using the Advanced selector type option in the New CSS Style dialog box. Generally speaking, it's common to apply unique identifiers to things like major page sections (navigation, content area, and so on), as in the following example, which would style a web page element (such as a div) with an ID value of "masthead" to be 700 pixels wide and 50 high.

```
#masthead {
width: 700px;
height: 50px;
}
```

> Class selectors can be used multiple times on a web page, but ID selectors cannot. Typically, IDs are used to define one-off page elements, such as structural divisions, whereas classes are used to define a style for multiple items.

Grouped selectors

Should you wish to set a property value for a number of different selectors, you can use grouped selectors, which take the form of a comma-separated list. For instance, the selector to define a style for several levels of headings may look like this: h1, h2, h3, h4, h5, h6 and a rule may look like this:

```
h1, h2, h3, h4, h5, h6 {
font-family: Arial, Helvetica, sans-serif
}
```

Note that grouped selectors needn't all be tag selectors—you can group tag selectors, class selectors, ID selectors, contextual selectors (discussed next), or any combination of these. Here's an example:

```
p, #masthead, .whiteBackground {
background-color: #ffffff;
}
```

It's also worth noting that CSS enables you to style an element more than once. Therefore, you can style common properties using a grouped selector and then style element-specific properties using a stand-alone selector. However, when doing so you need to be aware of the cascade, discussed shortly.

```
/* rule for all headings */
h1, h2, h3, h4, h5, h6 {
font-family: Arial, Helvetica, sans-serif
color: #000000;
}

/* over-ride rule for level-six headings only */
h6 {
color: #555555;
}
```

In Dreamweaver, grouped selectors are added by using the Advanced selector type in the New CSS Style dialog box.

> Note that some of the preceding code shows CSS comments, which are added /* like this */.

Contextual selectors

Contextual selectors style elements depending on context. This is handy when you need to style an element in one area of your web page, but don't want that style to affect the same element when used elsewhere. For instance, it's common to have navigation bar links styled very differently from links elsewhere on the web page. If the navigation links are housed within an HTML div element that has a unique ID of "navigation", you can use the contextual selector #navigation a to style links within that div. Links elsewhere on the page will not be affected. Here's an example:

```
/* rule for navigation links only */
#navigation a {
font-size: 80%;
color: #222222;
text-decoration: none;
}
```

By working with contextual selectors, it's possible to get very specific with regard to styling things on your website, and I'll be using these selectors regularly. In Dreamweaver, contextual selectors are added using the Advanced selector type in the New CSS Style dialog box.

> There are some other types of selectors used for specific tasks. These will be covered when we come to them later in the book.

The cascade

It's possible to define the rule for a given element multiple times: you can do so in a single style sheet, and several style sheets can be attached to a single HTML document. It's also possible to create inline styles and directly apply them to a tag on a web page. The **cascade** is a way of dealing with conflicts, and its simple rule is this: *The value closest to the element in question is the one that is applied.*

In Dreamweaver terms, this means the style applied last is the one that's used. It's good to have at least some understanding of how CSS code works, because sometimes you may need to reorder elements to avoid later rules overruling earlier ones.

Also note that CSS uses the concept of **inheritance**. A document's HTML elements form a strict hierarchy, beginning with <html>, then branching into <head> and <body>, each of which has numerous descendant elements (such as <title> and <meta> for <head> and <p>, and <img> for <body>). When a style is applied to an element, its descendants—those elements nested within it—often (although not always) take on the parent element's CSS property values, unless a more specific style has been applied. In other words, apply a font to the <body> tag, and all text on the page will use the same font unless otherwise overridden by another rule that's "closer" to the elements in question.

> *For more information on working directly with CSS, check out* Web Designer's Reference *by Craig Grannell (friends of ED, ISBN: 1590594304) and* Web Standards Solutions *by Dan Cederholm (friends of ED, ISBN: 1590593812).*

Working with CSS

As I've already mentioned, CSS workflow in Dreamweaver 8 is now almost entirely centered around the CSS Styles panel. At the bottom of the panel is a toolbar with a number of icons. Of the four to the right, the first, Attach Style Sheet, was looked at in the "Attaching CSS files" section earlier in this chapter. The second, New CSS Rule, opens the dialog box you use to create a new CSS rule, while the third, Edit Style, enables you to edit an existing style. The final icon deletes a CSS property.

Creating and editing a CSS style

This section will take you through the steps of creating and editing CSS styles. To start with, create a new HTML document and save it as creating_and_editing_css.html. Then create a new CSS document, save it as creating_and_editing_css.css, and attach it to the web page.

To create a CSS style, ensure that the HTML document is the active document, and then click the New CSS Rule button. The New CSS Rule dialog box will appear.

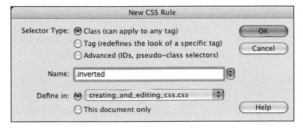

The Define in options enable you to specify whether the rule for the style you're about to create should be defined in the current document only or in an external file. It's a bad idea to define CSS in the current document only—much of the power of CSS comes from its ability to style an entire site (and manage those styles) by using a single, external document. If you start adding styles to individual documents, managing them becomes much harder, and consistency tends to be lost. Therefore, always choose your CSS document for the Define in option.

Which Selector Type option you should choose depends on the element or elements you're intending to style. The "Understanding CSS" section earlier in this chapter provided an overview of the various selector types and their uses. For now, select Class, which enables you to define a class that can be applied to multiple elements on the page.

In the Name field, type .inverted. Click OK to continue.

> *Classes require a period before the class name, so don't forget to include one, or your style won't work.*

The CSS Rule Definition dialog box should then appear, with the name of your style and the location where it's to be defined in the title bar. Select a category in the Category list, and you can set values for related properties. It's a good idea to familiarize yourself with which properties are found in each category.

For now, select Type from the Category list. This category, unsurprisingly, has options to do with typography. Use the Color pop-up color picker to select white (which should then insert #FFFFFF—the hex value for white—in the Color field).

Next, select the Background category, and select black from the pop-up color picker next to Background color (when you do so, #000000 will appear in the Background color field). Click OK to close the dialog box. You've just created a style rule.

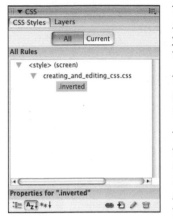

To view your style rule, click the All button in the CSS Styles panel, and in the All Rules area you'll see a collapsible list. Open <style> and the CSS list, and you'll see the rule you just created. Select the rule, and you'll see its properties in the Properties section of the CSS Styles panel.

To edit a style, select it and then use the Properties section of the CSS Styles panel to add or change values by clicking the area to the right of the relevant property and choosing a new value.

The three icons at the bottom left of the CSS Styles panel provide you with three ways of viewing your CSS styles. The first, Show category view, creates a collapsible list view, where properties are grouped into related fields (Font, Background, Block, and so on). The second, Show list view, offers a straight A–Z list of properties, while the third, Show only set properties, does exactly what you'd expect—it restricts the properties displayed in the Properties section of the CSS Styles panel to only those that you've already set a value for.

If you find the CSS Styles panel restrictive or difficult to work with, even with all these viewing options, you can return to the CSS Rule Definition dialog box by selecting a rule in the CSS Styles panel and clicking the Edit Style button. (This assumes that you have When double-clicking in CSS panel set to Edit using CSS dialog in the CSS Styles category of Dreamweaver's preferences.)

Applying a style

There are several ways to apply a style to elements in a web page. In Design view, type a few lines of dummy text to represent a few paragraphs, and we'll look at the different methods.

Click anywhere inside one of the paragraphs of text, and then click the Style drop-down menu in the Properties panel—you should see the style you created earlier (along with a basic preview of the style). To apply the style to the selected element, just choose the style from the Style menu. In this case, the paragraph of text should have inverted colors (white on black).

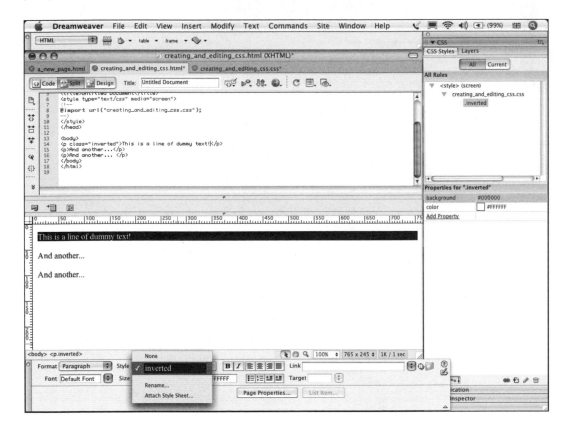

Alternatively, you can click inside the element you want to apply the style to and then select the relevant tag from the toolbar at the bottom of the document window. In this case, click inside one of the paragraphs and then Ctrl-click or right-click <p>, select Set Class, and choose the style from the submenu.

Similarly, it's possible to use Dreamweaver's context menu to choose a CSS style. Ctrl-click or right-click on the element you want to style, and select your style from the CSS Styles submenu).

> *Dreamweaver's context menus are extremely useful time-saving devices.*
> *Get used to using them, in order to speed up your work.*

Classes needn't be applied to entire elements, though. You can also select just a word or two—or even a single character—and apply the style to just that selection.

If you look in Code view, you'll see that class="inverted" has been added to the start tags of the elements the style was applied to, and if you applied the style to just a few words, they are now wrapped in a <span> element.

To view the CSS associated with any element, select that element and click the CSS button in the Properties panel.

This opens the Current section in the CSS Styles panel, summarizing the properties associated with the selected item. (If the Current section is already displayed, the CSS button will be grayed out in the Properties panel.) Double-clicking any of the property/value lines in the Summary area opens the CSS Rule Definition dialog box, enabling you to edit the relevant rule.

Setting default margins for a web page

Before working on a web page's internal layout, you first need to set some page defaults. We've already created a blank HTML document, attached a CSS file to it, and added some content to the web page. If you look at the content in Design view, you can see a margin of blank space around the edge of the content, and this is also the case when previewing the page in a web browser. The margin has the potential to throw out carefully planned layouts, because the margin size varies among browsers. Therefore, we need to get rid of it.

To remove margins, access the New CSS Rule dialog box (see the earlier "Creating and editing a CSS style" section if you don't remember how). Select Tag as the Selector Type, and choose body from the Tag pop-up menu (or just type body into the field yourself). Ensure Define in is set to your style sheet, and click OK.

In the CSS Rule Definition dialog box, select the Box category. The section on the right will then show properties that deal with an element's box.

> When working on web design, you need to be aware that every element is effectively housed inside its own box. This box's dimensions (height and width) can be set, as can the padding and margin values at each edge of the box.

Ensure Same for all is checked under both Padding and Margin, and then type 0 in each of the Top fields, as shown. Because Same for all has been checked in both cases, the value placed in the Top field is then applied to all other edges of the box (which Dreamweaver shows on screen in grayed-out fashion). Click OK and you should see the margins disappear in Design view.

This is the first CSS rule you should add for every web page you work on. Should you later decide that you need to change the padding or margin values, you can do so by editing the rule as explained earlier in the chapter. If the CSS file is attached to all of your web pages, any such amendment will be applied site-wide.

Adding backgrounds to web pages

While we're covering web page defaults, it makes sense to look at web page backgrounds. Although such things used to be commonplace, they became unpopular once designers figured out that visitors to web pages didn't like them. With text being hard to read on screen as it is, it's adding insult to injury to inflict some nasty paisley mosaic background (or worse) on the poor reader, too.

But, as affordable monitors continue to increase in size and resolution, designers face a conundrum. If they're creating a liquid design that stretches to fit the browser window, text can become unreadable in wide windows, because the eye finds it easier to scan text in narrow columns. And if they're creating a fixed-width design, large areas of the screen can end up blank. It's for this fixed-width design style that backgrounds can be useful, both in drawing the eye to the content and providing some visual interest outside the content area.

Like most things related to design, the use and style of backgrounds is subjective, but some rules are worth bearing in mind. The most obvious is that a background should not distract from your content. If you're using images, keep them simple, and when you're using color, keep contrast and saturation fairly low. Unless you're using a subtle watermark, it's bad form to put images underneath text—the relatively low resolution of computer monitors means it will be harder to read than a printed equivalent. Also, because backgrounds are not main site content, loading times should be kept as low as possible.

Using CSS to add backgrounds to web pages

To add backgrounds to a web page, you apply styles to the body tag, primarily by using properties found within the Background category of the CSS Rule Definition dialog box. The options work as follows:

- Background color: This sets a background color for the web page. You can use the pop-up color picker to select a color, or type a hex value into the adjacent field. Remember that if you type a hex value, it must be preceded by a hash sign (#).

- Background image: Use the Browse button to select an image for the background.

- Repeat: If you omit a value in this field (or select repeat from the drop-down list), the background image will tile indefinitely. This is only acceptable if you have created an interlocking pattern. Tiling and repeating photographs or other individual design elements will drive a reader batty. The repeat-x and repeat-y values restrict tiling to horizontal and vertical respectively. The no-repeat value sets the background to not repeat at all—in other words, it displays the chosen background image once only.

- Attachment: This property has two values: scroll and fixed. The default is scroll, which means the background works as normal, scrolling with the rest of the page. If fixed is used, the background image remains stationary while the rest of the page scrolls.

- Horizontal position: Entering a value (a percentage or a pixel value) defines the horizontal origin point of the background image. The keyword values left, center, and right are also available, and they set the background's horizontal position to the left, center, or right of the browser window respectively.

- Vertical position: Entering a value (a percentage or a pixel value) defines the vertical origin point of the background image. The keyword values top, center, and bottom are also available, and they set the background's vertical position to the top, center, and bottom of the browser window respectively.

> *Keywords should not be mixed with other values, but it is acceptable to mix percentages and pixel sizes (so you could have* 50% *for the horizontal position and* 100 pixels *for the vertical position, but you should avoid* center *for the horizontal position and* 100 pixels *for the vertical position). This shouldn't really cause a problem, because keyword positioning can be emulated with numbers anyway—for instance,* left, top *is the same as* 0, 0.

```
CSS Rule Definition for body in setting_default_margins.css

Category              Background
  Type
  Background            Background color:  [ ]  [              ]
  Block
  Box                   Background image:  [              ] [≑] ( Browse... )
  Border
  List                          Repeat:  [        ] [≑]
  Positioning
  Extensions               Attachment:  [        ] [≑]

                    Horizontal position:  [        ] [≑] ( pixels [≑] )

                      Vertical position:  [        ] [≑] ( pixels [≑] )


  ( Help )                                    ( Apply )  ( Cancel )  ( OK )
```

Remember that techniques in CSS often work on any element. Therefore, the background techniques mentioned here actually work for applying a background to any web page element, including divs, tables, paragraphs, and headings.

Creating Web page backgrounds

This section of the chapter will show you how to create a few different web page backgrounds that you can adapt for use on your own websites. We'll look at how to use tiled background images to create striped backgrounds and pages with drop shadows, and how to use a couple of GIF images to add subtle watermarks to your web pages.

There are some files you can download from the friends of ED website (www.friendsofed.com) for this section. They are all within the Chapter 4 folder:

- backgrounds folder: This contains a number of graphics that can be used in the examples in this section.
- backgrounds_blank.html: This is a web page that contains a single div element populated with some paragraphs. If you click within the div in Design view, you'll see from the document toolbar that it has an ID value of content (this is shown as <div#content>).
- backgrounds.css: This is a blank CSS document that's been attached to the web page.

> dolor. In eget metus. Praesent at augue in diam
> ultricies eget, neque. Lorem ipsum dolor sit am
>
> Pellentesque rutrum fringilla orci. Praesent ege
>
> `<body> <div#content> <p>`

Before we start adding backgrounds, the web page needs some basic styles.

First, create a body rule, as shown earlier in the "Setting default margins for a web page" section. In the Box category of the CSS Rule Definition dialog box, set the Padding and Margin values to 0.

Next, create a new rule: access the New CSS Rule dialog box, choose Tag as the Selector Type and p as the Tag. Click OK.

In the CSS Rule Definition dialog box, choose the Box category. Deselect Same for all under Margin, and type 0 into the Top field. Click OK.

What this does is set the top margin of the paragraph element to zero, which ensures that no extra padding is placed at the top of the content. Text elements in HTML tend to come with default margins, which vary from browser to browser, and these margins can—and often should—be overridden by using CSS. (There will be more about styling text in Chapter 5.)

Now create another new CSS rule, but this time select Advanced as the Selector Type. Here, we're going to be styling the div that has an ID value of content. You may remember that when we styled the class, the selector name had to be preceded by a period. ID selectors also require a character prior to the name, and the character used is a hash sign (#). Therefore, to create a rule to style our div with an ID value of content, we need to type #content in the Selector field. Once you've done that, click OK.

In the CSS Rule Definition dialog box, select the Background category and then choose white for the Background color (#ffffff is hex for white, and you can just type the value yourself).

In the Box category, set Width to 500 pixels, thereby restricting the content div's width. Set Padding to 10 pixels, thereby ensuring the content div's content won't hug its edges. Deselect Same for all under Margin, and set Top and Bottom to 0 and Left and Right to auto. This removes the top and bottom margins, but sets the left and right ones to auto, which automatically places the div centrally in the browser window regardless of the browser window's width. Click OK.

Version 5 of Internet Explorer for Windows doesn't correctly deal with the auto *value when it's applied in this way. You can get around this by setting* Text align *in the* Block *category to* center *in the* body *rule, and* Text align *to* left *in the* #content *rule. This is something of a hack, albeit a widely used one.*

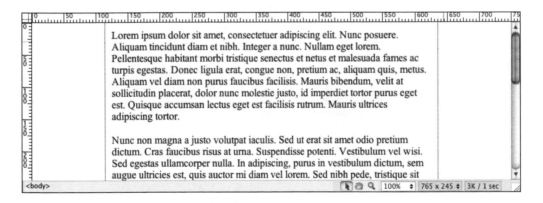

Select File ➤ Save All to ensure all your files are saved before proceeding. Your page should look something like this now:

Striped background tiles

In order to add a background to the web page, you need to edit the body rule. As you may recall, you access rules by opening the CSS Styles panel and double-clicking the rule's selector name.

This opens the now-familiar CSS Rule Definition dialog box. Click the Background category, and use the Browse button to choose striped_background.gif from the backgrounds folder you copied from the friends of ED site.

Select File ➤ Save All to save your files. In Design view (or when previewing the page in a web browser), you should now see the background applied.

Drop shadows

Now let's apply a background that leaves the page content area white, but that casts a drop shadow on a striped background. To achieve this, we'll use the drop_shadow.gif image. If you open this file in an image editor, you'll see that the image has a white center section with drop shadows on either side, and underneath there's a striped background. The image is wider than a typical monitor resolution, in order for the background not to run out on larger monitors.

To apply the background, edit the body rule. Change the background image to drop_shadow.gif and then set Horizontal position in the CSS Rule Definition dialog box to 50%. This horizontally centers the background image, ensuring that the white portion appears behind the content div and that the drop shadows in the image appear just to the sides of the content area.

Click OK, and you should see the background applied to your page in Design view.

Applying watermarks

In this final example of web page backgrounds, the page will be left-aligned instead of centered, a graphic will be applied to the background to the right of the content area, and a subtle watermark will be applied to the content area itself. Obviously, this requires a few more changes than for the drop shadows.

First, we'll deal with the content div. Double-click #content in the CSS Styles panel to access the #content rule that styles the content div. Click the Box category, and check the Same for all check box under Margin. This should set all the margin values to 0, so when you click Apply, you should see the content div become left-aligned instead of centered (assuming you can see enough of Design view behind the CSS Rule Definition dialog box).

Next, in the Background category, set Background image to background_watermark.gif (from the backgrounds folder), set Repeat to no-repeat, and set both Horizontal position and Vertical position to 20 pixels. Click OK and you should see a subtle, gray watermark behind the text in the content area, offset from both edges by 20 pixels.

Next, the body element's background needs updating for the new design. Access the body rule and in the Background category change the Background image value to the background_star.gif file (again, from the backgrounds folder). Set Repeat to no-repeat, Horizontal position to 520 pixels, Vertical position to 0, and Background color to #8b8b8b.

When you check out Design view, you should see a quarter star on the background, to the right of the content area.

The Repeat setting is set to no-repeat because we don't want the image to tile. The background's horizontal and vertical positions are set to 520 pixels and 0 to correctly position it on the screen: the 0 vertical setting means it hugs the top of the browser window (the default would otherwise vertically center the image), while the 520 pixels horizontal setting means the image is placed 520 pixels from the left of the window. This is because we earlier defined the content area as 500 pixels wide with 10 pixels of padding: 500 + 10 + 10 = 520.

In CSS, each element is considered to be a rectangular box that is surrounded by padding, borders, and margins. The rules for how these are described—referred to as the CSS box model—explicitly state that padding should be added to the outside of a box's defined dimensions. In other words, if you set the width of an element to 500 pixels and then add 10 pixels of padding, it ends up taking 520 pixels of space in width (10 + 500 + 10). Internet Explorer 5 and 5.5 for Windows (but not Internet Explorer 6) get this wrong, instead placing padding inside the defined dimensions. This means sites with fixed-width elements and padding on those elements may not display as intended in that browser. You can use various hacks to deal with such problems; the most common of these is Tantek Çelik's box model hack, which is introduced in the next chapter.

Adding comments

If you're working on a project that someone else may have to edit at a later date, or creating something new where you need to remind yourself of what's going on at various points on the page, you need to make use of HTML comments. These are invisible to the end user viewing your site, but they can be accessed by looking at a page's source code (Code view in Dreamweaver, or via a browser's view-source command).

Comments can be added by selecting a point in Design or Code view where you want the comment to be inserted, and clicking the Comment button in the Common section of the Insert bar.

This brings up the Comment dialog box. Enter your comment, and click OK to add it to your page.

In Code view, comments look like this:

```
<!-- This is a comment -->
```

In Design view, they remain invisible unless you check the Comments check box in the Invisible Elements category of Dreamweaver's preferences, and then ensure that View ➤ Visual Aids ➤ Invisible Elements is checked.

Preferences

Category | Invisible Elements

General
Accessibility
Code Coloring
Code Format
Code Hints
Code Rewriting
Copy/Paste
CSS Styles
File Compare
File Types / Editors
Fonts
Highlighting
Invisible Elements
Layers
Layout Mode
New Document
Preview in Browser
Site
Status Bar
Validator

Show: ☑ Named anchors
☐ Scripts
☑ Comments
☐ Line breaks
☐ Client-Side image maps
☑ Embedded styles
☑ Hidden form fields
☑ Form delimiter
☐ Anchor points for layers
☐ Anchor points for aligned elements
☑ Visual Server Markup Tags (ASP, CFML, ...)
☐ Nonvisual Server Markup Tags (ASP, CFML, ...)
☐ CSS display: none

Show dynamic text as: {Recordset.Field}

Server-Side includes: ☑ Show Contents of Included File

Help   Cancel   OK

When comments are turned on in this way, they appear in Design view. Selecting a comment then enables you to edit its content in the Properties panel. Note, however, that when comments are visible in Design view, the flow of the document is amended to accommodate them, and the display is therefore a little less accurate at representing the final result—after all, comments aren't displayed in a browser.

| 0 | 50 | 100 | 150 | 200 | 250 | 300 | 350 | 400 | 450 | 500 | 550 | 600 | 650 | 700 | 75 |

Lorem ipsum dolor sit amet, consectetuer adipiscing elit. Nunc posuere. Aliquam tincidunt diam et nibh. Integer a nunc. Nullam eget lorem. Pellentesque habitant morbi tristique senectus et netus et malesuada fames ac turpis egestas. Donec ligula erat, congue non, pretium ac, aliquam quis, metus. Aliquam vel diam non purus faucibus facilisis. Mauris bibendum, velit at ⬚ sollicitudin placerat, dolor nunc molestie justo, id imperdiet tortor purus eget est. Quisque accumsan lectus eget est facilisis rutrum. Mauris ultrices adipiscing tortor.

Nunc non magna a justo volutpat iaculis. Sed ut erat sit amet odio pretium dictum. Cras faucibus risus at urna. Suspendisse potenti. Vestibulum vel wisi. Sed egestas ullamcorper nulla. In adipiscing, purus in vestibulum dictum, sem augue ultricies est, quis auctor mi diam vel lorem. Sed nibh pede, tristique sit amet, dignissim vitae, pulvinar eu, dolor. In eget metus. Praesent at augue in diam faucibus bibendum. Ut massa ante, consequat ut, aliquet eget, ultricies eget, neque. Lorem ipsum dolor sit amet, consectetuer adipiscing elit. Aenean lacinia mattis purus.

Pellentesque rutrum fringilla orci. Praesent eget sem nec felis ultricies dictum. Donec sapien. Nullam commodo

`<body> <div#content> <p>`   100%   765 x 245   3K / 1 sec

Along with enabling you to document portions of your work, comments can also be used to temporarily disable areas of code. To do this, access Code view and surround the code you want to disable with comment tags.

If you're working in Code view, you can also use the Coding toolbar's Apply Comment button to add a comment to your code.

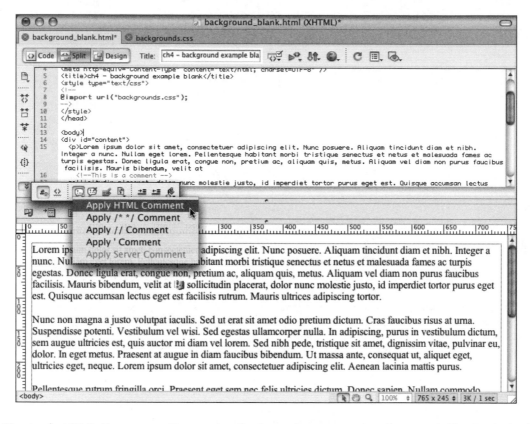

The Apply HTML Comment option creates the type of comment already covered. The Apply /* */ Comment option is for adding comments to CSS documents or multi-line JavaScript and PHP comments. The Apply // Comment option is for adding single-line comments to JavaScript or PHP files, while the Apply ' Comment option is for adding comments to VBScript documents.

> *In addition to explaining the code, comments in CSS documents are useful for splitting the document into sections for ease of editing later on. For instance, you could add /* navigation */ before your rules that deal with navigation styles.*

Adding Design Notes

Dreamweaver's Design Notes feature is primarily intended for those people working in a collaborative environment, enabling you to leave notes for colleagues. To ensure Design Notes is active for a particular site, go to Site ➤ Manage Sites, select the relevant site, and click Edit. Select the Advanced tab in the Site Definition dialog box, click the Design Notes category, and ensure that Maintain Design Notes is checked.

Site Definition for Snub Communications

Basic   Advanced

Category

Local Info
Remote Info
Testing Server
Cloaking
Design Notes
Site Map Layout
File View Columns
Contribute

Design Notes

Design notes: ☑ Maintain Design Notes   Clean Up...

Design Notes let you add, edit, and share extra information associated with a file, such as comments on its status or the name of its original source file.

Dreamweaver also uses Design Notes for integration with Fireworks and Flash.

☐ Upload Design Notes for sharing

This option lets you share Design Notes and File View columns with others working on the site.

Help   Cancel   OK

Adding a design note to a file is a simple process: right-click or Ctrl-click a file in the Files panel, and select Design Notes. This brings up the Design Notes dialog box. On the Basic info tab, you can assign a status to the file by using the Status drop-down menu, and you can add notes using the Notes field. Clicking the small calendar icon adds the current date to that field. If you check Show when file is opened, the Design Notes dialog box will appear as soon as the file is opened.

The All info tab enables you to fine-tune the information for a file, adding specific key/value pairs. You could, for instance, add Author in the Name field, which is used to define the key's name, and your name in the Value field, which is used to define the key's value.

> *While Design Notes is primarily used by those working in collaborative environments, it can still be of use to the solo Dreamweaver user, enabling you to leave notes for yourself inside the application itself, rather than on easy-to-lose scraps of paper.*

Summary

In this chapter, you've taken a big step towards working using modern methods. Along with learning how to set up web page defaults, including a number of extremely important elements that many web designers wrongly ignore, you should now be familiar with the workings of CSS and be able to create and edit CSS rules. Make sure you're familiar with the sections on creating and editing CSS styles from this chapter, because this book returns to the same dialog boxes numerous times in the chapters that follow.

Next, we're going to continue working with web page content, concentrating on web page text.

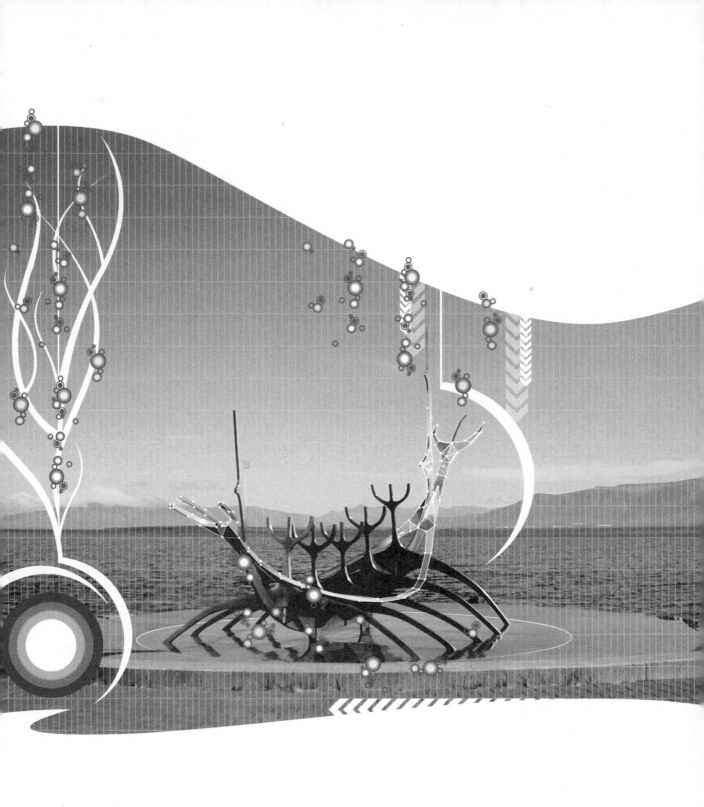

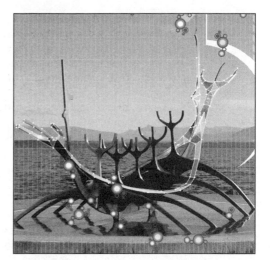

Chapter 5

WORKING WITH TEXT

In this chapter . . .

- Creating and styling text
- Setting advanced text properties
- Creating and styling lists
- Creating drop caps and pull quotes
- Understanding text differences between Mac and Windows

Unless you're creating a very image-heavy website, it's likely that most of your content will be text. One of the things you need to do when working on text for websites (especially if you're coming from designing for other media) is unlearn a lot of whatever you already know. Text on the Web works very differently from text in other media, due to the way that it is displayed and the limitations of the medium itself. However, in recent years, text styling has improved by leaps and bounds—whereas in the 1990s, you had to struggle for site-wide consistency by slavishly applying the exact same style values to every relevant element on your site, now you can use CSS to style elements site-wide, all from an external document. Dreamweaver, of course, makes this process as straightforward as possible.

Semantic markup

A phrase that's often bandied about in the context of web design is **semantic markup**—it refers to using tags that describe what each item in the design is, rather than describing what you want it to look like. (Presentation, of course, should be done using CSS.) If you want to create a list, for example, use an HTML list element—don't just create a paragraph and separate the items with line breaks; if you want to create a heading, use a heading element and don't use a styled paragraph. Doing so means that it'll later be much, much easier to change how the elements appear: if your lists are composed of HTML lists, you can directly style them in CSS, changing the type of bullet point, the spacing, and more. If you've specified the details of the appearance in the HTML, on the other hand, you'll have to change all the HTML.

If you're thinking that you're using Dreamweaver, not editing HTML, you need to keep in mind that working semantically is just as important when you're working with a visual design tool, such as Dreamweaver. Always think about what each element is supposed to be before you style it using Dreamweaver's built-in tools.

Adding text elements

Some of the most common text styles are paragraphs, headings, preformatted text, and bold and italic text. All these elements can be formatted using Dreamweaver's Properties panel, as we'll see in the following sections.

Creating paragraphs, line breaks, and headings

Type a few lines of text into Design view so that you have a few paragraphs to play with. You should find that Dreamweaver automatically formats the lines into paragraphs (with a gap between each one) as soon as you press the Enter key the first time. If you want to create a line break instead of a paragraph break, hold the Shift key down when pressing Enter.

Do not use line breaks instead of paragraphs—some designers advocate this on the basis that it removes the default margins of paragraph elements, or because it enables you to have "paragraphs" without gaps between them. Both of those perceived problems are simple enough to deal with in CSS, so think semantically, and ensure that your paragraphs are formatted as paragraphs.

Headings are created by clicking inside an existing text element and using the Properties panel's Format menu to choose a heading level. HTML allows for six levels of headings, and these are all available in the Format menu. Although browsers have their own ideas about heading font sizes and margins, remember that every aspect of heading styles can be styled site-wide using CSS.

Note that some people incorrectly assume that level 5 and 6 headings, which are, by default, usually displayed smaller than paragraph text, are to be used for small text. This isn't the case—they are merely the fifth and sixth levels of headings and should be used as such. Use headings for headings and paragraphs for paragraphs, and then use CSS to sort out how they end up being displayed on the web page.

Specifying preformatted text

There are occasions where it can be useful to have text displayed in a monospace font, just as it's shown in Code view. For instance, application code and movie scripts tend to require very specific formatting; this can be achieved by using the Preformatted option in the Format menu.

Making text bold and italic

In the middle of the Properties panel is a set of six formatting buttons, the first two of which display a bold B and an italic I. If you've ever worked with a word processor, you know what to expect: when you select some text in Design or Code view and then click the B button, the text is emboldened, and when you click the I button, the text is italicized. To make text both bold and italic, click both buttons. Each style can be removed by clicking the relevant button again.

> If you're using Code or Split view, you'll notice that the Bold and Italic buttons don't actually add <b> and <i> elements—they instead add <strong> and <em> elements. This has been the case in Dreamweaver since Dreamweaver MX, and it is an example of the application's preference for using logical style elements, which determine what content actually is, rather than physical style elements, which only describe what content looks like. For instance, screen readers may ignore <b> or <i> elements, but they will emphasize content within <em> tags and strongly emphasize content in <strong> tags.
>
> In a standard web browser, the two methods of styling look identical, so it's recommended you stick with logical styles. However, should you choose otherwise, you can go back to the old way of creating bold and italic text by unchecking Use <strong> and <em> in place of <b> and <i> in the General section of Dreamweaver's preferences.

Aligning text

The buttons next to the Bold and Italic ones are (in order) Align Left, Align Center, Align Right, and Justify. These do pretty much what you'd expect—click inside a text element, and then click one of the buttons to align your text.

> While you can use these buttons to align text, they add code to your document that is classed as deprecated by the web standards body, W3C (www.w3.org). This means it is scheduled to be removed from the specifications, and support can therefore not be guaranteed in future browser releases. (The code in question is the align attribute, which can be seen in the start tags of elements where you've amended the alignment.) For that reason, W3C recommends avoiding such code and instead using CSS to align elements. In the "Using the CSS Styles panel to style text" section, later in the chapter, you'll find out how to align text using the CSS text-align property.

Styling text elements

In this section, we're going to take a look at how to style text in Dreamweaver. You'll find out how to use the Properties panel, what the various field values mean, and how to style text using CSS.

Using the Properties panel to style text

The Properties panel can be used in two ways to style text, one of which is recommended, and the other which very definitely isn't.

The method you shouldn't use is to select some text in Design view and then use the Properties panel to set its font, size, and color (using the fields of the same name). While this seems to work well enough, a quick glance at Code view once you've made a few changes tells a different story: the styles are added to the <head> section of the web page rather than to an external style sheet, meaning the styling can't be used site-wide.

However, the Properties panel isn't to be entirely ignored when styling text—you can use its Style menu to access any styles that you've previously created. To apply one of your existing styles, click inside a text element and choose a value from the menu to style the entire element, or select a piece of text and choose a value from the menu to create a styled span (that is, a style that's applied to specific characters rather than to an entire element).

Using the CSS Styles panel to style text

The best method for styling text is to use the CSS Styles panel. You've already seen how to attach a CSS file to your web page (see the "Attaching CSS files" section in the previous chapter). After attaching a CSS file to your web page, you simply click the New CSS Rule button to bring up the New CSS Rule dialog box. Then you can choose what selector type you want—Class for creating a style to be used on multiple elements; Tag to affect a specific element (such as h1 to create a style to affect all level-one headings); or Advanced for contextual selectors (targeting those within specific divs); or grouped selectors (comma-separated selectors, to apply a style to more than one element, or more than one other selector type).

```
                          New CSS Rule

Selector Type:  ● Class (can apply to any tag)           ( OK )
                ○ Tag (redefines the look of a specific tag)
                                                        ( Cancel )
                ○ Advanced (IDs, pseudo-class selectors)

      Name:   [                                    ] ⊟

   Define in: ● [ 5_pull_quotes.css              ] ⊟
              ○ This document only                      ( Help )
```

Once the options within the New CSS Rule dialog box are set, click OK and you'll see the CSS Rule Definition dialog box. Most of the properties that relate most specifically to text are found in the Type and Block categories.

```
                  CSS Rule Definition for .text in 5_pull_quotes.css

Category              Type

Type
Background            Font:  [                              ] ⊟
Block
Box                   Size:  [     ] ⊟ [ pixels ⊟ ]   Weight:  [        ] ⊟
Border
List                  Style: [          ] ⊟            Variant: [        ] ⊟
Positioning
Extensions      Line height: [     ] ⊟ [ pixels ⊟ ]     Case:  [        ] ⊟

                 Decoration:  ☐ underline               Color:  ☐ [      ]
                             ☐ overline
                             ☐ line-through
                             ☐ blink
                             ☐ none


               ( Help )              ( Apply )( Cancel )( OK )
```

As you can see, the Type category includes the following properties:

- Font: This enables you to choose from a list of predefined web-safe font collections, or to add your own to the list by selecting Edit Font List. Note that you can type directly into the field to choose something other than what's in the pop-up list.

CSS fonts work by enabling you to define fall-back fonts. If the first choice isn't available on a user's system, the browser keeps looking through the list until it finds a font that's available. If nothing from the list is available, a default font is used, so it's good practice to end a list with a generic value, such as sans-serif, serif, or monospace. Dreamweaver's default font sets provide the most commonly used lists, which should be suitable for the majority of web pages—after all, although you can choose any font for your page, other users will only see it if they have that font installed too. Therefore, sticking to standard web fonts is a good idea.

- Size: This enables you to set the size of your text. The drop-down menu provides a list of options for units, including the commonly used pixels and %. Print-based measurements such as points, cm, and mm should generally be avoided as they have no relevance onscreen.

- Weight: Various values are available to set the weight of text, but browsers tend to ignore most of them, so just stick to using normal and bold.

- Style: This is used to make text italic, although most browsers treat the italic and oblique values the same way.

- Variant: This enables you to render text in small-caps.

- Line height: This sets the leading for text—essentially, the higher the value, the bigger the gaps between lines of text. On the Web this can be a particularly important thing to get to grips with, because tightly packed text can be a nightmare to read.

- Case: This field sets the CSS text-transform property, enabling you to change the case of a piece of text. Along with none, available values are capitalize, uppercase, and lowercase. The capitalize value capitalizes the first letter of each word (Rather Like This), whereas uppercase and lowercase force all characters to UPPERCASE and lowercase, respectively.

- Decoration: Various options are available to decorate text. Underline adds the standard underline that you see on links (and, as such, shouldn't be used for body text), while overline adds a line above the text. The line-through value creates a strike-through effect, with a line through the vertical center of the text. The other two values are none, which removes decoration from the text, and blink, which is a hangover from the old Netscape days and a value that browsers are not required to support; needless to say, it's best ignored.

- Color: Enables you to set the color of your text by typing a value directly into the field, or by selecting a color by using the pop-up color picker.

The Block category also contains a number of useful properties when working with text.

- Word spacing and Letter spacing: These fields enable you to amend the spacing between words and letters, respectively. However, do take care when using these properties, because any reduction in the default values can result in unreadable text. Also, be aware that spacing is often not consistent across platforms, so you'll need to do extra testing when using these properties.

- Vertical alignment: This is the rough equivalent of the deprecated valign in HTML, setting the vertical alignment of inline elements and of those within table cells.

- Text align and Text indent: These enable you to define text alignment (left, center, right, justify) and indent, respectively.

CSS Rule Definition for .text in 5_pull_quotes.css

Category	Block

Type
Background
Block
Box
Border
List
Positioning
Extensions

Word spacing: [   ] [⇅] [ems ⇅]
Letter spacing: [   ] [⇅] [ems ⇅]
Vertical alignment: [   ] [⇅] [% ⇅]
Text align: [   ] [⇅]
Text indent: [   ] [pixels ⇅]
Whitespace: [   ] [⇅]
Display: [   ] [⇅]

(Help)   (Apply) (Cancel) (OK)

Applying styles to multiple elements and selections

Earlier in this chapter, I said you could create a style to be used for multiple elements. This can be useful when you need to create a style that's used occasionally on multiple pages, or if you want to create a "modification" style to be applied to a number of elements.

1. Create new XHTML and CSS documents, and link the CSS file to the web page. Add some text to the page, making sure that you include at least one heading along with a couple of paragraphs.

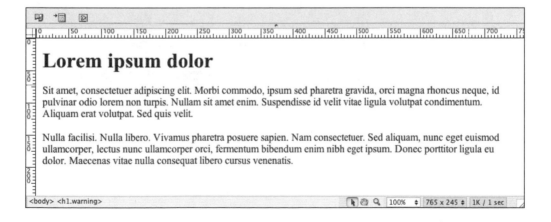

Lorem ipsum dolor

Sit amet, consectetuer adipiscing elit. Morbi commodo, ipsum sed pharetra gravida, orci magna rhoncus neque, id pulvinar odio lorem non turpis. Nullam sit amet enim. Suspendisse id velit vitae ligula volutpat condimentum. Aliquam erat volutpat. Sed quis velit.

Nulla facilisi. Nulla libero. Vivamus pharetra posuere sapien. Nam consectetuer. Sed aliquam, nunc eget euismod ullamcorper, lectus nunc ullamcorper orci, fermentum bibendum enim nibh eget ipsum. Donec porttitor ligula eu dolor. Maecenas vitae nulla consequat libero cursus venenatis.

`<body>` `<h1.warning>`   100% ⇅ 765 x 245 ⇅ 1K / 1 sec

2. Click the New CSS Style button in the CSS Styles panel to bring up the New CSS Rule dialog box. Choose Class as the selector type, and type .warning in the Name field. Ensure Define in is set to your CSS document and not to This document only. Click OK.

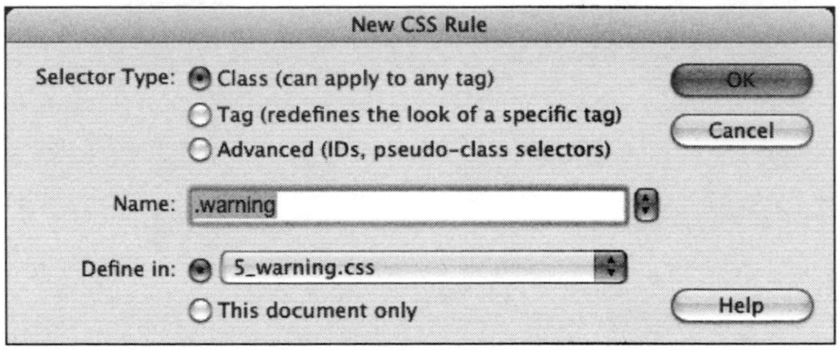

New CSS Rule

Selector Type: ⦿ Class (can apply to any tag)
○ Tag (redefines the look of a specific tag)
○ Advanced (IDs, pseudo-class selectors)

Name: .warning

Define in: ⦿ 5_warning.css
○ This document only

OK   Cancel   Help

3. In the Type category, set Weight to bold and Style to italic. Choose red from the Color pop-up selector (or enter #FF0000 in the Color text field).

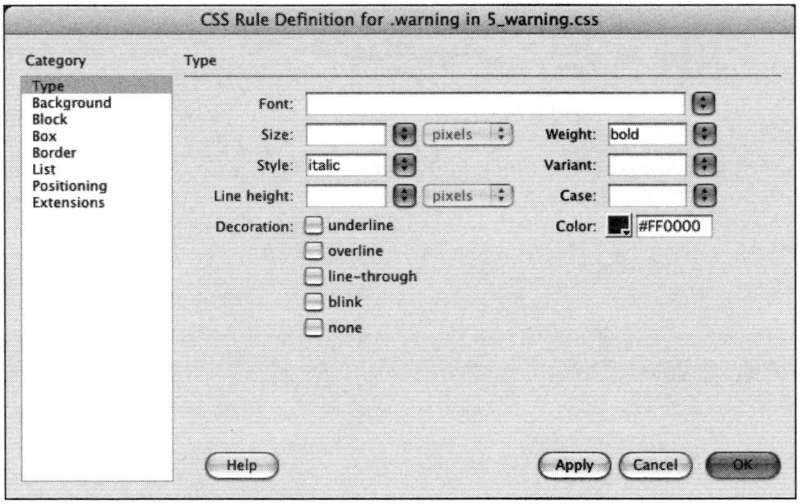

CSS Rule Definition for .warning in 5_warning.css

Category   Type
Type
Background   Font:
Block
Box   Size: pixels   Weight: bold
Border
List   Style: italic   Variant:
Positioning
Extensions   Line height: pixels   Case:

                  Decoration: ☐ underline   Color: ▮ #FF0000
                              ☐ overline
                              ☐ line-through
                              ☐ blink
                              ☐ none

Help   Apply   Cancel   OK

4. In the Border category, deselect all of the Same for all check boxes, and for Bottom set Style to dotted, Width to 1 pixel, and Color to red (again, by using the pop-up selector, or by typing #FF0000 into the Color field). Click OK.

> *Solid underlines aren't generally used on the Web, apart from for links, which is why we're using a dotted underline for this style.*

5. The style can now be applied to entire elements by clicking inside them and selecting warning from the Properties panel's Style menu, or by going to CSS Styles ➤ warning in the contextual menu. To apply the rule to a section of text, select the relevant characters and then apply the style in the same way as for an entire element.

The completed files for this exercise are available in this book's download archive on the friends of ED website. They are named 5_warning.html and 5_warning.css and can be found in the Chapter 5 folder.

Working with lists

Although lists are extremely common on the Internet, a surprisingly large number of them aren't correctly structured. Web designers often use line breaks and inline images to create something that looks like a list, but when you look at the source, it's merely a paragraph with a load of line breaks.

"So what?" you might be thinking. "If it looks OK, why not just use this method?" Well, not only does HTML provide you with a perfectly good way to rapidly create lists and CSS provide a perfectly good way to style them, but Dreamweaver also enables you to add lists to your pages quickly and efficiently, as you'll see in this section.

Creating a list

The Properties panel has a set of four buttons dedicated to list creation. They are, in order, Unordered List, Ordered List, Text Outdent, and Text Indent. By default, the Unordered List button creates a bullet-point list, whereas the Ordered List button creates a numbered list.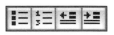

To make a standard bullet-point list, click the Unordered List button and type the first list item. Press Enter when you're done, and another bullet point automatically appears. Repeat this process until the list is complete. Should you wish to add content underneath the list, simply press Enter twice to terminate the list. (This creates a blank paragraph under the list, ready for you to add content to. You can use the Properties panel's Format menu to adjust this formatting as necessary.)

```
• Item one
• Item two
• Item three
• Item four
```

`<body> <ul> <li>`   100%   765 x 245   1K / 1 sec

To add an item between two existing ones, place the cursor after one of the list items, and press Enter to create a new, blank list item, ready for content.

To create a nested list, just enter the list items as usual, and select the points that should be nested. Then, click the Text Indent button to indent those points further.

Changing a list's type

If you create an unordered list, but later want to change it to an ordered one, Dreamweaver offers a simple process for doing so. First, select the list that needs to be changed. You'll see the <ul> tag appear in the status bar. Right-click or Ctrl-click that tag and choose Quick Tag Editor.

In the resulting pop-up dialog box, replace ul with ol (because <ol> is the HTML start tag for an ordered list).

103

Click back on Design view, and the list will immediately change.

Styling lists

Like any other web page element, Dreamweaver makes it fairly simple to style lists. For this exercise, copy the following files from the downloads section of the friends of ED website (www.friendsofed.com) to your hard drive: 5_list.html, 5_list.css, and 5_bullet.gif, all of which are found in the Chapter 5 folder for this book.

1. The CSS file you've downloaded is already attached to the web page. Click the New CSS Rule button on the CSS Styles panel to open the New CSS Rule dialog box. Choose Tag as the selector type, and type ul into the Tag field. Ensure Define in is set to 5_list.css.

2. Choose the List category, and click the Browse button next to Bullet image. Navigate to and select 5_bullet.gif. This changes the default bullet point to the selected graphic.

CSS Rule Definition for ul in 5_list.css

Category | List

Type
Background
Block
Box
Border
List
Positioning
Extensions

Type: [ ] ◉

Bullet image: [5_bullet.gif] ◉ (Browse...)

Position: [ ] ◉

(Help)   (Apply) (Cancel) (OK)

3. In the Box category, set Padding to 0, and then deselect Same for all under Margin. For the margins, set Top and Right to 0, Bottom to 1 ems, and Left to 10 pixels. This removes default browser margins, setting explicit values for each edge of the containing boxes of the lists.

CSS Rule Definition for ul in 5_list.css

Category | Box

Type
Background
Block
Box
Border
List
Positioning
Extensions

Width: [ ] ◉ [pix... ◉]   Float: [ ] ◉

Height: [ ] ◉ [pix... ◉]   Clear: [ ] ◉

Padding_____   Margin_____

☑ Same for all   ☐ Same for all

Top: [0] ◉ [pix... ◉]   Top: [0] ◉ [pix... ◉]

Right: [0] ◉ [pix... ◉]   Right: [0] ◉ [pix... ◉]

Bottom: [0] ◉ [pix... ◉]   Bottom: [1] ◉ [ems ◉]

Left: [0] ◉ [pix... ◉]   Left: [10] ◉ [pix... ◉]

(Help)   (Apply) (Cancel) (OK)

Browsers tend to disagree about whether list bullet points are in the list margins or padding area. Therefore, it's a good idea to set one of the Left values to 0 and then use the other to add the indent; otherwise you may end up with an inconsistent display across browsers.

4. Click OK and then create another new rule, this time with li as the tag. In the Box category, deselect Same for all under Padding, and set Bottom to 3 pixels. In the Border category, deselect the Same for all check boxes, and set the Bottom values to solid, 1 pixel, and #cccccc. Click OK.

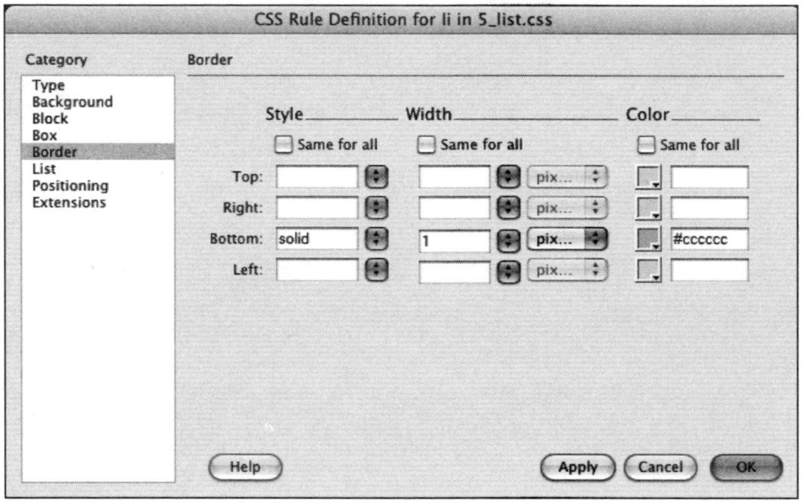

The padding setting places a gap between each list item, and the border setting adds a bottom border to each list item. At this point, the list should look rather like the one depicted here:

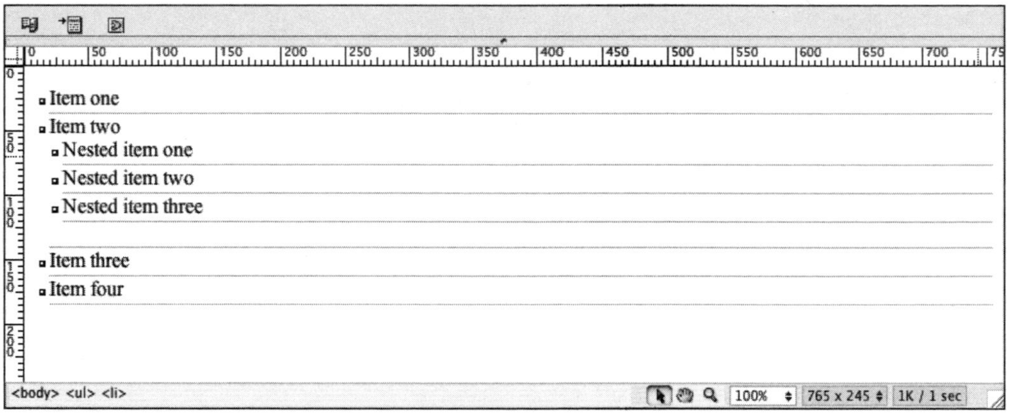

As you can see, some of the settings have had undesired effects: the bottom margin is also applied to the nested list, creating an ugly gap, and the list is somewhat cluttered, due to the nested list items being underlined. To fix this, we'll use some contextual selectors to make some amendments.

5. Create another CSS rule, but this time choose Advanced as the Selector Type and type ul ul in the Selector field. This selector—ul ul—specifies unordered lists inside unordered lists—in other words, the style will be applied only to nested unordered lists, and not to top-level ones.

New CSS Rule

Selector Type: ○ Class (can apply to any tag)
  ○ Tag (redefines the look of a specific tag)
  ● Advanced (IDs, pseudo-class selectors)

Selector: ul ul

Define in: ● 5_list.css
  ○ This document only

OK
Cancel
Help

6. In the CSS Rule Definition dialog box, choose the Box category and deselect Same for all under Margin. Set Bottom to 0 and click OK.

CSS Rule Definition for ul ul in 5_list.css

Category
  Type
  Background
  Block
  Box
  Border
  List
  Positioning
  Extensions

Box

Width: pix...   Float:
Height: pix...   Clear:

Padding
  ☑ Same for all
  Top: pix...
  Right: pix...
  Bottom: pix...
  Left: pix...

Margin
  ☐ Same for all
  Top: pix...
  Right: pix...
  Bottom: 0   pix...
  Left: pix...

Help   Apply   Cancel   OK

7. Create another new rule, like in step 5, but this time type li li into the Selector field. In the Border category, set Style to none and click OK. The nested bottom borders will disappear, resulting in a more logical and navigable list.

```
  □ Item one
  □ Item two
    □ Nested item one
    □ Nested item two
    □ Nested item three
  □ Item three
  □ Item four
```

107

By using more contextual selectors, you can take things much further, creating ever increasingly complex list styles. For instance, by using the selector ul ul ul li, you could define settings only for list items within nested lists within nested lists that won't affect the list items up the hierarchy. We'll be making more use of advanced list styling in Chapter 7, which covers website navigation.

Creating inline lists

Although people generally think of lists as vertically oriented, it's possible (and, indeed, often useful) to create horizontal lists. These can be used for things like breadcrumb navigation, which we'll look at in Chapter 7. However, we'll cover the basics of creating an inline list right now.

Once you've created a list as usual, you only need to create two rules in CSS to turn it into an inline list. The first should be a class rule with the name .inlinelist.

In the List category, set Type to none, removing the default bullet points entirely. Click OK.

Next, create another rule, this time with an advanced selector, .inlinelist li (which will mean the style is only applied to list items within an element that has the class inlinelist applied to it).

```
                         New CSS Rule

Selector Type: ○ Class (can apply to any tag)          ( OK )
               ○ Tag (redefines the look of a specific tag)
               ● Advanced (IDs, pseudo-class selectors)  ( Cancel )

     Selector: .inlinelist li                    ◆

    Define in: ● 5_inline_list.css           ◆
               ○ This document only                ( Help )
```

In the Block category, set Display to inline, and in the Box category, deselect Same for all for Padding, and set the Right value to 10 pixels.

Click somewhere in your list, and you'll see its tag appear in the status bar. Right-click or Ctrl-click the tag and use the contextual menu to select inlinelist.

```
<body> <ul>                                          100%  765 x 245  1K / 1 sec
        Remove Tag
 Format Quick Tag Editor...        ◆  CSS  B I        Link
 Font   Set Class            ▶  None        Target
        Set ID               ▶  inlinelist
                                             Page Properties...   List Item...
            ▼
```

The resulting list should look rather like this:

```
    0    50    100   150   200   250   300   350

    List item one   List item two   List item three
```

You can tidy this up further by messing around with the margin and padding settings in the .inlinelist and .inlinelist li rules already created. Completed files for this exercise can be found in the Chapter 5 folder of the download files—the files in question are 5_inline_list.html and 5_inline_list.css.

Text styling examples

In this section, you'll work through some exercises that will show you how to create great-looking type on a website. The examples are simple and modular, so you can mix and match to create many variations!

Sizing text: pixels versus keywords

In theory, defining font sizes should be easy enough. You just use a tag selector for each element you want to set the size of, and then set a value for Size in the CSS Rule Definition dialog box's Type category. The thing is, there are various units available. Most, as I briefly mentioned earlier, are unnecessary—there's little point, for instance, in using any print-oriented unit when a site is only going to be used on screen. However, that still leaves a number of options, including pixels, ems, and percentages.

Pixels are the unit of choice for many web designers, because pixels are the only measurement that enables you to know, with a large degree of certainly, that your text will look pretty much identical wherever it's viewed. Unfortunately, unlike every other major browser, Internet Explorer for Windows can't resize pixel-based text, and this creates an accessibility problem (although a user can chose to ignore font sizes via the little-known accessibility controls).

Therefore, if you decide to size text in pixels, ensure your text is very readable. Test it on various people, and listen to feedback. If you hear that someone "had trouble reading the words," or that another rooted around for a microscope before giving up and playing solitaire, you need to increase your pixel size settings. Sure, the resulting page might not look quite as "designery," but at least people will be able to read it.

Some designers battle with ems and percentages for sizing text, and end up bashing their head against nearby objects when cascading values multiply in unruly browsers, creating either massive or tiny text. Keywords are a better alternative for setting a default size of text in CSS, even though these aren't available from Dreamweaver's menus. The available values are xx-small, x-small, small, medium, large, x-large, and xx-large—pretty straightforward, unless you can only think in numbers these days. Keyword values don't compound, and most modern browsers set a lower limit, even on xx-small, so text never enters the realms of the illegible.

Styling headings and paragraphs

In this exercise, we're going to make use of the files 5_styling_headers_and_paras.html and 5_styling_headers_and_paras.css, which are found in the Chapter 5 folder of the file archive that you can download from the friends of ED website.

The CSS file is initially empty and connected to the web page, which has three levels of headings and some paragraphs. The headings are set out in a fairly standard manner: the level-one heading is intended as the article title; the level-two heading is a strap-line; the level-three headings are cross-heads, used to introduce subsections of an article. During the exercise, you'll find out how easy it is to use CSS to style these elements—the text will look much nicer, the headings will stand out, and the page will be easier to read and use.

Lorem ipsum dolor

Sit amet, consectetuer adipiscing elit. Morbi commodo, ipsum sed pharetra gravida

Orci magna rhoncus neque, id pulvinar odio lorem non turpis. Nullam sit amet enim. Suspendisse id velit vitae ligula volutpat condimentum. Aliquam erat volutpat. Sed quis velit. Nulla facilisi. Nulla libero.

Vivamus pharetra

Posuere sapien. Nam consectetuer. Sed aliquam, nunc eget euismod ullamcorper, lectus nunc ullamcorper orci, fermentum bibendum enim nibh eget ipsum. Donec porttitor ligula eu dolor. Maecenas vitae nulla consequat libero cursus venenatis. Lorem ipsum dolor sit amet, consectetuer adipiscing elit.

Morbi commodo

Ipsum sed pharetra gravida, orci magna rhoncus neque, id pulvinar odio lorem non turpis. Nullam sit amet enim. Suspendisse id velit vitae ligula volutpat condimentum. Aliquam erat volutpat. Sed quis velit. Nulla facilisi. Nulla libero. Vivamus pharetra posuere sapien. Nam consectetuer.

Sed aliquam, nunc eget euismod ullamcorper, lectus nunc ullamcorper orci, fermentum bibendum enim nibh eget ipsum. Donec porttitor ligula eu dolor. Maecenas vitae nulla consequat libero cursus vnenatis.

`<body> <h1>`   100%   765 x 458   1K / 1 sec

1. The first thing to do is to set a default font size for the document. Click the New CSS Rule button on the CSS Styles panel to create a new rule. Select Tag for the Selector Type and then type body into the Tag field. Ensure your CSS file is selected in Define in, and then click OK.

New CSS Rule

Selector Type: ○ Class (can apply to any tag)
       ● Tag (redefines the look of a specific tag)
       ○ Advanced (IDs, pseudo–class selectors)

     OK
     Cancel

Tag: body

Define in: ● 5_styling_headings_and_paras.css
        ○ This document only

     Help

111

2. Select the Type category, and choose Verdana, Arial, Helvetica, sans-serif for its value. (Verdana is a good choice for body copy, because it's a very readable font, even at small sizes.) In the Size field, type small. Finally, set the color to #333333. While it's always a good idea to ensure there's plenty of contrast between the text and background, black on white can look very harsh, so softening the text color slightly often improves readability and its visual appearance.

3. Create another new rule, this time for the tag selector h1. In the Type category, set Font to Arial, Helvetica, sans-serif. (While Verdana is good for body copy, its roundness makes it suspect for headings—the blockier Arial is often a good choice for headings.) Set Size to 125%, Weight to bold, and Case to uppercase.

4. In the Border category, deselect all three Same for all check boxes, and then set Left to solid, 18 pixels, and #cccccc. This will create a solid rectangle next to the heading, thereby drawing attention to it.

5. In the Box category, deselect both Same for all check boxes. Set the Left value of Padding to 10 pixels. This ensures the heading content doesn't hug the border created in the previous step. Under Margin, set Bottom to 10 pixels and all other values to 0. Click OK.

6. Create a new rule, this time with h2 as the tag selector. Again, access the Type category and set Font to Arial, Helvetica, sans-serif, set Weight to bold, and set Case to uppercase. This time, however, set Size to 100%. In the Border category, deselect Same for all and set Bottom to dotted, 1 pixels, and #666666. This creates a subtle underline underneath the strap. Finally, in the Box category, deselect the Same for all check boxes. Set the Bottom value of Padding to 5 pixels. Under Margin, set Bottom to 5 pixels, set Left to 28 pixels, and set the other values to 0. Click OK.

7. Create another rule, this time with h3 as the tag selector. This time, in the Type category, set Weight to bold and Size to 85%. In the Border category, deselect Same for all and set Left to solid, 18 pixels, and #eeeeee. This mirrors the level-one heading border, but the color is lighter—it doesn't distract from the content, but it still enables easy navigation to the subsections of an article. Finally, in the Box category, deselect the Same for all check boxes. Set the Left value of Padding to 10 pixels. Under Margin, set Top to 1.6 ems, set Right and Left to 0, and set Bottom to 2 pixels. Click OK.

8. The last rule we need to create uses the tag selector p, in order to style the paragraphs. Only two properties need defining: in the Type category, set Size to 85%, and in the Box category, deselect Same for all under Margin, and set Top and Right to 0, Bottom to 0.8 ems, and Left to 28 pixels. Click OK.

> *If you look through the settings we've defined so far, you'll see that the margin-bottom setting on paragraphs is 0.8 ems (one "em" being the height of a character) and the margin-top setting for level-three headings is 1.6 ems. Logically, you might therefore think that if a level-three heading follows a paragraph, the margin between the two would be 2.4 ems (1.6 + 0.8). However, margins collapse in CSS, so the larger one simply overrides the smaller, leading, in this case, to a margin of 1.6 ems between a paragraph and a following level-three heading.*

And here's the completed text design:

The completed version of this exercise can be found in the Chapter 5 folder of the download files. The filenames to look for are 5_styling_headings_and_paras_1.html and 5_styling_headings_and_paras_1.css.

Restyling text using the CSS Styles panel

Rarely does a design work right away, so it's great to know that Dreamweaver provides you with an excellent method of rapidly editing CSS styles. Although you can use the collapsible rules list at the top of the CSS Styles panel to directly access a style in the CSS Rules Definition dialog box (just double-click a selector to open the dialog box), you can edit property values directly in the panel. Click on a selector, and in the Properties area of the CSS Styles panel you'll see the defined property values at the top of the subsequent list for easy access. Click on a value to bring up fields and menus that enable you to edit the values.

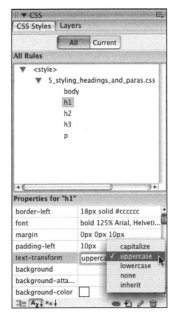

Note that in some cases the CSS values are grouped under common headings. For instance, in the top-right image, all of the margin settings are grouped in margin, *rather than showing separate values for* margin-top, margin-right, margin-bottom, *and* margin-left. *This is because in Chapter 2 we told Dreamweaver to use shorthand for CSS. This makes CSS files shorter by grouping rules wherever possible. In addition to margins, CSS shorthand can also be applied to padding (using the* padding *property), font values (using the* font *property), borders (using the* border *property), and several others. For more information about CSS shorthand, see* Web Designer's Reference *by Craig Grannell (friends of ED, ISBN: 1-59059-430-4).*

Rapidly restyling headings and paragraphs

In this exercise we'll restyle the page created in the last exercise using only the CSS Styles panel. You'll see the Design view update automatically as changes are made, making it easier to experiment.

1. Select the body selector in the All Rules section of the CSS Styles panel. Click the font value and change it to small Georgia, "Times New Roman", serif.

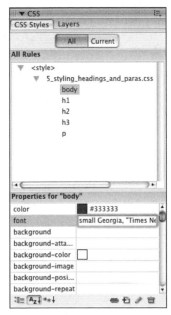

2. Select the h1 selector. Change text-transform (which controls the case of text) to lowercase. Change the value of font to normal 150% Arial, Helvetica, sans-serif. Set margin to 0px 0px 5px. (The margin settings are shorthand—when there are only three values, the first sets margin-top, the second sets both margin-left and margin-right, and the third sets margin-bottom; therefore, in this case all margins are set to 0 apart from the bottom one, which is set to 5 pixels.)

Properties for "h1"	
border-left	18px solid #cccccc
font	normal 150% Arial, Hel...
margin	0px 0px 5px
padding-left	10px
text-transform	lowercase
background	
background-atta...	
background-color	

The reason for using the normal *value for* font *is that in some browsers, headings are displayed in bold by default. Therefore, you need to set the weight to* normal *to override this.*

3. We'll now delete a couple of properties and add some new ones. This is simple enough to do: to delete a property, select it and click the trash can icon at the bottom-right of the panel. Do this to remove border-left and padding-left. To add new properties, just scroll down the list until you find the ones you want, and enter values in the standard way (by clicking to the right of the relevant property, and entering a value). We need to add the following: set color to #666666, set padding to 0 0 5px, and set border-bottom to 1px dotted #666666.

Initially, these newly defined properties won't move to the top of the list. However, if you choose a different selector and then return to the one you were editing, those with values will all appear at the top of the Properties *area.*

4. For the h2 selector, set text-transform to lowercase, set padding-bottom to 10px, delete margin-left, and then set margin to 10px 0 10px. Scroll to color and set it to #666666.

5. For the h3 selector, delete the border-left property, set font-size to 90%, set padding-left to 1.35 ems, and add a font-family property, with a value of Verdana, Arial, Helvetica, sans-serif.

6. For the p selector, set margin to 0 0 0.8em, set font-size to 90%, and add the following two rules: set line-height to 1.4em (to increase readability, which is especially important when using a serif font on the Web), and set padding-left to 1.4em.

The final result should look something like this:

The completed files for this exercise can be found in the Chapter 5 folder of the downloads archive. They are named 5_styling_headings_and_paras_2.html and 5_styling_headings_and_paras_2.css.

Creating print-like paragraphs

It's pretty standard to have gaps between paragraphs of online text. This largely stems from browser defaults, which put default margins around most block elements. However, if you're aiming for a more print-like style for a particular design, you can ape the look of a newspaper or book easily enough.

1. Create new XHTML and CSS documents, and link the CSS file to the web page. Add some paragraphs of text to the page and then create a new CSS rule by clicking the New CSS Rule button on the CSS Styles panel. Select Tag for the Selector Type, and then type p into the Tag field.

2. In the Box category of the CSS Rule Definition dialog box, set Margin to 0. Then select the Block category and set Text indent to 20 pixels. Click OK, and your paragraphs will look like those shown here.

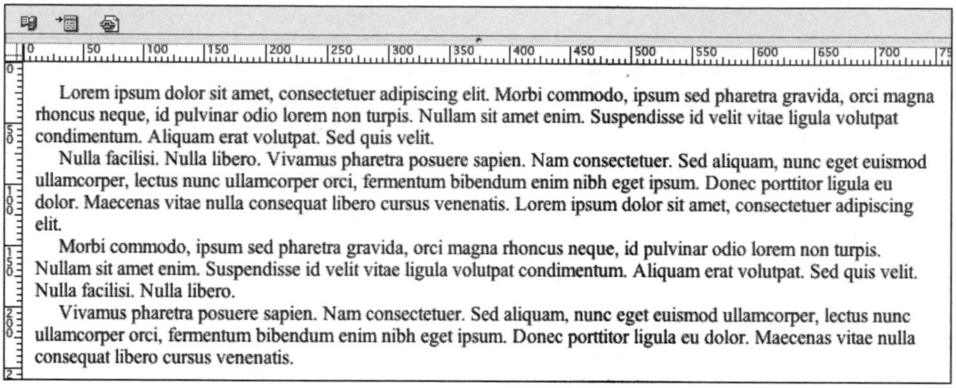

3. Many publications don't indent the first paragraph, however, so we can create a class rule to deal with that. Create a new rule—this time use a Class selector and type .noindent into the Name field.

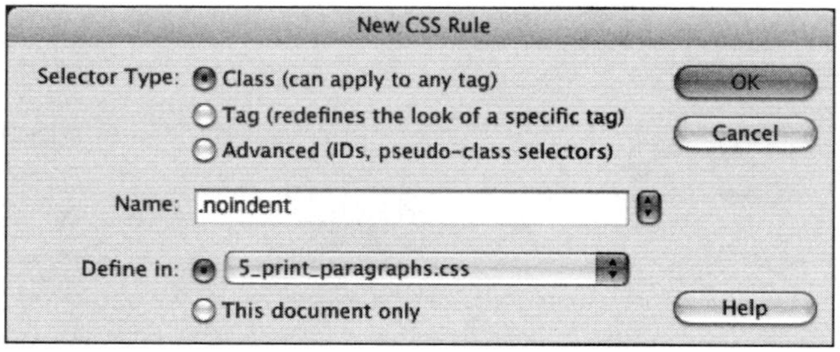

4. In the Block category, set Text indent to 0 and click OK. Click inside the first paragraph, and use either the Properties panel's Style menu to apply this style (or right-click or Ctrl-click inside the paragraph and select CSS Styles ➤ noindent).

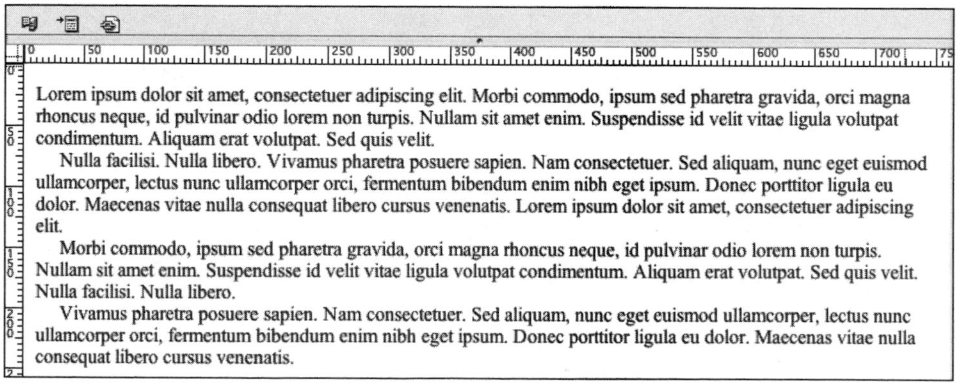

The primary reason why designers tend to stick with the usual gaps between paragraphs on the web, rather than using print-style paragraphs, is because they make text more readable. However, you can actually have the best of both worlds by integrating the two approaches—in the preceding exercise simply change the Bottom *setting in* Margin *(in step 2) to* 0.5 *ems.*

Creating drop caps

Drop caps are common in print publications, and they can look good online, too.

1. Create new XHTML and CSS documents, and link the CSS file to the web page. Add some text to the page.

2. Click the New CSS Rule button on the CSS Styles panel to access the New CSS Rule dialog box. Choose Tag as the Selector Type, and type .body into the Tag field. Ensure your CSS document is selected for the Define in option. Click OK.

3. In the CSS Rule Definition dialog box, select the Type category. Set Font to Verdana, Arial, Helvetica, sans-serif, and set Size to small. Click OK.

4. Create another tag rule, this time for the selector p. In the CSS Rule Definition dialog box, select the Type category and set Size to 85%. Click OK.

5. Create another new rule, but this time choose Class as the Selector Type and type .dropcap into the Name field. Ensure your CSS document is selected for the Define in option.

119

6. In the CSS Rule Definition dialog box, choose the Type category. Set Font to Arial, Helvetica, sans-serif, set Size to 60 pixels, set Line height to 53 pixels, set Weight to bold, and set the color to #444444. Note that there's nothing scientific about these sizes—I came up with them via trial and error.

CSS Rule Definition for .dropcap in 5_drop_cap.css

Category

Type
Background
Block
Box
Border
List
Positioning
Extensions

Type

Font: Arial, Helvetica, sans-serif

Size: 60 pixels   Weight: bold

Style: Variant:

Line height: 53 pixels   Case:

Decoration: ☐ underline   Color: #444444
☐ overline
☐ line–through
☐ blink
☐ none

Help   Apply   Cancel   OK

Although you should generally avoid using pixels to set font sizes, it matters less with a drop cap, because the character is several lines high and is very unlikely to need to be zoomed. Note, however, that this setting will mean a difference in display if browsers aren't using their default text sizes: Internet Explorer won't zoom the drop cap, but all other browsers will.

7. In the Box category, set Float to left, set Padding to 0, uncheck Same for all for Margin and set Right to 2 pixels and Bottom to -5 pixels. Click OK and return to Design view.

CSS Rule Definition for .dropcap in 5_drop_cap.css

Category

Type
Background
Block
Box
Border
List
Positioning
Extensions

Box

Width: pix...   Float: left

Height: pix...   Clear:

Padding   Margin

☑ Same for all   ☐ Same for all

Top: 0   Top: pix...

Right: 0   Right: 2 pix...

Bottom: 0   Bottom: -5 pix...

Left: 0   Left: pix...

Help   Apply   Cancel   OK

8. Select the first letter of the initial paragraph of text, right-click or Ctrl-click and go to CSS Styles ➤ dropcap to apply the newly created style to this character (or choose dropcap from the Properties panel's Style menu).

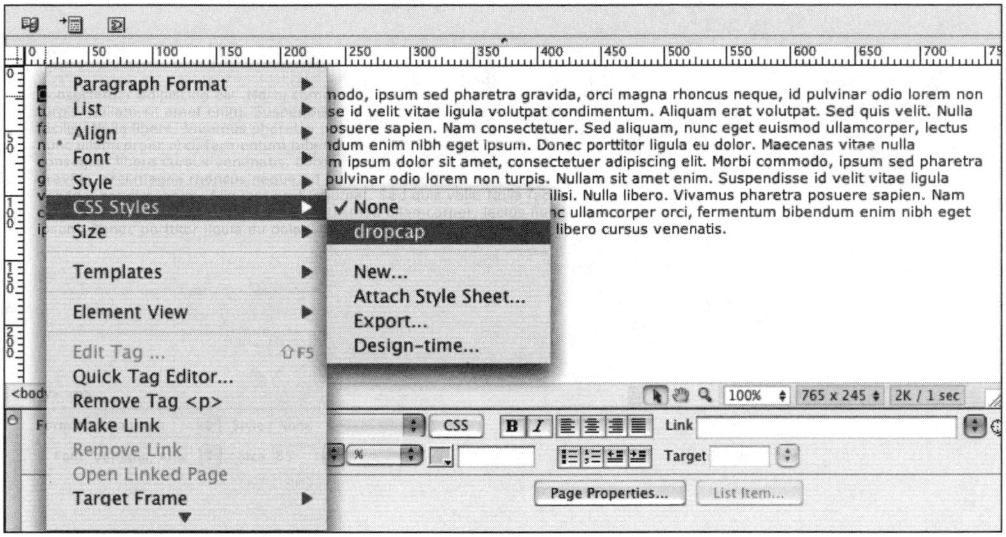

9. The character should be transformed, taking on the appearance of a drop cap, as shown in the following image. Because this style has been created in an external style sheet, it can be applied to multiple pages on your websites, or several times on the same document. Also, updating it is a quick and painless process—just double-click the rule in the CSS Styles panel to open up the CSS Rule Definition dialog box, and edit the values accordingly.

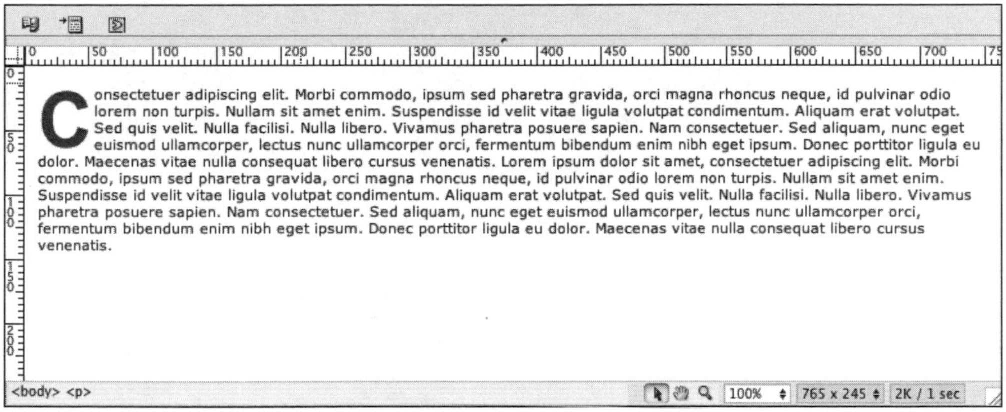

The completed files for this exercise are available in this book's download archive on the friends of ED website. They are found in the Chapter 5 folder and are named 5_drop_cap.html and 5_drop_cap.css.

Creating pull quotes

Like drop caps, pulls quotes are regularly used in print publications, but they work well online, too, enabling you to draw the reader's attention to a particular snippet of information, along with providing some typographical interest to the page.

1. Create new XHTML and CSS documents, and link the CSS file to the web page. As with the drop cap example, add some text to the page—this time add a few paragraphs.

2. Create a new CSS rule, and set the Selector Type to Class. In the Name field, type .pullquote. Make sure the Define in selection points to the CSS document you created in step 1. Click OK.

3. In the CSS Rule Definition dialog box, choose Type from the Category list. Set Font to Arial, Helvetica, sans-serif, set Size to 110%, set Weight to bold, and set Color to #666666.

> *Pull quotes need to be easy to distinguish from the standard body copy, hence setting the pull quote's font family, size, color, and weight to something different from that used for the body copy.*

4. In the Box category, set Float to right and set Width to 180 pixels. This provides the pull quote with a fixed width, aligns it to the right, and enables the other text to wrap around it. Deselect both Same for all check boxes, and set Top and Bottom under Padding to 10 pixels, set Bottom and Left under Margin to 10 pixels, and set Top under Margin to 0.

5. In the Border category, deselect Same for all under Style, and set Top and Bottom to solid. Set Width to 2 pixels and Color to #cccccc. Click OK.

6. In Design view, click inside the paragraph of text, and then either use the Properties panel's Style menu or the context menu's CSS Styles submenu to apply the pullquote style.

The resulting pull quote should look rather like that shown here, standing out from the other text and drawing the reader's attention:

Lorem ipsum dolor sit amet, consectetuer adipiscing elit. Morbi commodo, ipsum sed pharetra gravida, orci magna rhoncus neque, id pulvinar odio lorem non turpis. Nullam sit amet enim. Suspendisse id velit vitae ligula volutpat condimentum.

Aliquam erat volutpat. Sed quis velit. Nulla facilisi. Nulla libero. Vivamus pharetra posuere sapien. Nam consectetuer. Sed aliquam, nunc eget euismod ullamcorper, lectus nunc ullamcorper orci, fermentum bibendum enim nibh eget ipsum. Donec porttitor ligula eu dolor. Maecenas vitae nulla consequat libero cursus venenatis.

Nullam sit amet enim. Suspendisse id velit vitae ligula volutpat condimentum. Aliquam erat volutpat. Sed quis velit.

Lorem ipsum dolor sit amet, consectetuer adipiscing elit. Morbi commodo, ipsum sed pharetra gravida, orci magna rhoncus neque, id pulvinar odio lorem non turpis. Nullam sit amet enim. Suspendisse id velit vitae ligula volutpat condimentum. Aliquam erat volutpat. Sed quis velit. Nulla facilisi. Nulla libero. Vivamus pharetra posuere sapien. Nam consectetuer. Sed aliquam, nunc eget euismod ullamcorper, lectus nunc ullamcorper orci, fermentum bibendum enim nibh eget ipsum. Donec porttitor ligula eu dolor. Maecenas vitae nulla consequat libero cursus venenatis.

Because the quote's presentation is all driven by CSS, it's easy to rapidly experiment by editing the rule. For instance, in the Block category of the CSS Rule Definition dialog box, you could try experimenting with text alignment and letter spacing, in the Background category you could add a background image behind the quote, and so on. If you can see Design view behind the CSS Rule Definition dialog box, you can see how a change to a rule affects your document by simply clicking Apply. This enables you to make quick tweaks without exiting the dialog box.

The completed files for this exercise are available in the Chapter 5 folder of this book's download archive on the friends of ED website. They are named 5_pull_quotes.html and 5_pull_quotes.css.

Fixing text sizes in IE 5 for Windows

If you've tested the heading and paragraph examples in a range of browsers, you may have noticed some slightly odd things happening in older versions of Internet Explorer (IE). That browser got CSS keywords wrong before version 6—fonts defined using keywords are displayed too large in IE version 5 and before. You have two choices here: one is to just let people using an obsolete browser put up with wrongly sized fonts, but that's not a terribly good idea when a significant number of people still use the browser; the other is to implement a "hack" in the CSS.

Tantek Çelik's box model hack exploits a bug in IE before version 6, enabling you to have one set of values to cater solely for it, and let well-behaved browsers get on with displaying the correct values. An example looks like this:

```
body {
font-size: x-small;
voice-family: "\"}\"";
voice-family: inherit;
font-size: small;
}
```

Here, all browsers "see" the first font-size property, but the two voice-family lines trip IE versions earlier than 6, causing them to terminate the rule and go on to the next one. Compliant browsers, however, go on to see the second font-size property, which overrides the first. The upshot is that all versions of IE end up setting the font size correctly (as do other browsers). The only downside is that you have to use Code view to put this hack in place; however, it's only a few extra lines in your CSS file, so it's no great hardship!

Cross-platform issues

As a quick final word in this chapter, it's worth noting two aspects of fonts that differ on the Mac OS and Windows. The first is leading/line-height, which tends to be slightly larger in Windows-based browsers than in Mac-based browsers, unless the value is set in pixels. This isn't generally a problem, unless you're designing a pixel-perfect layout, in which case you're most likely using pixels to set text sizes anyway.

More noticeable is the Mac's tendency (as of Mac OS X) to anti-alias onscreen text, which affects spacing (in fact, various anti-aliasing algorithms can cause text to look slightly different in each browser on the Mac). On Windows, aliased text makes for jagged edges. This isn't a major problem for body copy (in fact, many people prefer aliased text when reading onscreen); however, set a heading to 40 pixels and you'll discover the results are less than visually pleasing.

The difference is hard to get across in words, so I've enlarged some text. In the images below, you can see Windows text on the left and Mac text on the right.

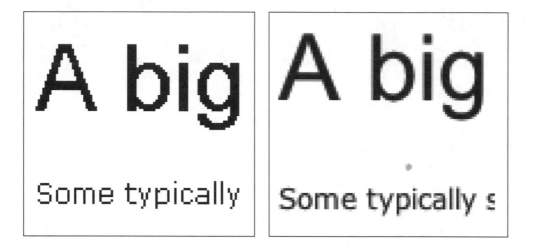

Windows displays a simpler version of the original font, reduced to a black and white bitmap, whereas the Mac attempts to emulate the soft curves of the original by introducing gray pixels at the edges.

Although arguments rage regarding which is the best method of displaying fonts on screen, this is a moot point for web designers, because you don't control the end user's setup and therefore must be aware of every possibility. For instance, Mac-based designers must take care not to use large text that looks great on their system without checking how it looks on Windows, too.

To complicate matters more, Windows-based laptops often have font-smoothing technology that approximates the Mac's anti-aliasing. Also, Windows XP has a technology called ClearType that more or less does the same thing but, for a reason I've never managed to fathom, it's turned off by default.

In conclusion, you can't be as precious about web-based text as you can with print-based copy. (The same, in fact, goes for the majority of web design—try to get into the habit of a "good enough" aesthetic, rather than trying to get everything exact on all platforms and in all browsers, for that way lies madness.

Summary

In this chapter you've learned how to work with website text, ensuring that it's structurally sound and logically marked-up, and that it looks good. The exercises have shown you how to make sure text remains accessible, while still maintaining a good degree of control as a designer. You should now be comfortable experimenting with the various text-oriented elements of the CSS Style Definition dialog box, so try creating a number of variations on the exercises in this chapter, combining different elements to create brand-new results.

In the next chapter, we will take a look at the other main component of website content: images.

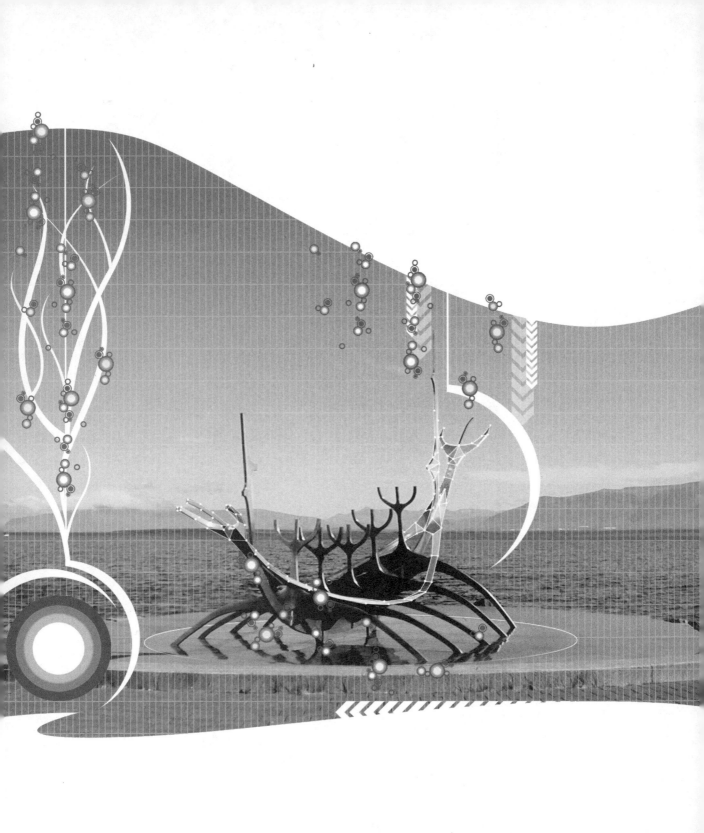

Chapter 6

WORKING WITH IMAGES

In this chapter . . .

- Choosing the best image format
- Avoiding common errors
- Adding images to web pages
- Editing images
- Styling images

Although text makes up the bulk of the Web's content, it's inevitable that you'll end up working with images at some point, unless you favor extremely basic websites akin to those last seen in 1995. These days, the bulk of interfaces are composed of images, as is a considerable amount of actual content. As the Web continues to barge its way into every facet of life, this trend will continue—visitors to sites expect a certain amount of visual interest and flair, just as readers of a magazine expect illustrations or photographs.

Like anything else, how you use or misuse images can make or break a website, so before we get into how to use Dreamweaver to add images to your website, we'll take a brief look at how best to work with images, and at some common mistakes you should avoid.

Choosing formats for images

When exporting images from a graphics package, it's essential to pick the best file format and amount of compression. With most such applications providing a huge list of formats, you'll be relieved to know that web design is generally only concerned with two: JPEG and GIF.

JPEG

The Joint Photographic Experts Group (JPEG) format is used primarily for images that require smooth color transitions and continuous tones, such as photographs. JPEG supports millions of colors, and very little image detail is lost even when compression settings are fairly high. This is because the format uses **lossy compression**, which removes information that the eye doesn't need. As the compression level increases, this becomes increasingly obvious—at extreme levels of compression, a JPEG will appear to be composed of linked blocks.

In general, 50 percent compression is the highest level you should use—less if the image in question is particularly important (for instance, it makes sense to use less compression if you're a graphic designer presenting a portfolio). If the download time for an image is unacceptably high, reduce its dimensions, if possible, rather than increasing compression—a small, detailed image tends to look better than a large, heavily compressed image.

> *Be aware that applications have different means of referring to compression ratios. For example, Fireworks and Photoshop both use a quality scale, in which 100 is uncompressed and 0 is the maximum level of compression. However, Paint Shop Pro uses compression values in which higher numbers indicate increased compression. Always be sure you know what scale you're using.*

Some applications have the option to save **progressive JPEGs**. Typically, this format results in larger file sizes, but it's useful because it enables your image to download in multiple passes. This means that a low-resolution version will display rapidly, and it will gradually progress to the quality you saved it at, allowing viewers to get a look at a simplified version of the image without having to wait for it to load completely.

GIF

The Graphics Interchange Format (GIF) is in many ways the opposite of JPEG: the GIF format is **lossless**, meaning that there's no color degradation when images are compressed. The format is also restricted to a maximum of 256 colors, thereby rendering it ineffective for color photographs. Using GIF for such images usually results in banding, in which colors are reduced to the nearest equivalent. A fairly extreme example of this is shown in the following illustration.

The GIF format is useful for displaying images with large areas of flat color, such as logos, line art, and type. Although you should generally avoid using graphics for text on your web pages, GIF is the best choice of format if you do.

Although GIF is restricted to 256 colors, you don't have to use the *same* 256 colors every time. Most graphics applications provide various palette options, such as **perceptual**, **selective**, and **web**. A perceptual palette prioritizes colors that the human eye is most sensitive to, providing the best color integrity. A selective palette works in a similar fashion, but balances its color choices with web-safe colors, creating results more likely to be consistent across platforms. A web palette is a 216 color so-called web-safe palette—this used to be popular online, but it has decreased in usage now that the vast majority of monitors are capable of displaying millions of colors (or thousands at the very least). Additionally, you can use applications to lock colors, forcing important colors to stay as they are and not be altered due to the restrictions of a limited 256-color palette.

Images can also be **dithered**, which prevents continuous tones from becoming bands of color. Dithering simulates continuous tones, using the available (restricted) palette. Most graphics editors allow for three different types of dithering: **diffusion**, **pattern**, and **noise**—all of which have markedly different effects on an image. Diffusion dithering applies a random pattern across adjacent pixels, whereas pattern dithering applies a half-tone pattern, rather like that seen in low-quality print publications. Noise dithering works rather like diffusion, but without diffusing the pattern across adjacent pixels.

Transparent GIFs

The GIF89 file format is identical to GIF, with one important exception: you can remove colors, which provides a very basic means of transparency and enables the background to show through. Because this is not alpha transparency (a type of transparency that enables a smooth transition from solid to transparent, allowing for many levels of opacity), it doesn't work in the way many graphic designers expect. You cannot, for instance, fade an image's background from color to transparent and expect the web page's background to show through—instead, GIF89's transparency is akin to cutting a hole with a pair of scissors: the background shows through the removed colors only. This is fine when the "hole" has flat horizontal or vertical edges, but if you try this with irregular shapes, you end up with ragged edges. (A way around this is to export the image with the same background color as that of the web page, but this is only possible if the web page's background is a plain, flat color.)

Because of this restriction, GIF89s are seldom used. They cling on in one area of web design, though—as spacers for stretching table cells, in order to lay out a page. However, even this is falling into disuse as more web designers move to using CSS to lay out web pages.

PNG

Although JPEG and GIF are the main formats used online, another is potentially useful and may become increasingly popular in coming years. The Portable Network Graphics (PNG) format comes in two flavors and can be used as a replacement for both GIF and JPEG. It enables full alpha transparency, thereby enabling all manner of fancy graphical effects. Unfortunately, Internet Explorer version 6 (and earlier) doesn't support this feature, rendering the most useful aspect of the format useless on the majority of PCs. For more information about this format, check out the PNG website at www.libpng.org/pub/png.

> You may be wondering about other formats, including BMP or TIFF, which are occasionally used on the Web. These are nonstandard formats, and although they work fine in some cases, they require additional software in order to render in some browsers (in many cases, they won't render at all, or they'll render inconsistently across browsers). Furthermore, JPEG, GIF, and PNG are well-suited to web design because they enable you to present a lot of visual information in a fairly small file. Presenting the same information in a TIFF or BMP file won't massively increase the image's quality (when taking into account the low resolution of computer monitors), but it will increase download times. The choice is simple: don't use any formats other than JPEG, GIF, or PNG for your web images (and if you decide to use PNG transparency, be sure that your target audience will be able to see it).

Web image mistakes to avoid

The same mistakes tend to crop up again and again when designers start working with images. We've covered the choice of file formats already; the following sections identify other common mistakes and how to avoid them.

Using graphics for body copy

Using graphics for body copy causes your text to print poorly—much worse than HTML-based text—and it also means your text can't be read by search engines or screen readers (thereby effectively locking out the visually impaired), can't be copied and pasted, and can't be enlarged (unless you're using Opera—and even then it will be pixelated). Also, if you need to update graphical text, you must rework the original image, re-export it, and reupload it. To some extent, the same is true for any graphical copy on websites, so wherever possible, use HTML-based text for headings, too.

Not working from original images

Say you have a high-quality TIFF file and then turn it into a compressed JPEG for your web page, but then need to change it slightly. You should start again from the original source material, because resaving an already compressed image reduces its quality each time you do so. Also, under no circumstances whatsoever should you increase the size of a compressed JPEG. Doing so leads to abysmal results every time.

Using too little contrast

Many designers use pale text on an only slightly darker background, and this lack of contrast often finds its way into other things, such as interface elements. In some cases, this isn't a problem: such designs can look stylish if a subtle scheme is used with care. You should, however, ensure that usability isn't affected—it's all very well to have a subtle color scheme, but it's not so great if it stops visitors from being able to easily find things like navigation elements, or from being able to read the text.

Resizing images using Dreamweaver

If you use Dreamweaver to resize an image, chances are it'll become distorted (even more so if you resize it nonproportionately. If you need to resize an image, rework it in a graphics package and then bring the new version back into Dreamweaver.

> *There are exceptions to this rule, although they are rare. For instance, if you work with pixel art, you can proportionately enlarge an image, making it large on the screen. Despite the image being large, the file size will be tiny.*

Not balancing quality and file size

Bandwidth can be a problem in image-heavy sites—both in terms of the host getting hammered when visitor numbers increase, and in terms of the visitors (many of whom may be stuck with dial-up modems) having to download the images. Therefore, always be sure that your images are highly optimized, in order to save on hosting costs and to ensure that your website's visitors don't have to suffer massive downloads. (In fact, they probably won't suffer—they'll more than likely go elsewhere.)

However, this doesn't mean that you should compress every image on your website into a slushy mess (and there are a *lot* of sites out there where the creator has exported JPEGs at what looks like 90 percent compression—"just in case").

Err on the side of caution, but remember that common interface elements are cached, so you can afford to save them at a slightly higher quality. Any image that someone requests (such as via a thumbnail on a portfolio site) is something they *want* to see, so these too can be saved at a higher quality, because the person is likely to wait. Also, there is no such thing as an "optimum" size for web images. If you've read in the past that no web image should ever be larger than 50K, it's hogwash. The size of your images depends entirely on context, the type of site you're creating, and the audience you're creating it for.

> *If you're wondering about the size of one of your web pages—assets and all—try running it through the "webpage size checker" at* www.searchengineworld.com/cgi-bin/page_size.cgi.

Using text overlays

There are many sites where perfectly good images are ruined by garish text overlays, proudly exclaiming who holds the copyright to the image. Although anyone can download images from your website to their hard drive, any reuse is prohibited by law, and you can deal with such (incredibly rare) occurrences accordingly. (Also, if they link directly to images on your server, just try changing the affected images to something text-based, stating "the scumbag whose site you're visiting stole images from me.") If you're worried about someone downloading your images and using them offline, that's not going to happen—a 72 dpi compressed JPEG isn't going to set the world on fire when appropriated for a brochure.

If you do decide on a text overlay—and this can occasionally be useful, such as for identifying the artist—make it succinct and small, and ensure that it doesn't distract from the image—otherwise the image perhaps shouldn't be there in the first place.

Stealing images and designs

Related to the previous tip, remember that copyright exists on the Web just like everywhere else. Unless you have permission to reuse an image you've found online, you shouldn't do so. If discovered, you may get the digital equivalent of a slap on the wrist, but you could also be sued for copyright infringement.

Although it's all right to be influenced by someone else's design, you should also ensure you don't simply rip off a creation found on the Web—otherwise you could end up in legal trouble, or the subject of ridicule as a feature on Tim Murtaugh's excellent website, www.pirated-sites.com.

Adding an image to a web page

Before you add an image to your page, ensure your image is in the correct folder within your website (commonly, designers tend to place images within a folder called assets or images). Then, choose how you want to add your image. Dreamweaver offers a few methods for doing so:

- Code the relevant HTML in Code view.
- Drag and drop the image from Windows Explorer (or Finder on Mac) onto Design view.
- Use Dreamweaver's Insert bar to add an image using dialog boxes.

> *If you choose the drag and drop method, and the image you're trying to add lies outside of your defined site folder, Dreamweaver will ask if you want to copy it across.*

To use the Insert bar method, you need to first select the Common category from the pop-up menu. This provides a number of common tools, including the Image menu.

135

Selecting Image from the menu brings up the Select Image Source dialog box, which is used to choose the image you want to add to your page.

Select an image and click OK (Choose on Mac) and the Image Tag Accessibility Attributes dialog box will appear (assuming you have the accessibility options set as shown in the "Web page editing preferences" section of Chapter 2). In the Alternate text field, type a succinct description of the image you're placing on the page. If the image is to be used as a means of accessing other content, instead type its function, because that will be more useful to people surfing the Web with assistive devices. (For instance, if you're going to add a logo to the page, which will eventually become a link to the site's home page, it makes more sense to enter "Back to home page" for the Alternative text than "logo".)

Click OK, and the image will be added to your web page. In Code view, the image is represented by the `<img>` element, while in Design view, you'll see the image appear as is, complete with drag handles.

However, avoid using these handles to resize the image (even though this is possible in Dreamweaver), because your image will become distorted. If you need to resize an image, edit it in your graphics application.

Editing an image

Unless your planning is always impeccable, you'll now and again need to edit images you've already added to your web page. Some such changes may be minor, while others will require completely replacing the image file. In this section, we'll look at various edits you can make to images directly in Dreamweaver.

Changing an image's source

The most drastic edit you can make to an image is to replace it with an entirely different one. The most efficient way of replacing an image is to bring the Select Image Source dialog box back up, which can be done by clicking the folder icon next to the Src field in the Properties panel, or simply by double-clicking the image itself in Design view.

Once the dialog box has appeared, use it to select a new file to replace the existing one, and then click OK (Choose on Mac). When you do so, Dreamweaver automatically updates the page's code, creating a path to the new image and also changing the height and width settings as necessary. Note, however, that Dreamweaver doesn't update the alt attribute value (for alternate text); if this needs amending, you need to do so manually by changing the value in the Alt field within the Properties panel.

Integrating with Fireworks

When you select an image, the Properties panel provides a number of options for image editing, which are accessed by clicking the icons next to the word Edit. The first two icons offer integration with Fireworks:

- The first, which is the Fireworks logo, enables you to edit the selected image in that application. Click the icon, and you are asked whether you want to work directly with the image or to use a separate PNG file, to avoid changing the original. You're then presented with your image inside the standard Fireworks user interface, except that the document window has Editing from Dreamweaver under the toolbar, and a Done button, which completes the edit and sends you back to Dreamweaver.

- The second, whose tooltip says Optimize in Fireworks, enables you to recompress an image using the Fireworks Optimize dialog box.

Although both tools are handy, it's perhaps best to go back to your original image when you want to make changes—recompressing an image will create a worse result than setting the same level of compression from the original file that the web image is based on.

If you don't have Fireworks installed, you cannot use the Optimize in Fireworks *tool, but the* Edit *tool will work, launching whatever image editor you have on your computer, such as Photoshop. Note, however, that there's no other integration between such applications.*

Cropping an image

If you need to crop an image, you can do so directly in Dreamweaver, rather than opening up the likes of Photoshop or Fireworks.

To crop an image, select it and then click the Crop tool icon on the Properties panel. If this is the first time you've used the tool, a warning dialog box appears, saying that any changes you make to the image are permanent. (Therefore, if you're not sure what you're doing, work on a backup copy!) Any crops can be undone, however, by using the standard Edit ➤ Undo menu selection.

> Dreamweaver 8
>
> (!) The action you are about to perform will permanently alter the selected image. You can undo any changes you make by selecting Edit > Undo.
>
> ☐ Don't show me this message again.
>
> OK

Click OK and a crop outline will appear inside your image. Use the drag handles to define new edges for the image, and then either double-click inside the crop or press Enter on your keyboard, and the changes will take effect.

Resizing and resampling an image

It's recommended that you work solely in an image editor when creating optimized images for a website. If you need to resize something, go back to the original source image and recreate the web version. However, if you're working on a rough visual for a client, it's a lot quicker to resize an image directly inside Dreamweaver.

To resize an image, click on it, and then drag the grab handles that appear at the image's edges. To resize proportionately, Shift-drag the bottom-right grab handle.

After an image is resized, it will look jagged, because although the original source file has certain pixel dimensions, the HTML is now forcing the image to display at a different size. This can be dealt with by clicking on the Resample icon, which reworks the image, smoothing out the wrinkles.

Setting brightness, contrast, and sharpening

While you should generally do your image editing in graphics editors, there are occasions when you see your web page and think that an image could do with being just a touch brighter, or a tad sharper (the latter is often the case with images you've reduced in dimensions for viewing on the Web, because reducing images tends to blur them). The two icons next to the Crop icon are Brightness and Contrast (the circle) and Sharpness (the triangle). Like the Crop tool, using these tools permanently alters your image, so take care, and use a backup of your image if you're not absolutely sure of what you're doing.

Clicking the Brightness and Contrast button brings up its associated dialog box, complete with two controls—one to adjust brightness and the other to edit the contrast of the image. Unless your aim is to create wacky effects, go easy when using these controls; otherwise your photographs will end up looking very fake. However, a relatively small boost in contrast can often add a lot to photographs that have slightly dull colors.

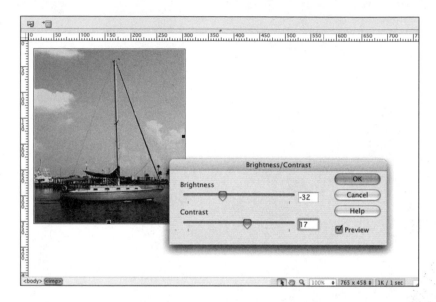

The Sharpen tool is pretty basic as sharpening tools go, offering a single slider that has values from 0 to 10. At the top end, the effect wrecks most images, producing ugly artifacts, so it's unlikely that you'll ever set this slider to higher than 4. That said, I actually recommend using your graphics application's unsharp mask filter instead, because it'll give you more control than Dreamweaver's built-in tool.

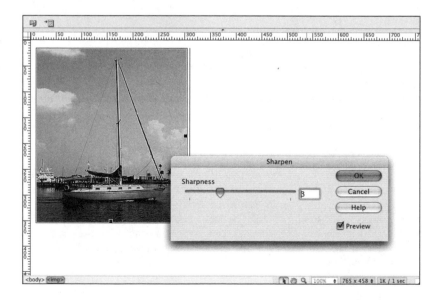

Creating image maps

Image maps have fallen out of favor with most web designers, but they still have occasional uses. If you're not familiar with the terminology, an **image map** is essentially a system of making specifically defined areas, often referred to as **hotspots**, within an image act as links to other pages. You could, for example, have a map of the UK, and have links for each of the various counties leading to a separate HTML document.

Dreamweaver makes creating image maps a simple process.

Adding an image map to your web page

1. First, select your image, and then choose the hotspot type you want to use from the Image menu in the Common category of the Insert bar, or from the set of icons below Map in the Properties panel.

2. Drag out your hotspot directly on the image itself. When you're done, add some content to the Link field, to say where the hotspot should lead to when it's clicked on the web page (if this is an external URL, type it in, including http://; if not, click the folder icon and choose a file from your website). Also add content to the Alt field, describing where the hotspot leads to—this helps those using screen readers to navigate the image map.

3. If you need to edit the hotspot, don't drag the drag handles while the hotspot icon is still active in the Properties panel, otherwise you'll end up dragging out another hotspot. Instead, click the Pointer Hotspot Tool icon (the arrow directly under Map in the Properties panel) and use it to drag the various points of the hotspot (which you can do when the arrow turns white). You can also click and hold inside the hotspot and drag it around, should you need to.

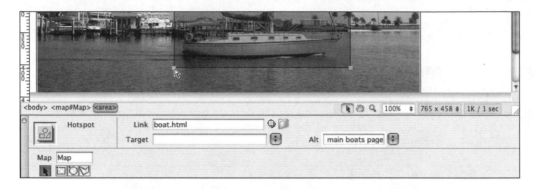

This exercise shows only the rectangular hotspot type, but Dreamweaver also offers oval and polygonal hotspots. The latter can have as many points as you wish; using Dreamweaver's new zoom feature, it's possible to create highly accurate image map hotspots (although you should avoid doing terribly complex image maps, because each hotspot adds code to your page—hundreds of hotspots could increase the download time of your page considerably).

Styling images using CSS

Like any other web page element, images can be rapidly styled with CSS. In the following exercises you'll see how to add borders to web page images, how to wrap text around an image, and, finally, how to make use of contextual selectors to affect all images within specific web page divs.

As I've already shown, there are various ways of styling web page elements, and images are no exception. You can style an individual element by applying a style directly to it, you can style all similar elements on a web page by applying a style to a tag, or you can style elements within a specific area of a page by applying a style to a contextual selector. All three methods are used in the exercises that follow.

Adding borders to all web page images

In this exercise, we'll run through the process for adding a border to all of your web page images using CSS. The advantage to adding borders with CSS, rather than directly in the image, are that the border will be a solid color (as opposed to the borders on a JPEG, which may be composed of a variety of shades, due to the format's compression), and they can be applied and edited site-wide in minutes.

1. Create a new web page, and add a few images to it. Attach a CSS document to the web page.

2. Create a new CSS rule by clicking the New CSS Rule button in the CSS Styles panel. Choose Tag for the Selector Type, and enter img in the Tag field. Ensure that Define in is set to your attached style sheet, and click OK.

3. When the CSS Rule Definition dialog box appears, choose the Border category. Set Style to solid, Width to 2 pixels, and Color to black (use the color picker or just type #000000 in the field). Click OK.

4. Any images on the page will have a border styled using the settings defined in the previous step. To edit this style, just double-click it in the CSS Styles panel. Because this style is applied site-wide, borders for every image on every page of your site can be changed in seconds.

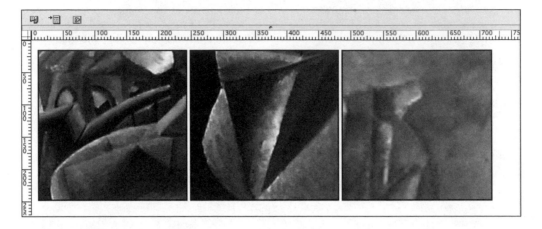

Completed files for this exercise can be found in the Chapter 6 folder of this book's download files: 6_adding_borders_to_all_images.html, 6_adding_borders_to_all_images.css, painting.jpg, painting2.jpg, and painting3.jpg.

Adding a border to a single image only

The previous exercise added the same border to all images on the website. This exercise will show you how to apply a border to a single image.

1. Create a new web page, and add some images. Attach a CSS document to it.

2. Create a new CSS rule, and choose Class as the Selector Type. In the Name field type .imgBorder, and make sure Define in is set to your attached style sheet. Click OK.

3. Define your style in the CSS Rule Definition dialog box the same way you did in step 3 of the previous exercise: in the Border category, set Style to solid, Width to 2 pixels, and Color to black. Click OK.

4. Apply your style to the relevant image or images by right-clicking the image and choosing the style from the CSS Styles menu, or by selecting the image and choosing the style from the Properties panel's Style menu, or by one of the other methods.

Completed files for this exercise can be found in the Chapter 6 folder of the book's download files: 6_adding_borders_to_one_image.html, 6_adding_borders_to_one_image.css, painting.jpg, painting2.jpg, and painting3.jpg.

Wrapping text around an image

It's common in print publications to have text wrapping around images, and a similar effect is simple enough to create in Dreamweaver.

1. Create a new web page and attach a style sheet to it. Add a single image to the web page; for this purposes of this exercise, make the image fairly small—less than 250 pixels per side. (You can use painting.jpg from the Chapter 6 folder of the book's download files if you like.) Underneath the image, add a few paragraphs of text. Dreamweaver will likely place the image inside a paragraph, so select the image, right-click or Ctrl-click the <p> tag in the status bar and choose Remove Tag from the pop-up menu.

2. Create a new style, and set Class as the Selector Type. Type .floatRight into the Name field, and click OK.

New CSS Rule

Selector Type: ● Class (can apply to any tag)
○ Tag (redefines the look of a specific tag)
○ Advanced (IDs, pseudo-class selectors)

OK
Cancel

Name: .floatRight

Define in: ● 6_wrapping_text_around_an_im...
○ This document only

Help

---

3. In the CSS Rule Definition dialog box, select the Box category and set Float to right. Because we don't want the text to hug the image, we also need to set margins around any image styled using this rule, so deselect Same for all under Margin, and set Bottom and Left to 10 pixels. Click OK.

CSS Rule Definition for .floatRight in 6_wrapping_text_around_an_image.css

Category
Type
Background
Block
Box
Border
List
Positioning
Extensions

Box

Width: [   ] pix...   Float: [right]
Height: [   ] pix...   Clear: [   ]

Padding   Margin
☑ Same for all   ☐ Same for all
Top: [   ] pix...   Top: [   ] pix...
Right: [   ] pix...   Right: [   ] pix...
Bottom: [   ] pix...   Bottom: [10] pix...
Left: [   ] pix...   Left: [10] pix...

Help   Apply   Cancel   OK

---

4. In Design view, apply the floatRight style to your image, and it should then sit to the right of your paragraphs of text. If your text's height is larger than the image, the text will wrap around the image.

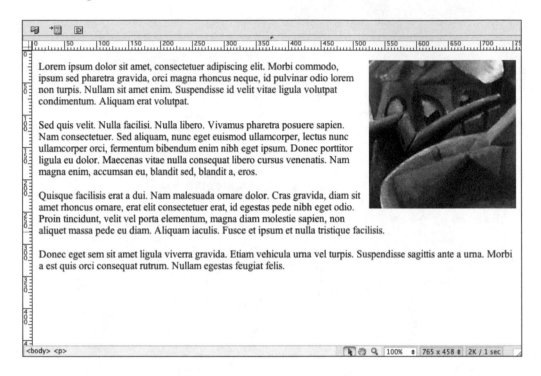

Completed files for this exercise can be found in the Chapter 6 folder of the book's download files: 6_wrapping_text_around_an_image.html, 6_wrapping_text_around_an_image.css, and painting.jpg.

Styling images using contextual selectors

Earlier, we made all images within a site have a border. However, in most websites, there are certain areas of the page where borders aren't required. For instance, I've created numerous sites where borders are used in the entire content area, but are not needed within the masthead and navigation areas. While it would be possible to style such images separately, applying a style to turn off the border, it's better to use contextual selectors. As long as the images that need to be borderless are within a div with a known ID value, you can create a rule that essentially says "ensure all images within the navigation div don't have a border," even if there's a rule elsewhere stating that all images have a border. This is making use of the CSS cascade referred to in "The cascade" section in Chapter 4.

1. Start with the completed files from the previous exercise, "Wrapping text around an image." Click at the top left corner of Design view, and use the cursor arrows to move the cursor up and left until it won't move any further. This ensures the cursor is placed at the start of your web page's content area. (You can double-check this by looking at the cursor position in Code or Split view—the cursor should be positioned right after the <body> tag.) Click Insert Div Tag from the Layout section of the Insert bar to bring up the Insert Div Tag dialog box. Type navigation in the ID field, and click OK.

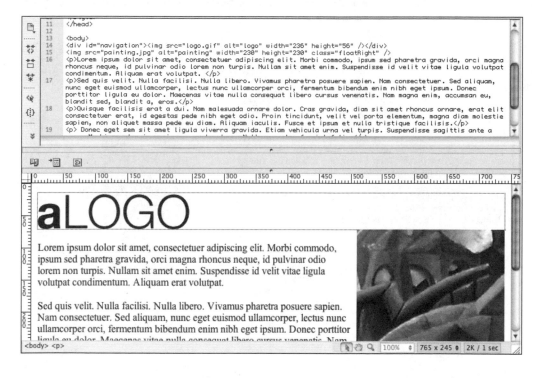

2. Replace the default content of the div with an image, such as logo.gif from the Chapter 6 folder of the book's download files.

3. Create a new CSS rule. Choose Tag as the Selector Type, and type img in the Tag field. Click OK.

4. In the Border category, set Style to solid, Width to 2 pixels, and Color to black. Click OK, and both of the images on the page will have borders.

5. To remove the border from the logo *without* applying a rule to the image itself, you can use a contextual selector. Create a new CSS style, and choose Advanced as the Selector Type. Type #navigation img in the Selector field. This means that any property values defined for this rule will only affect images within the navigation div.

6. In the CSS Rule Definition dialog box, choose the Border category and set Style to none. Click OK, and the border around the logo should disappear—as would any borders around other images placed inside the navigation div.

Completed files for this exercise can be found in the Chapter 6 folder of the book's download files: 6_contextual_selectors.html, 6_contextual_selectors.css, painting.jpg, and logo.gif.

Creating a thumbnails area

Another useful tip involving contextual selectors and images relates to creating an area on a web page to house image thumbnails (for a gallery). Rather than using a table to format the thumbnails, you can just add a bunch of images to a div, and then use CSS to add borders to the images and separate them.

1. Create a new web page and attach a style sheet to it. Also ensure that you have a thumbnail image handy, or just use thumbnail.jpg from the Chapter 6 folder of the book's download files.

2. Click Insert Div Tag from the Layout section of the Insert bar to bring up the Insert Div Tag dialog box. Type thumbnails in the ID field, and click OK. Inside this div, add 20 instances of your image by copying and pasting. (Of course, a real site would use lots of different thumbnail images, but this is just a layout example! Feel free to use lots of different thumbnail images if you have time!)

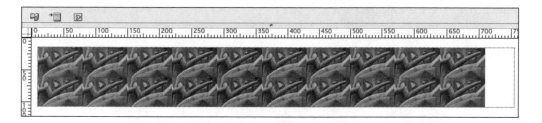

3. Create a new style, and in the New CSS Rule dialog box choose Advanced as the Selector Type. In the Selector field, type #thumbnails img and click OK.

4. In the CSS Rules Definition dialog box, select the Border category and set Style to solid, Width to 1 pixels, and Color to black—this adds a border around all of the thumbnail images.

5. In the Box category, set Float to left, and set the Bottom and Left settings under Margin to 10 pixels. This floats all of the thumbnails and sets a margin between them. Click OK, and you should see something like the following image.

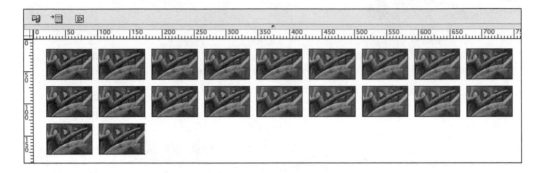

If you save your files and preview your web page, you'll see that the images all line up as expected, with the margins defined in the previous step. Borders have also been applied because of this style. However, if you add more thumbnails in Dreamweaver and refresh the page in a browser, you'll note that the images automatically reflow, depending on the width of the browser. This automatic reflow also occurs if the thumbnails div's width is restricted and fixed. Old methods would have you using line breaks or tables to deal with this kind of layout, but now we have bordered, neatly arranged thumbnails, with the presentation all controlled by CSS. If we remove some images and place others there, they will all automatically pick up the style and reflow, potentially saving you lots of time.

> *Chapter 8, which concentrates on web page layout, has plenty more about working with floated elements, and also about the important **clear** CSS property, which is used to ensure that content that comes after floated elements ends up positioned in the manner you require.*

Summary

In this chapter, you've learned how to approach using images on your web pages, found out about the different image formats available, discovered various means of adding images to pages and editing them in Dreamweaver, and you also now know a number of ways to style them using CSS. In combination with the previous chapter, you now have the means to create the bulk of your website's content.

In the next chapter, we'll explore the main area of web page interactivity, by looking at how to create navigation for your websites.

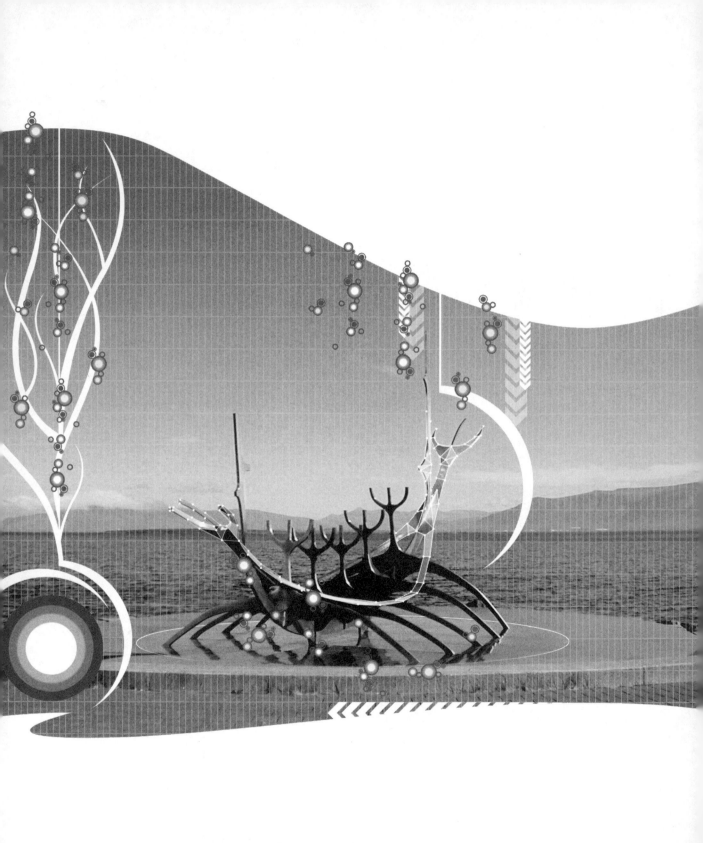

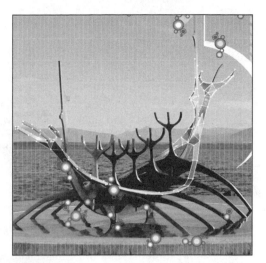

Chapter 7

CREATING NAVIGATION FOR YOUR WEBSITE

In this chapter...

- Introducing web navigation
- Creating links
- Styling links in CSS
- Creating pop-up windows
- Using links to switch images
- Creating navigation bars
- Creating rollover links

The primary concern of most websites is the provision of information. The ability to enable nonlinear navigation via the use of links is one of the main things that sets the Web apart from other media. But without organized, coherent, and usable navigation, even a site with the most amazing content will fail.

In this chapter, we'll look at how to create various types of navigation. Instead of relying on large numbers of graphics and clunky JavaScript, we'll create rollovers that are largely driven by CSS rules. And rather than using pop-up windows to display large graphics when a thumbnail image is clicked, you'll see how to do everything on a single page.

Navigation types

There are essentially three types of navigation on the Web:

- **Inline navigation:** General links within web page content areas
- **Site navigation:** The primary navigation area of a website, commonly referred to as a **navigation bar**
- **Search-based navigation:** A search box that enables you to search a site using terms you input yourself

Although the distinctions between these three categories seem clear enough in this list, lines blur, and not every site includes all the different types of navigation. Also, various designers call each type of navigation different things, and there's no official name in each case. In the following sections, I'll expand a little on each type.

Inline navigation

Inline navigation used to be the primary way of navigating the Web, which, many moons ago, largely consisted of technical documentation. Oddly, inline navigation—links within a web page's body copy—has become increasingly rare. Perhaps this is due to the increasing popularity of visually oriented web design tools, leading designers to concentrate more on visuals than usability. Maybe it's because designers have collectively forgotten that links can be made anywhere and not just in navigation bars. In any case, links—inline links in particular—are the main thing that differentiates the Web from other media, making it unique.

For instance, you can make specific words within a document link directly to related content. A great example of this is Wikipedia (www.wikipedia.org), the free encyclopedia.

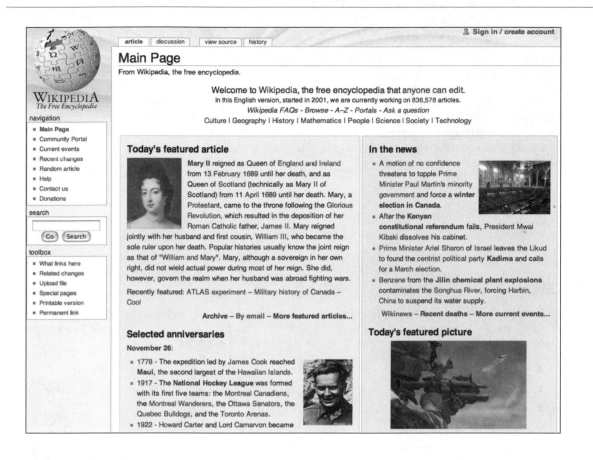

Site navigation

Wikipedia showcases other types of navigation. To the left, underneath the logo, is a navigation bar that is present on every page of the site, allowing users to quickly access each section. This kind of navigation tool is essential for most websites—long gone are the days when users were happy to keep returning to a homepage to navigate to new content. (Actually, to be fair, they weren't ever too happy about it, but there you go.)

As Wikipedia proves, just because you have a global navigation bar, that doesn't mean you should skimp on inline navigation. In recent times, I've seen a rash of sites that say things like Thank you for visiting our website. If you have any questions, you can contact us by clicking the contact details link on our navigation bar. Quite frankly, this is bizarre. A better solution is to say Thank you for visiting our website. If you have any questions, please contact us, and to turn contact us into a link to the contact details page. This might seem like common sense, but not every web designer thinks in this way.

Search-based navigation

Wikipedia has a search box below the navigation bar on each page. It's said there are two types of web users: those who eschew search boxes, and those who head straight for them. The thing is, search boxes are not always needed, despite the claims of middle managers the world over. Indeed, most sites get by with well-structured and coherent navigation. However, sites sometimes grow very large (typically those that are heavy on information and that have hundreds or thousands of pages, such as technical repositories, review archives, or large online stores). In such cases, it's often not feasible to use standard navigation elements to access information. Attempting to do so leads to users getting lost trying to navigate a huge navigation "tree."

Unlike other types of navigation, search boxes aren't entirely straightforward to set up yourself, and they require server-side scripting for their functionality. *Foundation ASP for Dreamweaver 8* by Omar Elbaga and Rob Turnbull (friends of ED, ISBN: 1590595688) shows how to create a search function, and a quick trawl through a search engine should provide you with various other sources.

Creating and targeting links

The simplest way to create a link in Dreamweaver is by making use of the Properties panel. First, select the element on the web page that you want to make into a link (commonly some text, but you can also turn images into links). Next, you have several ways to define what the link accesses:

- Click the folder icon in the Properties panel and browse to the page you want to link to
- Drag the "point to file" icon (which is next to the folder icon) to a document in the Files panel
- Drag a document from the Files panel to the Link field in the Properties panel
- Use the pop-up menu next to the Link field to select a previously used link
- Simply type a location directly into the Properties panel's Link field

If you're familiar with the structure of your site and how various link types work, it generally is faster to type locations directly into the Link field. However, if you wouldn't know a relative link from a cucumber, or have never seen the characters ../ before, it's perhaps best to initially stick to Dreamweaver's automated methods of linking to files. However, if you are curious to learn, the following three sections provide an overview of the three different ways of linking to web documents.

> *If you're wanting to link to a document on an external website, simply type the URL into the* Link *field as you would into a web browser, taking care not to omit* http://.

Absolute links

A link like those used to access a website in a web browser is typically known as an **absolute link**, sometimes called a **full URL**. When you're working in Dreamweaver, this kind of link is typically used when linking to external files—other websites. This type of link provides the entire path to a destination file, including the file transfer protocol, domain name, any directory names, and the filename itself. Here's an example of such a link:

```
http://www.wireviews.com/lyrics/instar.html
```

In this case, the file transfer protocol is `http://`, www indicates that the page is part of the World Wide Web, the domain is `wireviews.com`, the directory is `lyrics`, and the filename is `instar.html`.

> *Depending on how the target site's web server has been set up, you may or may not have to include www prior to the domain name when creating this kind of link. When linking to a home page that is merely a domain and a domain suffix (such as google.com or bbc.co.uk), it's best to include the www; however, when linking to subdomains, such as news.bbc.co.uk, adding the www will break the link. Therefore, always ensure you check absolute links in a web browser before adding them to a web page.*

If you're linking to a website's homepage, you can usually leave out a filename, and the server will automatically pick up the default document (assuming one exists), which can be index.html, default.htm, index.php, index.asp, or some other name, depending on the server type. However, adding a trailing slash after the domain is beneficial (for example, http://www.wireviews.com/).

Relative links

A relative link is one that locates a file in relation to the current document. Taking the Wireviews example, if we were on the `instar.html` page, located inside the `lyrics` directory, and we wanted to link back to the homepage via a relative link, we could use the following link:

```
../index.html
```

The index.html filename is preceded by `../`, which tells the web browser to move up one directory prior to looking for index.html. Moving in the other direction is done in the same way as with absolute links: by preceding the filename with the path. Therefore, to get from the homepage back to the instar.html page, which is in the lyrics directory, you can use the following link:

```
lyrics/instar.html
```

In some cases, you need to combine both methods. For instance, this website has HTML documents in both the `lyrics` and `reviews` directories. To get from the `instar.html` lyrics page to a review, you have to go up one level, and then down into the relevant directory to locate the file. This would be done by using the following link:

```
../reviews/alloy.html
```

To dissect this, `../` moves up one level, `reviews/` moves into the `reviews` directory, and `alloy.html` picks the document of that name.

Root-relative links

Root-relative links work much like absolute links, but from the root of a website instead of from your current location. They ensure you point to the relevant document without your having to type an absolute link or mess around with relative links. For instance, regardless of how many directories deep you are in the Wireviews website, a root-relative link to the homepage always looks like this:

```
/index.html
```

And a link to the instar.html page within the lyrics directory always looks like this:

```
/lyrics/instar.html
```

The initial forward slash tells the browser to start the path to the file from the root of the current website.

> *All link paths must contain forward slashes only. Some software—notably some by Microsoft—both creates and permits backward slashes (such as* lyrics\wire\154.html*), but this is nonstandard and does not work in non-Microsoft web browsers. Ensure that whenever you type your links in Dreamweaver, you only ever use forward slashes.*

Targeting links

Targeting a link is when you specify in the link itself where the link should be opened. The Target field is found in the Properties panel underneath the Link field, and it provides you with a number of options for where the link is opened. The most popular value is _blank, which opens the target document in a new, blank web browser window.

However, targeting should be avoided wherever possible. While some argue that opening external links in a new window is beneficial, because it enables users to look at external content and then return to your site, what it actually does is take control of the browser *away* from the users (after all, if they want to open content in a new window, they can do so using keyboard commands or contextual menus). More important, opening documents in new windows breaks the history path. For many, this might not be a huge issue, but for those navigating the Web via a screen reader, pop-ups are a menace. New content opens up, is deemed to not be of interest, and the Back function is invoked. But this is a new window, with its own *blank* history. Gnashing of teeth ensues.

There are exceptions to this rule—notably when using frames, as you'll see when we cover that technology in Chapter 8—but target is generally to be avoided. The W3C agrees: although the target attribute is valid when working with XHTML Transitional, it's not when using XHTML Strict.

Linking to elsewhere on a web page

As well as linking to other pages, you can link to other areas of the same web page. In this exercise, we'll create a simple system that could be used on a FAQ page. At the top of the page will be a list of links, and clicking a link will make the page "jump" to the relevant answer. After each answer will be a link that enables you to "jump" back to the questions list.

1. Create a new HTML document, and add a three-item list at the top, as shown.

2. Turn each of the list items into a link, and link Question one, Question two, and Question three to #answer1, #answer2, and #answer3 respectively.

3. Click somewhere inside the list. In the status bar, you'll see the start tag for a list (<ul>) appear (along with some others); right-click or Ctrl-click it and choose Quick Tag Editor from the contextual menu.

4. When the Quick Tag Editor appears, use it to amend the tag to read as follows: <ul id= "questions">. Press Enter to confirm the edit.

What you've done here is provided this particular list element with a unique ID, which can now be referenced in various ways. (Note how in the status bar <ul> has become <ul#questions> in response to the ID being defined.)

5. If the list is still selected, use the cursor keys to get to the end of it, and press Enter until a new, blank paragraph is created. Press Enter a bunch more times until the question list can no longer be seen.

6. Type The answer to question 1! and press Enter. Underneath this answer, in a new paragraph, type Back to questions. Turn the second line into a link, linking to #questions.

7. Click inside the "answer" paragraph, and use the status bar to access the Quick Tag Editor by right-clicking or Ctrl-clicking the <p> tag (in the same way that you did in step 4). Change the tag to read <p id="answer1">.

8. Repeat steps 6 and 7 for two more paragraphs, replacing question 1 in the paragraph of text with question 2 and question 3, and replacing id="answer1" with id="answer2" and id="answer3" in the Quick Tag Editor as appropriate.

9. Use File ➤ Preview in Browser to preview the page. Shrink the browser window down small for best effect, and try clicking on the question links. You should find the page jumps to the associated answer. Similarly, clicking on Back to questions jumps back up the page to the questions list. Note, though, that the page only jumps to a linked element if there's enough room underneath it. If the linked element is at the bottom of the web page, you'll see it plus a browser window's height of content above. This is the case with the third answer—to make the browser behavior similar to that of the other two questions, add a bunch of blank paragraphs under the Back to questions link under the third "answer" paragraph.

A completed version of this exercise can be found in the Chapter 7 folder of the book's download files. The file is 7_anchors.html.

Styling links using CSS

By default, links are underlined and displayed in blue when viewed in a web browser. However, links have four states, and their visual appearance varies depending on the current state of the link. The four states are

- **link:** The link's standard state, before any action has taken place. The default appearance is underlined and blue.
- **visited:** The link's state after having been clicked. The default appearance is underlined and purple.
- **hover:** The link's state while the mouse cursor is over it. Web browsers do not change the link's appearance on the hover state by default, but this state can be styled using CSS.
- **active:** The link's state while being clicked. The default appearance is underlined and red.

If every site adhered to this default scheme of link appearances, it would be easier to find where you've been and where you haven't on the Web. However, most designers prefer to dictate their own color schemes rather than having blue and purple links peppering their designs. In my view, this is fine.

Despite what some usability gurus claim, most web users these days probably don't even know what the default link colors are, and so hardly miss them. However, always ensure links are easy to differentiate from other text-based content on your page, or users won't be able to find and click them.

To create styles for a link state, create a new CSS rule as usual, select Advanced for the Selector Type, and then use the pop-up menu to select a state.

In the CSS Rule Definition dialog box, try experimenting with amending the color and background color of the text on the hover state, to provide user feedback, as shown in the following images. For the visited state, a subtly lighter version of your standard link state color is often a good choice. The depicted example shows a fairly radical change: on the hover state, the link's background turns a dark grey and the text turns white.

The files for this example can be found in the Chapter 7 folder of the book's download files, and they're named 7_styling_links.html and 7_styling_links.css.

Note that you need to define a:link, a:visited, a:hover, and a:active for each set of link styles on your website, otherwise defaults will be displayed for undefined states. Alternatively, you can set a style for all anchors (rather than just clickable links) using the a selector. To do this, choose Tag as the Selector Type in the New CSS Rule dialog box, and type a in the Tag field before proceeding to the CSS Rule Definition dialog box. However, even when doing this, it's highly recommended to still define a hover state, in order to provide user feedback when a link is moused over.

Multiple link states: the cascade

A common problem web designers come up against is multiple link styles within a document. Although you should be consistent with links, there are very specific occasions where it's okay to have different link styles. One of those is for site navigation. Web users are quite happy with navigation bar links differing from standard inline links. Other occasions that spring to mind are for a web page's footer, where links are often displayed in a smaller font than that of the other web page copy, and for areas where background colors are different and the standard link color wouldn't stand out (although in such situations it would perhaps be best to amend either the background or your default link colors).

Some designers apply a class to every link that should have a non-default style, but in doing so they end up with loads of inline junk that can't be easily amended at a later date. Instead, by the careful use of divs (with unique IDs) on the web page and contextual selectors in CSS, we can rapidly style links for each section of the web page.

Creating different link styles in two page areas

1. Create a new HTML document and link a CSS document to it. By using the Insert Div Tag button (in the Layout section of the Insert bar), add three divs to your web page, each one underneath the previous (done by using the After tag option in the Insert menu). When creating the divs, give them the following ID values, in order: navigation, content, footer.

   When adding the divs: for the navigation div, select At insertion point from the Insert menu; for the content div, select After tag from the Insert menu and select <div id="navigation"> from the menu to the right; and set the footer div to be inserted after the content div.

2. Replace the default content of each div with a list containing a few links. As these links are just "practice" ones, link them to # to create dummy links.

3. Create a new CSS rule, and in the New CSS Rule dialog box, select Tag as the Selector Type. In the Tag field, type a and click OK.

4. The property values used in this step will be the defaults for all links on the website. For this exercise, we'll keep things simple: in the Type category of the CSS Rule Definition dialog box, set Weight to bold and Color to red. Click OK, and all your links will turn red and be rendered in bold type.

5. Next, we'll create overrides for the links in the navigation area. Create a new CSS style, but this time choose Advanced as the Selector Type. In the Selector field, type #navigation a and click OK.

6. Let's make the navigation buttons very different from the standard ones: in the Type category of the CSS Rule Definition dialog box, set Decoration to none to remove the default underlines, set Case to uppercase, and set Color to #aaaaaa; in the Background category, set Background color to #333333.

7. Finally, create another new advanced CSS rule, this time with #footer a as the selector. Set Size to 80% in the CSS Rule Definition dialog box.

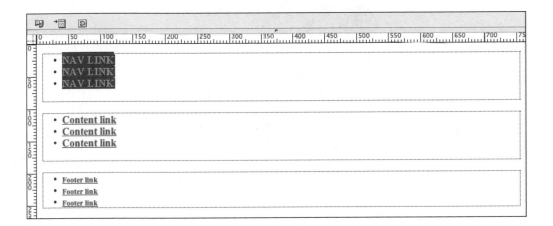

In Design view, you should see something like the previous image—three totally different link styles on the same page. Try taking this further, defining a hover state for each of the three different areas; you'll need to use the advanced selector a:hover for the default hover state, and the selectors #navigation a:hover and #footer a:hover for the navigation link hover state and footer link hover state respectively.

The completed files for this exercise can be found in the Chapter 7 folder of the book's download files: 7_multiple_states.html and 7_multiple_states.css.

Advanced link usage

We'll now look at two more advanced ways of working with links: creating pop-up windows and using links to switch an image that's on a web page.

Creating pop-up windows

Although pop-up windows are generally a pain in the backside, especially when automated, there are some occasions when they can be useful. For instance, if you want to provide a user with brief access to terms and conditions without interrupting an online store checkout process, you might open the terms in a pop-up window.

1. Create and save a new HTML document and a new JavaScript document. (To create a JavaScript document, go to File ➤ New, choose the General tab, and then select Basic page from the Category column. In the Basic page column, select JavaScript and click Create.) Bring the JavaScript document to the front, and delete any content within it. Drag the Pop-Up Window snippet from the Snippets panel (found in JavaScript ➤ windows) to the JavaScript document in Code view. Save and close the JavaScript document.

2. You should now have just the HTML document open. Ensure head content is visible between Code and Design view (check that View ➤ Head Content is checked) and double-click some blank space in this area (i.e., click to the right of the two default icons). This moves the cursor in Code view to inside the head area of the web page.

3. Choose the HTML section in the Insert bar, and click the Script button. Click the folder icon to browse to the JavaScript document created in step 1, and click Choose and OK.

4. Add some text in your web page, to be used as the trigger for the pop-up window. In order to create the link, select it and then type the following in the Link field:

```
javascript:popUpWindow('http://www.google.com','10','20','400','300')
```

As you can see, each of the five values is comma-separated and enclosed in single quotes. The values are, in order: the pop-up window's source (which can be an external website or a page elsewhere on your own site), the horizontal offset from the screen edge, the vertical offset from the screen edge, the width of the window, and the height of the window.

Click on the link to open the pop-up window. As you can see, the window itself is very definitely "bare bones," but by directly editing the script, you can specify which elements of the window are disabled and which are enabled. To do so, simply open up your JavaScript document and look for the string of values in the popUpWin line, changing no to yes or vice-versa, as appropriate. (For instance, if you want the status bar to be enabled, change status=no to status=yes.)

Completed versions of these files are in the Chapter 7 folder of the book's download files: 7_pop-up.html and 7_pop-up.js.

Using links to switch images

While working with JavaScript and snippets is fresh in your mind, let's take a quick look at how to create an image switcher in Dreamweaver. This exercise will show you how to create a basic image gallery, using two thumbnail images, two full-size images, a JavaScript document, and a single web page. Using this technique, you can rapidly get online galleries up and running.

For this exercise, you need to create two thumbnail images and two full-size images. If you don't have any at hand, use the files image_1.gif, image_2.gif, image_1_thumbnail.gif, *and* image_2_thumbnail.gif *from the book's download files, available from the friends of ED website.*

1. Create a new HTML document and a JavaScript document, and link the JavaScript document to the HTML as you did in the previous exercise.

2. Bring the JavaScript document to the front, delete all content, and then drag the Switch Image script into the document from the Snippets panel. (The Switch Image script is found in JavaScript ➤ images.)

3. Add the two thumbnails to the web page, using the Insert bar's Image button (found in the Common section—see Chapter 6 for more on adding images to a web page). Underneath, add one of the full-size images. Select it, and then give it the name mainPhoto by using the Properties panel.

4. Click on each of the thumbnails in turn, and turn them into links that will switch the main image by adding the following to the Link field:

```
javascript:switchImage('mainPhoto','image_name.jpg')
```

Replace 'image_name.jpg' with the filename of the image that replaces the main image when the thumbnail is clicked. (If you'd like to add more thumbnails to the gallery, just repeat this process in each case. And you can always add borders to the images by integrating the exercise shown in Chapter 6, "Adding borders to all web page images".)

The files for this exercise are in the Chapter 7 folder of the book's download files, and are named as follows: 7_image_swap.html, 7_image_swap.js, image_1.gif, image_2.gif, image_1_thumbnail.gif, image_2_thumbnail.gif.

Creating navigation bars

The final section in this chapter will show you how to create a number of different navigation bars, some of which are aligned vertically and some horizontally. Because the presentation aspects of these examples are driven by CSS, you should be able to use them as the basis for dozens of variations—in other words, each of the navigation bars in this section could provide the starting point for the navigation area of the majority of website projects you may happen to work on.

Vertical navigation bars

Vertical navigation bars are typically used on websites that have a lot of top-level links, or on those where the people creating and maintaining the site want the second-level links to also be visible and therefore immediately accessible. This exercise will show you how to create and style such a navigation bar.

> Note that because of bugs in Internet Explorer, this exercise as created in Dreamweaver won't initially display as intended. See the subsequent "Removing white space in Internet Explorer" section after the exercise for a fix.

Creating and styling a vertically aligned navigation bar

1. Create a new HTML document and CSS document, and link the latter to the former. Save the files on your hard drive.

2. Bring the HTML document to the front, and click the Insert Div Tag button in the Layout section of the Insert bar. In the ID field, type navigation, and then click OK. This creates a new div for the navigation bar to be placed within. This means that when it comes to styling the navigation elements, we can use contextual selectors so the styles will only affect elements within the navigation div.

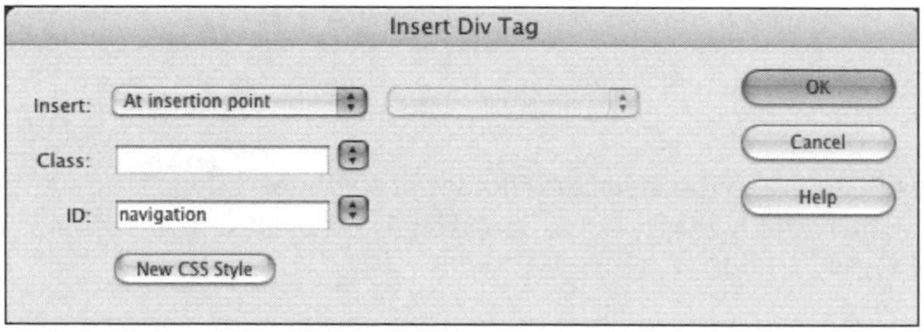

3. In Design view, replace the default content for the navigation div with a list, like the one shown in the following image. The Section items are intended to be top-level links, and the links shown as A link to a page are level-two links. The nested links are indented by selecting the relevant list items and clicking the Text Indent button in the Properties panel—see Chapter 5 for more information about working with lists.

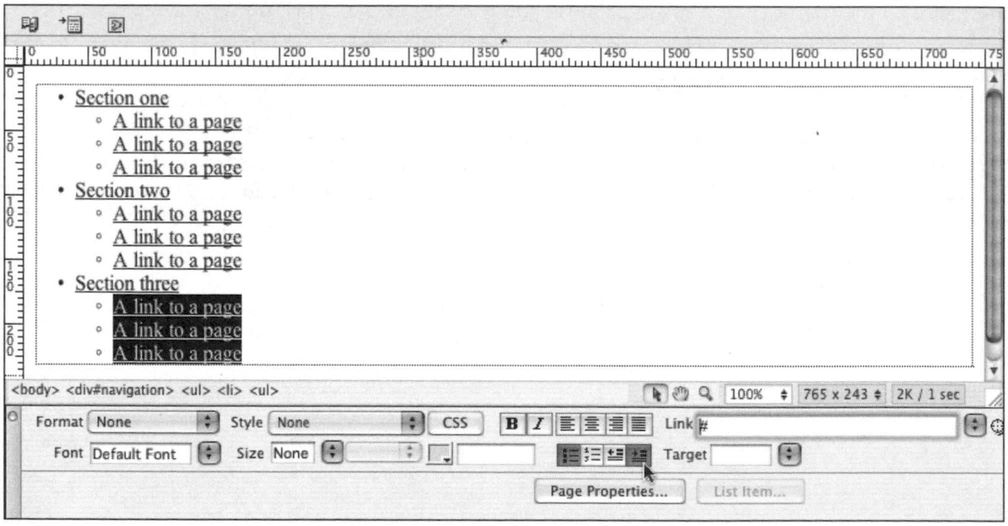

4. Create a new Tag rule that styles the body selector, ensuring it's defined in the style sheet created in step 1. In the Type category of the CSS Rule Definition dialog box, set Size to small; in the Background category, set Background color to #aaaaaa.

5. All other rules in this exercise use advanced selectors. First, create a rule for #navigation ul, and set the following: in the Type category of the CSS Rule Definition dialog box, set Font to Arial, Helvetica, sans-serif, and set Size to 100%; in the Box category, set Width to 140 pixels, Padding to 0, and Margin to 0; in the List category, set Type to none.

6. Create a rule for #navigation li, and in the Box category, set Margin to 0.

7. Create a rule for #navigation a, and set the following: in the Type category, set Weight to bold, Case to uppercase, Color to #ffffff, and Decoration to none; in the Background category, set Background color to #666666; in the Block category, set Display to block (which should make links fill their container, so that each navigation item looks more like a button); in the Box category, uncheck Same for all under Padding and set Top and Bottom to 3 pixels, Left to 8 pixels, and Right to 12 pixels; in the Border category, set Style to solid, set Width to 1 pixel, uncheck Same for all under Color and set Top and Left to #dddddd, and Right and Bottom to #333333 (this creates a kind of 3-D effect to the button borders, providing a highlight for the top and left borders, and a shadow for the right and bottom borders).

8. Create a highlight for the hover state by creating a rule for #navigation a:hover and setting Background color (in the Background category) to #777777.

9. Next, we need to style the active state. Because this navigation bar's items look like buttons, we're going to make the active (clicked) state look like the item being clicked is being pressed down. To do this, we need to reverse the border colors, darken the text and background, and move the text up and left slightly, to give the impression that it's moving into the screen.

   To start off, create a new rule for #navigation a:active. In the Type category, set Color to #eeeeee; in the Background category, set Background color to #444444; in the Box category, deselect Same for all under Padding and set Top to 2 pixels, Right to 13 pixels, Bottom to 4 pixels, and Left to 7 pixels; in the Border category, set Style to solid, set Width to 1 pixel, uncheck Same for all under Color, and set Top and Left to #333333 and Right and Bottom to #dddddd. (These are nearly the same border settings as in step 7—the top and left color settings in step 7 are used for the bottom and right here, and vice versa.)

10. At this stage, the navigation bar works fine, but it's not possible to differentiate between top-level and second-level links. Therefore, we need to create some override styles for nested link items. First, create a rule for #navigation li li a (which will affect links inside the navigation div that are within list items that themselves are within list items) and set the following: in the Type category, set Weight to normal, Case to lowercase, Color to #111111, and Decoration to none; in the Background category, set Background color to #999999; in the Box category, deselect Same for all under Padding and set Top, Right, and Bottom to 3 pixels and Left to 17 pixels.

11. Create a new rule for #navigation li li a:hover and set Background color (in the Background category) to #aaaaaa.

12. Create a final new rule, this time for #navigation li li a:active. Here, set the following: in the Type category, set Color to #000000; in the Background category, set Background color to #888888; in the Box category, deselect Same for all under Padding and set Top to 2 pixels, Right and Bottom to 4 pixels, and Left to 16 pixels; in the Border category, set the same settings as for #navigation a:active in step 9 (set Style to solid, set Width to 1 pixel, uncheck Same for all under Color, and set Top and Left to #333333 and Right and Bottom to #dddddd).

The navigation bar should look something like the following one, shown with a link in the three different states (link, hover, and active).

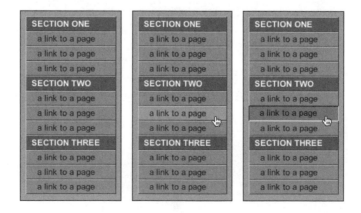

The completed files for this exercise can be found in the Chapter 7 folder of the book's download files, and are named 7_vertical_nav_bar.html and 7_vertical_nav_bar.css. Note that the download files have had a fix applied so that it displays properly in Internet Explorer. The fix is explained in the "Removing white space in Internet Explorer" section later in the chapter.

Using JavaScript to create collapsible sections

The navigation bar in the previous exercise can be taken in a different direction. By using a simple JavaScript, which is included in the files you can download from the friends of ED website, you can use the section links to toggle the visibility of the second-level links. This exercise continues from the end of the previous one.

1. Ensure head content is visible (View ➤ Head Content). Double-click the head content area (found directly above Design view) and then click the Script icon in the HTML section of the Insert bar. Use the folder icon to browse to and choose 7_toggler.js, and click OK to attach it to your web page.

2. Click on the first nested link in one of the sections. The status bar should show something like <div#navigation><ul><li><ul><li><a>. Right-click or Ctrl-click on the second of the <ul> links (which refers to the nested link) and choose Quick Tag Editor. Change <ul> to <ul id="sectionOneLinks" style="display:none;">. This provides the list with a unique ID and sets it by default to not be visible. Follow the same process with the other two nested lists, giving them ID values of sectionTwoLinks and sectionThreeLinks respectively.

> Edit tag: `<ul id="sectionOneLinks" style="display:none;">`

> *Should you want one of the nested lists to be visible by default, omit the style attribute.*

3. Click on the first of the section links. Right-click or Ctrl-click the <a> tag in the status bar, and again select Quick Tag Editor. Amend the link so that it looks like this: <a href="#" onclick="swap('sectionOneLinks'); return false;'>. Do the same with the other section links, amending the quoted value to sectionTwoLinks and sectionThreeLinks as appropriate.

> Edit tag: `<a href="#" onclick="swap('sectionOneLinks');return false;">`

> *If you're comfortable working directly with code, you can make the edits in this exercise in Code view, rather than using the Quick Tag Editor.*

175

Test the page in a web browser and you should find that clicking on the section links toggles the display of the second-level links.

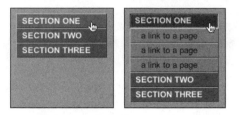

A word of warning, though: while this trick is nice enough in some circumstances, many users choose to surf the web with JavaScript disabled. Therefore, always ensure that you provide some means of allowing those people to access the links. For example, instead of linking to # in the section links, you could link to a non-JavaScript site-map page that you'd need to create separately.

The completed files for this exercise can be found in the Chapter 7 folder of the book's download files, and are named 7_vertical_nav_bar_toggle.html and 7_vertical_nav_bar_toggle.css. Note that the download files have had a fix applied so that it displays properly in Internet Explorer. The fix is explained in the following section.

Removing white space in Internet Explorer

If you test the completed page from either of the previous exercises in Internet Explorer, you may discover gaps between the navigation buttons. This is because IE frequently incorrectly displays white space in the HTML code. If this happens for you, go into Code view and delete the white space between various elements. When doing so, you may end up with code like the following, where list items appear with no white space between them. This code works fine in IE:

```
<ul>
  <li>
        <a href="#" onclick="swap➥
('sectionOneLinks');return false;">Section➥
 one</a><ul id="sectionOneLinks" style="➥
display: none;"><li><a href="#">A link to➥
 a page</a></li><li><a href="#">A link to➥
 a page</a></li><li><a href="#">A link to➥
 a page</a></li></ul>
  </li>
  <li>
     <a href="#" onclick="swap➥
('sectionTwoLinks');return false;">Section➥
 two</a><ul id="sectionTwoLinks" style="➥
display: none;"><li><a href="#">A link to➥
 a page</a></li><li><a href="#">A link to➥
 a page</a></li><li><a href="#">A link to➥
 a page</a></li></ul>
```

```
    </li>
    <li>
      <a href="#" onclick="swap➡
('sectionThreeLinks');return false;">Section➡
three</a><ul id="sectionThreeLinks" style=➡
"display: none;"><li><a href="#">A link to➡
 a page</a></li><li><a href="#">A link to➡
 a page</a></li><li><a href="#">A link to➡
 a page</a></li><li><a href="#">A link to➡
 a page</a></li></ul>
    </li>
</ul>
```

Horizontal navigation bars

Horizontal navigation bars are common on websites that have few top-level navigation links, or those where some links are removed from the standard navigation bar, to be placed somewhere more prominent. This is commonly referred to as **pull navigation** and may include important links, such as "contact details" and "about the company."

The basis for a horizontal navigation bar is still a list, but one where the list items are displayed inline, in order to switch the list's alignment from vertical to horizontal. Inline lists are covered in Chapter 5, so you may want to review that chapter's "Creating inline lists" section before tacking the following exercises.

Creating and styling a horizontal navigation bar

1. Create a new HTML document and CSS document, and link the latter to the former. Save both files somewhere on your hard drive.

2. Bring the HTML document to the front, and click the Insert Div Tag button in the Layout section of the Insert bar. In the ID field, type navigation, and then click OK. This creates a new div for the navigation bar to be placed within. This means that when it comes to styling the navigation elements, we can use contextual selectors so the styles will only affect elements within the navigation div.

3. Replace the default content of the navigation div with an unordered list containing a few typical navigation links. Just link to # in each case, if you're wanting to just create a sample navigation bar for experimenting with. (For more information on creating list items, see Chapter 5.)

- About the company
- Products
- Services
- Contact details

4. Create a new CSS rule, using an advanced selector #navigation ul, ensuring the rule is defined in the style sheet attached in step 1. In the CSS Rule Definition dialog box, set the following: in the Type category, set Font to Arial, Helvetica, sans-serif, set Size to 85%, set Weight to bold, set Line height to 1.5 ems, and set Case to uppercase; in the Box category, set both Padding and Margin to 0; and in the List category, set Type to none. This should result in something like the image to the right.

ABOUT THE COMPANY
PRODUCTS
SERVICES
CONTACT DETAILS

5. Create another new CSS rule, this time with the advanced selector #navigation li. In the CSS Rule Definition dialog box, set the following: in the Background category, set Background color to #666666; in the Block category, set Display to inline to make the list display horizontally; in the Box category, set Float to left and Margin to 0.

6. Now we need to create a rule to style the links in this list, so create another advanced CSS rule, with the selector #navigation a. In the CSS Rule Definition dialog box, set the following: in the Type category, set Color to #ffffff and set Decoration to none to turn off the default underline for links within the navigation area; in the Block category, set Display to block; in the Box category, deselect Same for all under Padding, and then set Top and Bottom to 2 pixels, and Right and Left to 10 pixels; in the Border category, deselect all Same for all check boxes, and set the Left values to solid, 3 pixels, and #333333.

ABOUT THE COMPANY | PRODUCTS | SERVICES | CONTACT DETAILS

In Dreamweaver, the resulting navigation bar looks a bit strange, with the text jutting out; however, this just shows that you can't always rely on Dreamweaver's Design view to show you exactly what a page will look like—it should be treated more as a rough guideline.

7. Next we need to create a rule for the hover state for the navigation bar links, to provide some user feedback when the mouse cursor is over a link. Create yet another advanced selector, #navigation a:hover. Then, in the CSS Rule Definition dialog box, set the following: in the Type category, set Color to #ffff00 (which is hex for yellow) and Decoration to underline (which will show the default underline when the link is moused over, thereby confirming to many that it's a link); in the Border category, deselect all the check boxes and then set Color in the Left row to #ffff00.

Although the navigation bar doesn't look quite right in Design view, preview the page in a browser and you should see something like the images below (the top one shows the default state, and the bottom one shows the hover state, with the color of the text, the underline, and the border all changing when the mouse cursor hovers over the link).

The completed files for this exercise are found in the Chapter 7 folder of the book's download files, and are named 7_horizontal_nav_bar.html and 7_horizontal_nav_bar.css.

Creating a "breadcrumbs" navigation area

Breadcrumbs are commonly used on large websites to show the path you've taken to the current page. For example, you might see something like Home > Products > Electronics > DVD Players at the top of the page when you're at an online store. In this exercise, we'll make use of an inline list and a background image (7_breadcrumb_bullet.gif, found in the Chapter 7 folder of the book's download files) to create an example of breadcrumb navigation.

1. Create a new HTML document and CSS document, and link the latter to the former. Save both files somewhere on your hard drive, and copy 7_breadcrumb_bullet.gif into the same folder.

2. Bring the HTML document to the front, and create a list for the bread-crumb links, as shown.

- Home page
- Products
- Electronics
- DVD players

3. Right-click or Ctrl-click the <ul> tag in the status bar, and select Quick Tag Editor.

4. In the tag editor, change <ul> to <ul class="breadcrumbs">. This will enable you to use CSS selectors to style lists used for breadcrumb navigation, without affecting lists elsewhere on the web page.

5. Create a new CSS rule, defined in the CSS file created in step 1. Use Advanced as the Selector Type, and type ul.breadcrumbs into the Selector field. Click OK.

6. In the CSS Rule Definition dialog box, set the following: in the Type category, set Size to 77% (breadcrumb text is commonly smaller than body copy text, to differentiate it and to not dis-tract from the main content); in the Box category, set Padding to 0, deselect Same for all under Margin, and set all margin values to 0 except for Bottom, which should be set to 1 ems (the padding and margin settings remove browser defaults, but the margin-bottom setting ensures the breadcrumbs won't hug subsequent content on the web page); in the List category, set Type to none to remove the default bullet points.

7. Create another CSS rule with an advanced selector, this time ul.breadcrumbs li. The styles defined here will affect any list items within a list that has the breadcrumbs class applied. In the CSS Rule Definition dialog box, set the following: in the Background category, set Background image to 7_breadcrumb_bullet.gif (use the Browse button to navigate to and choose it if you wish), set Horizontal position to 0 and Vertical position to 3 pixels; in the Block category, set Display to inline; in the Box category, deselect Same for all under Padding, and set Left to 12 pixels.

Again, Dreamweaver's Design view has a few quirks in displaying this list, notably leaving out the background image. Therefore, preview the page in a web browser, and you should see something like the following image.

>> Home page >> Products >> Electronics >> DVD players

Note that link styles for breadcrumb links are generally best driven by global link styles, so that they match the links in the body copy; however, if you want to create breadcrumb-specific link styles, you could do so by adding the advanced selectors ul.navigation a and ul.navigation a:hover and styling them as you see fit. Also note that because we've used a class to style the breadcrumbs list, you can apply the style to multiple lists on the same web page. For instance, if you want to include breadcrumb navigation at the top and the foot of the page, you'd only need this one set of CSS rules.

The completed files for this exercise can be found in the Chapter 7 folder of the book's download files, and they're called 7_breadcrumbs.html, 7_breadcrumbs.css, and 7_breadcrumb_bullet.gif.

Creating a horizontal navigation bar with rollover images

Navigation bars containing rollover images are common online, but they can be problematic. They often require a number of images that must be preloaded (something many browsers don't do, resulting in an awkward pause when your mouse cursor is over a link while the browser downloads an image state). They can also be time-consuming to update and JavaScript-heavy. The last of those points is also the case with Dreamweaver's built-in navigation-bar creation tool (accessed via Insert ➤ Image Objects ➤ Navigation Bar), so this is the last time you'll hear about that tool in this book. Instead, we're going to create a navigation bar using just a standard list, one image, and a bunch of CSS rules.

For this exercise, you'll need the image 7_rollover.gif, found in the book's download files.

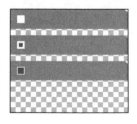

As you can see from the image to the right (from Photoshop), the 7_rollover.gif image includes three link states (for link, hover, and active). The way this exercise will work is to use this image as the background for each navigation link, only showing the relevant portion of the image for each state. Note that the hover state begins 40 pixels down and the active state begins 80 pixels down—these measurements will be important come steps 8 and 9 of this exercise.

1. Create a new HTML document and CSS document, and link the latter to the former. Save both files somewhere on your hard drive.

2. Bring the HTML document to the front, and click the Insert Div Tag button in the Layout section of the Insert bar. In the ID field, type navigation, and then click OK.

3. Replace the default content of the navigation div with an unordered list containing a few navigation links. As with previous exercises, just link to # in each case, if you're wanting to just create an example navigation bar to experiment with.

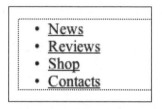

All subsequent steps in this exercise involve creating advanced CSS selectors in the New CSS Rule *dialog box and then styling them in the* CSS Rule Definition *dialog box. In each case, remember to define the rules in the style sheet created in step 1.*

New CSS Rule

Selector Type: ◯ Class (can apply to any tag)
◯ Tag (redefines the look of a specific tag)
◉ Advanced (IDs, pseudo-class selectors)

OK

Cancel

Selector: #navigation ul

Define in: ◉ 7_rollovers.css
◯ This document only

Help

4. The first CSS rule requires an advanced selector called #navigation ul. In the CSS Rule Definition dialog box, set the following: in the Box category, set Padding and Margin to 0; in the List category, set Type to none.

5. For the advanced selector #navigation li, set the following: in the Background category, set Background image to 7_rollover.gif, set Repeat to no-repeat, set Horizontal position to left, and set Vertical position to top (this sets and positions the default state of the rollover image); in the Block category, set Display to inline; in the Box category, set Padding and Margin to 0; and in the Border category, deselect all the Same for all check boxes, and then set the Bottom row to solid, 5 pixels, and #888888.

CSS Rule Definition for #navigation li in 7_rollovers.css	
Category	**Background**
Type Background Block Box Border List Positioning Extensions	Background color: ☐ Background image: 7_rollover.gif Browse... Repeat: no-repeat Attachment: Horizontal position: left pixels Vertical position: top pixels
Help	Apply Cancel OK

6. Next, we need to style links in the navigation bar using the selector #navigation a. Create the rule, and in the CSS Rule Definition dialog box, set the following: in the Font category, set Type to Arial, Helvetica, sans-serif, set Size to 13 pixels, set Weight to bold, set Case to uppercase, set Color to #ffffff, and set Decoration to none; in the Block category, set Display to block.

> *You may notice that we set the font size to pixels for this example. While pixel-based font sizing should generally be avoided, due to Internet Explorer versions 6 and lower not being able to resize such text, it's generally OK for things like navigation bars, so long as the text is perfectly readable. (Here, there's enough contrast and the font, which is in uppercase, is also sized at a large 13 pixels). Avoid pixel sizing for body copy, though.*

7. Still styling the same rule, access the Box category. We need to set the dimensions of the links to the same as those of the background image—185 × 30 pixels. However, we also want to add some padding around the link text, so that it doesn't hug the edges of the link, and also so the text doesn't sit over the square button decoration at the left of the background image.

First, define the Padding: deselect *Same for all* and set *Top* to 7 pixels and *Left* to 30 pixels. Because the CSS box model places padding on the outside of defined dimensions, we need to ensure that these padding settings plus the width/height settings add up to the actual dimensions of the image. Therefore, set *Width* to $185 - 30 = 155$ pixels, and *Height* to $30 - 7 = 23$ pixels. (If we'd set *Width* to 185 and *Height* to 30, the padding settings would be applied **outside** these dimensions, making the navigation bar break.)

8. Next, we need to define the hover state. Use an advanced selector, #navigation a:hover. In the *Background* category of the CSS Rule Definition dialog box, set *Background image* to `7_rollover.gif`, set *Horizontal position* to 0, and set *Vertical position* to -40 pixels. What this effectively does is move the background image up 40 pixels during the hover state, showing just the hover portion of the image.

9. The active state is styled in much the same way. This time create the advanced selector #navigation a:active. In the CSS Rule Definition dialog box, select the Background category, and set Background image to `7_rollover.gif`, Horizontal position to 0, and Vertical position to -80 pixels.

And here are the resulting three link states in a browser:

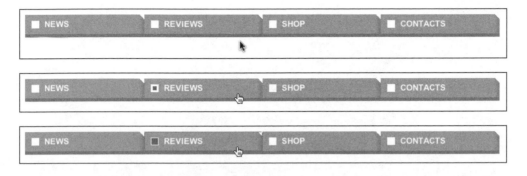

The advantage of this system over Dreamweaver's built-in one is that the CSS-based system can be updated in seconds. Want a new rollover image? Just swap the image `7_rollover.gif` for a new one! Want to change the link text for a link? Just edit it in Design view, rather than having to create three new images as you would if you were using Dreamweaver's built-in tool.

The completed files for this exercise are in the Chapter 7 folder of the book's download files, and are named `7_rollovers.html`, `7_rollovers.css`, and `7_rollover.gif`.

Summary

If you've worked through this entire chapter, you'll now have the knowledge to create arguably the most important interactive element of any website: its links. You should now be comfortable with creating typical web page links, but also a number of different navigation bars. In addition, you have also learned how to use links for creating some dynamic on-page content: swapping an image by clicking a thumbnail. Try experimenting with the different exercises, adding your own styles and images. Remember that this book aims to teach in a modular manner—once you've created a single rollover navigation bar that works, you should be able to rapidly adapt it to work on *any* website, rather than always having to start from scratch.

The next chapter is the final piece in learning how to create the bulk of website pages—you've already learned about typography, images, links, and navigation, so now it's time to deal with general web page layout, so you can position on the screen all the elements you've learned how to create so far.

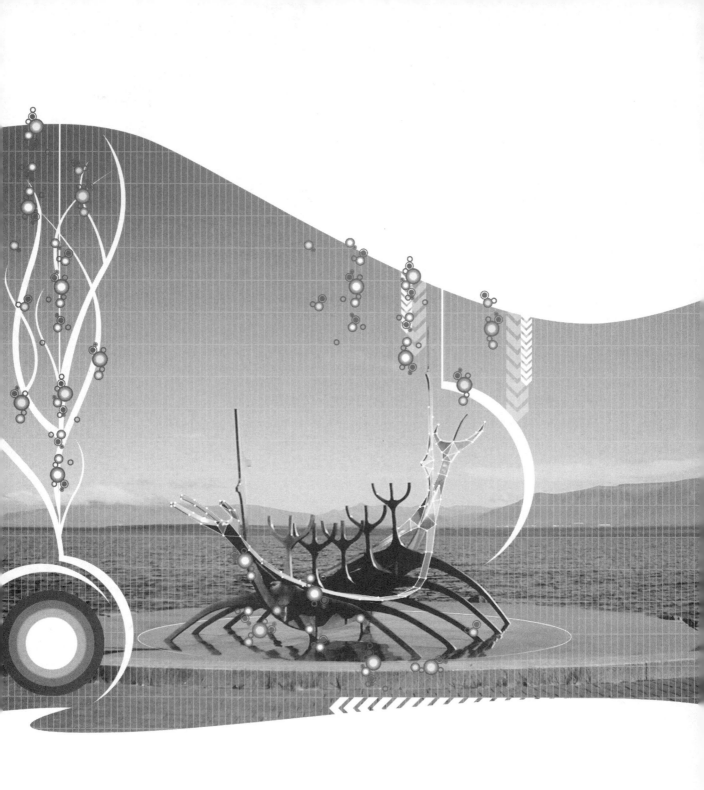

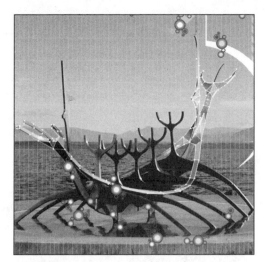

Chapter 8

WEB PAGE LAYOUTS

In this chapter . . .

- The CSS box model
- Creating column-based web page layouts
- Creating mastheads and footers
- Working with tables
- Adding scrollable areas to a web page

Many designers use CSS for styling fonts, but few venture further. This chapter shows how straightforward it can be to create CSS layouts in Dreamweaver, so long as you carefully plan what you're going to do. As you work through the chapter, the benefits of a CSS-based system over a table-based layout will become obvious, notably how rapidly such layouts can be put together and how much control you have over them, enabling rapid edits and updates.

Before we begin, it is worth mentioning that some browsers have problems with CSS, and this is often given as a reason to not use CSS-based layouts. Of those browsers still in fairly widespread use, Internet Explorer 5 (and the 5.5 update) for Windows causes the most frustration. In most cases, there are simple workarounds, leading me to believe that many naysayers of CSS are negative simply because they don't have the skill to create such layouts. Certainly, if you learn how to use Tantek Çelik's box model hack (a full explanation of which is found at www.tantek.com/CSS/Examples/boxmodelhack.html), you'll find very few problems when creating your CSS-based layouts.

Creating a structure

I mentioned semantic markup earlier in this book—that is, using HTML elements that describe what each item in the design is, rather than describing what you want it to look like. This approach should also be followed when working with CSS-based layouts. When you use tables for layout, cells are merged, split, chopped, and changed until everything works *visually*. But when working with CSS, you need to be aware of the *struc*ture of your web page. That way, you can create structural elements with IDs that relate to their purpose, and then style them to suit.

For basic page structure, you mostly tend to work with divs, which are added to your web pages via the Insert bar's Insert Div Tag button (found in the Common and Layout sections).

In CSS-based layouts, divs are pivotal: divs are added to the web page in logical order, creating the basic structure. Each is provided with a unique ID relating to its purpose, and the divs can then be styled to provide spacing, padding, backgrounds, and so on.

All this will become apparent as you continue through this chapter.

Box formatting

The box model is something you need to understand when working on CSS-based layouts. In CSS, every element is considered to be within its own box, and you can define its dimensions and then add padding, a border, and a margin to each edge, as required, as shown in the following image.

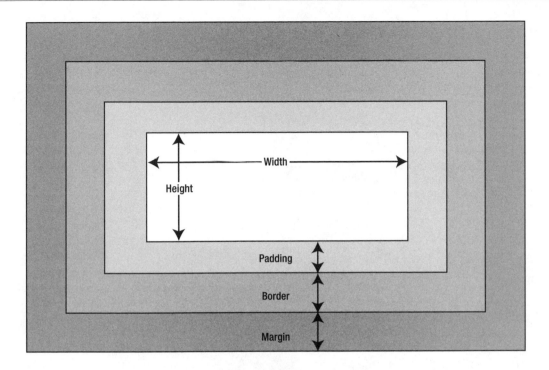

This is one of the trickiest things to understand about CSS: padding, borders, and margins are *added to the element's dimensions* (its width and height settings), so the sum of these measurements is the overall space that the element takes up. For example, if you set the width of a div to 200 pixels and then the padding to 50 pixels, the overall width the element takes up would be 50 + 200 + 50 = 300 pixels.

> *Note that the top and bottom margins on adjacent elements collapse, meaning that the overall box dimensions aren't necessarily fixed, depending on your design. For instance, if you set the bottom margin to 50 pixels on an element, and you have a top margin of 100 pixels on the element below it, the effective margin between the two elements will be 100 pixels, not 150 pixels.*

Some browsers—notably Internet Explorer 5 and 5.5 for Windows—don't display the box model correctly, placing padding and borders *inside* the defined dimensions of an element. However, the aforementioned box model hack can be used to deal with this issue.

Creating page layouts in Dreamweaver

In this section, we'll show how to create a number of skeleton layouts for web pages, which you can then use as the basis for countless pages. Along with learning how to create boxouts and sidebars, you'll find out how to create web page columns, and how to work with both fixed and liquid design.

Boxouts and sidebars

Boxouts and **sidebars** are design elements commonly used in magazines, but they can, in principle, also be used on the Web. A boxout is a box separate from other page content that is often used to house images, captions, and other ancillary information. Sidebars are (usually) thin bars of content that run alongside the main page content. In magazines, these may be used for supporting text, alternative features, or magazine mastheads (with contributor information). Online, both have similar uses, enabling you to immediately present separate content that's complementary to the main text.

For example, in the following screenshot from the Snub Communications website (www. snubcommunications.com), the sidebar on the right side of the page is used to house supplementary copy that supports the main content to the left.

And in the following screenshot of one of the reviews on the Wireviews website (www.wireviews.com), a boxout is used to house cover art, identifying information about the album being reviewed, and links to associated content.

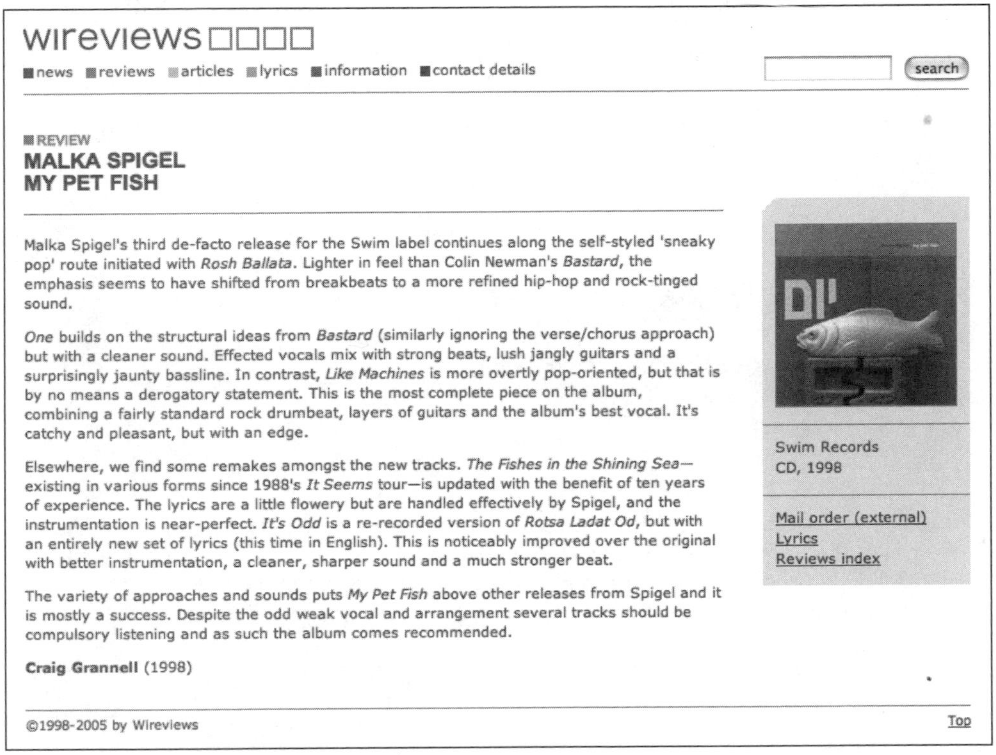

Creating either of these elements in Dreamweaver is done in much the same way, and the method is similar to one covered in Chapter 5. You may remember working on a drop cap in that chapter, to float and style a specific character. For boxouts and sidebars, you instead float an entire div.

The float property

Mastering the float property (usually accessed via the Box section of the CSS Rule Definition dialog box) is key to creating cutting-edge web page layouts. It allows you to float an element left or right of other web page content, which then wraps around it. This enables you to do away with ugly hacks such as fixed-width tables aligned right to create a boxout. In the previous screenshot of the Wireviews website, a div for the boxout was created and floated right of the other page content.

The benefit of using the float property over older methods is the ability to control its appearance site-wide from the CSS document.

Creating a boxout

This exercise requires the files 8_artwork.jpg and 8_boxout_corner.gif, which can be found in the Chapter 8 folder of this book's download files, available from the friends of ED website.

1. Create a new web page and a new CSS document, link the latter to the former, and save them in a folder. Place the files 8_artwork.jpg and 8_boxout_corner.gif in the same folder.

2. Click the Insert Div Tag button in the Common section of the Insert bar to add a div to the web page. In the ID field, type boxout. Click OK.

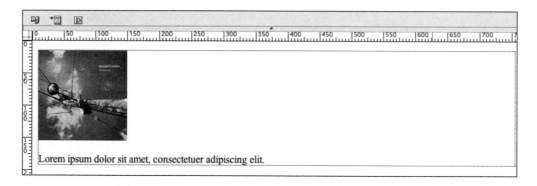

3. Replace the default content for the boxout with the image 8_artwork.jpg. (Use the Image button in the Common section of the Insert bar to add the image.) Add some alternative text in the Image Tag Accessibility Attributes dialog box, and click OK. Press Enter and then add a short paragraph of text (which is intended to be a caption for the image).

4. At this point, the image will be formatted as a paragraph (Dreamweaver will have done this when you pressed Enter). However, we don't want the image to be within a paragraph, because it will take on properties associated with paragraphs when we style the p selector later. Therefore, move the cursor to the side of the image (but don't select the image), and use the Format menu in the Properties panel to change the image's formatting to None. Alternatively, select the image, right-click or Ctrl-click <p> in the status bar, and select Remove Tag from the pop-up menu.

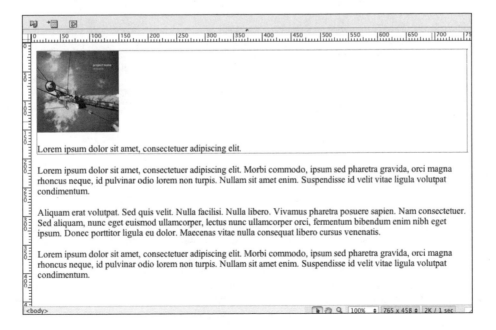

> You should be able to see a dotted line in Design view—this is a visual aid, showing the outline of the div element. If you can't see this, select CSS Layout Outlines *from the* Visual Aids *menu, which is the "eye" icon to the right of the toolbar at the top of the* document window. (Alternatively, go to View ➤ Visual Aids ➤ CSS Layout Outlines.

5. Click underneath the div added earlier, and add some more dummy text. Then format it as a series of paragraphs. If you check Code view, you will see your new text appear after the div's end tag (</div>).

6. Create a new CSS rule. Choose Tag for the Selector Type and type body in the Tag field. Ensure Define in is set to your CSS file.

7. In the CSS Rule Definition dialog box, set the following: in the Type category, set Font to Verdana, Arial, Helvetica, sans-serif, set Size to small, and set color to #000000; in the Box category, set Margin to 0 and Padding to 30 pixels.

8. Create another tag selector, this time to style the p tag. In the CSS Rule Definition dialog box, set the following: in the Type category, set Size to 90% and Line height to 1.4 ems; in the Box category, deselect Same for all under Margin and set Top to 0 and Bottom to 1 ems.

9. Create an advanced selector, typing #boxout in the Selector field of the New CSS Rule dialog box. In the CSS Rule Definition dialog box, set the following: in the Background category, set Background color to #e6e6e6, Background image to 8_boxout_corner.gif, Repeat to no-repeat, and both Horizontal position and Vertical position to 0. This sets the background to a light grey, but effectively removes a triangular piece from the top-left corner by using the image 8_boxout_corner.gif. In the Box category, set Width to 162 pixels and Float to Right. Uncheck both Same for all check boxes, and set the Top value of Padding to 20 pixels (thereby creating padding at the top of the boxout), the Left value of Margin to 30 pixels (so there will be 30 pixels of space between the edge of the boxout and other page content), and the Bottom value of Margin to 20 pixels (again, so the boxout doesn't hug other page content).

10. We now need to use the CSS cascade to style images and paragraphs within the boxout div, to improve the visual appearance of the web page. First, create an advanced rule #boxout img and set the following: in the Border category, set the values to solid, 1 pixel, and #818181; and in the Box category, deselect Same for all under Margin, and set the Bottom value to 1 ems.

11. Create another advanced rule: #boxout img, #boxout p. This style's values will be applied to both images and paragraphs within the boxout. In the CSS Rule Definition dialog box, deselect the Same for all check box under Margin in the Box category, and set the Left and Right values to 10 pixels. Click OK.

12. Finally, create another advanced rule: #boxout p. In the CSS Rule Definition dialog box, set the following: in the Type category, set Weight to bold, Size to 80%, Line height to 1.2 ems, and Color to #333333. These settings differentiate text in the boxout from that in the main content area.

Dreamweaver's Design view doesn't display this page entirely accurately, so preview it in a browser and you should see something like the following screenshot:

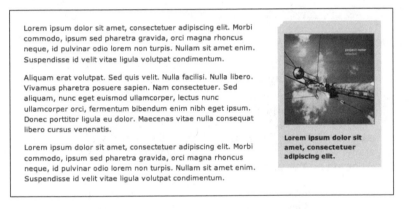

The completed files for this exercise can be found in the Chapter 8 folder of the book's download files, available from the friends of ED website. The files are 8_boxout.html, 8_boxout.css, 8_artwork.jpg, and 8_boxout_corner.gif.

> The use of an ID for the boxout means that we're assuming only one boxout will appear on each page. However, should you want the option of using multiple boxouts, you can instead use a CSS class. The quickest way to do this is directly in Code view: change id="boxout" to class="boxout" in the HTML, and change all instances of #boxout to .boxout in the CSS.

Creating a sidebar

The process for creating a sidebar in CSS is pretty similar to creating a boxout, so we'll be reusing many of the elements from the previous exercise.

1. Create a new web page and a new CSS document, link the latter to the former, and save them in a folder. Place the files 8_artwork.jpg and 8_boxout_corner.gif in the same folder.

2. Follow steps 2 through 5 of the previous exercise, but substitute sidebar for boxout when creating the div. When you've added the paragraphs of text, select them, and click the Insert Div Tag button. Set Insert to Wrap around selection, and type content in the ID field.

3. For the various CSS rules, follow steps 6 through 12 in the previous exercise, substituting #sidebar for #boxout. The exception is that for the #sidebar rule, no Background settings need be set, and the Padding values should all be set to 0.

4. Create a new advanced CSS rule, #content. In the CSS Rule Definition dialog box, set the following: in the Border category, deselect the Same for all check boxes and set the values to solid, 1 pixel, and #222222; in the Box category, deselect the Same for all check boxes and set the Right value of Margin to 162 pixels and the Right value of Padding to 10 pixels. The margin value sets a margin to the right of the content div, meaning that it effectively stops 162 pixels short of the browser window. The width setting of the sidebar is, of course, 162 pixels, which is why this margin measurement was chosen. The padding setting ensures that the content of the content div doesn't butt up against the border at its right side.

The completed files can be found in the Chapter 8 folder of the book's download files, available from the friends of ED website. The files are 8_sidebar.html, 8_sidebar.css, and 8_artwork.jpg.

Note that although this method works well, it's not a perfect solution. The line is applied to the content div, which is fine when it takes up more vertical space than the sidebar. But if the sidebar content is longer than the body content, the stripe stops short. An alternative method would be to use a web page background image to create the stripe.

To switch from a border to a background image in the previous exercise, you need to copy the file 8_sidebar_background.gif from the download files to the folder where your exercise files are. This image is a 193-pixel-wide image that has a one-pixel line at its left. This measurement is made up from the 162-pixel width of the sidebar, the one-pixel width of the line, and the 30 pixels of padding applied to the body of the web page. When set at the very right of the web page (and then tiled vertically), the line will appear in the correct position).

Open up the #content rule by double-clicking it in the CSS Styles panel, and delete the settings in the Border category. Then open up the body rule, and in the Background category, set Background image to 8_sidebar_background.gif, Repeat to repeat-y, and Horizontal position to 100%.

If all's gone to plan, the amended web page should look like the screenshot below.

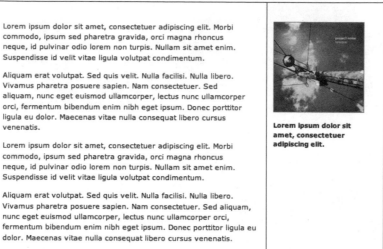

The completed files for this amendment are in the Chapter 8 folder of the book's download files, and are called `8_sidebar_alt.html`, `8_sidebar_alt.css`, and `8_artwork.jpg`.

> *Always strive for uncluttered pages to avoid making the design feel claustrophobic. If you're using boxouts and sidebars, ensure the content isn't being crammed in and that it has enough space to "breathe." Also, if these areas are to be populated with text-based content, ensure that the widths are large enough to cater for this; it's rather pointless to set text within a sidebar that has room for only one or two words on each line.*

Working with columns

Although columns of the sort found in newspapers and magazines should be avoided online, columns can be useful when you're working with various types of content. For instance, the Snub Communications homepage (`www.snubcommunications.com`) has two columns: the left one shows current news, while the right one provides an introduction to the organization and also a means to contact it. The use of columns makes both sets of information immediately available. If this kind of site used a one-column structure, the designer would have had to decide which information the user should see first and which information would initially be hidden (and perhaps never—or rarely—seen).

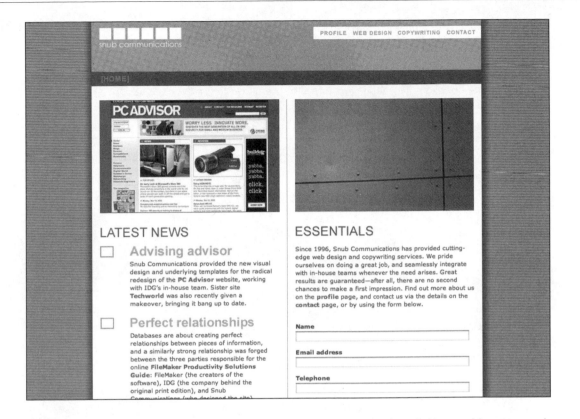

The general principle of columns applies to more than text content, though. You could use one column to house a vertical navigation bar, another to house the site's content area, and a third to contain thumbnail images relating to an article. In this section, we'll look at various column-based layouts, and we'll also tweak some rules along the way to show how flexible they can be.

Creating a two-column layout

The two-column layout is versatile and forms the basis for many CSS layouts. In fact, although it may not be immediately apparent, we've already created one in this chapter: the sidebar. However, in that case we worked on a page created for a boxout, so we'll start from scratch to make the general rules for creating column layouts more obvious.

> *Although this exercise does, as its heading and the previous paragraph suggest, concentrate on two-column layouts, you should be able to take the theory presented here and apply it to a layout with any number of columns.*

1. As usual, create a new web page and a new CSS document, link the latter to the former, and save them in a folder.

2. Use the Insert Div Tag button (in the Common section of the Insert bar) to add a div to the web page. Type wrapper in the ID field, and click OK. This will act as a container for other page content—for example, enabling us to set an overall width for the page design.

3. Delete the div's default content and click the Insert Div Tag button again. This time type newsColumn in the ID field. Click OK.

> Although you can use ID values such as leftColumn and rightColumn, it's best in most cases to use values that relate to the content inside the divisions you're adding to the page.

4. We now will add another div for the second column. Click the Insert Div Tag button again, but this time set Insert to After tag. Because we want this column to sit next to the one created in step 3, the second pop-up menu needs to be set to <div id="newsColumn">. In the ID field, type infoColumn, and click OK.

5. In both columns, add some text. Include a heading and a couple of paragraphs in each case.

6. Create a CSS rule with a tag selector, typing body in the Tag field. As always, ensure Define in is set to your style sheet, and click OK. In the CSS Rule Definition dialog box, select the Box category and set both Margin and Padding to 0, to remove the page's default padding settings.

7. Create a new CSS rule, using the advanced selector #newsColumn, #infoColumn. In the CSS Rule Definition dialog box, select the Box category and set Float to left.

8. Add a new advanced CSS rule for #newsColumn. In the CSS Rule Definition dialog box, set the following: in the Background category, set Background color to #cccccc; in the Box category, set Width to 300 pixels.

201

9. Add another advanced CSS rule, this time for #infoColumn. Use the same settings as for #newsColumn, but change the Background color setting to #999999. The resulting page should look like this:

The background colors were primarily added to make it easier for you to see what's going on in these exercises. However, Dreamweaver 8's enhanced Design view also has a number of useful visual aids that you should get used to using: CSS Layout Outlines *adds dotted lines around CSS elements, while* CSS Layout Backgrounds *adds temporary color backgrounds to CSS boxes, to make it easy for you to see their boundaries. The keyboard shortcut Shift+Ctrl+I (Shift+Cmd+I on Mac) toggles visual aids, which is useful when you want to temporarily remove or see them all. Also, all visual aid options can be accessed via* View ➤ Visual Aids, *or via the document window's* Visual Aids *menu.*

Adding padding and spacing

1. Following on from the previous exercise (or using the files 8_2_col.html and 8_2_col.css from the Chapter 8 folder of the book's download files), double-click newsColumn in the CSS Styles panel. In the Box category, set Padding to 10 pixels. Deselect Same for all under Margin, and set Right to 10 pixels.

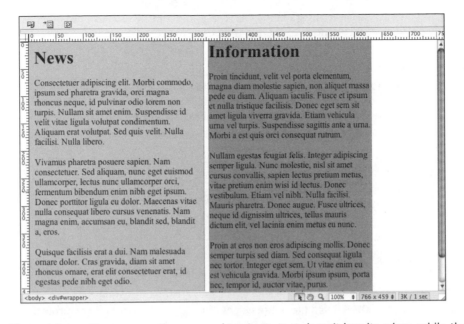

The padding setting ensures the news column's content doesn't hug its edges, while the margin setting adds a gap to the right of the news column, thereby separating the two columns. The use of background colors also helps show an important difference between padding and margins: backgrounds extend to the edge of the padded area, but backgrounds for an element end before margins. Also, as I've mentioned previously, padding is added to the defined dimensions of a CSS box. Therefore, the news column now effectively takes up 320 pixels of horizontal space—300 pixels for the defined width, and 10 pixels of padding at each side.

2. Now double-click infoColumn in the CSS Styles panel. Again, set Padding to 10 pixels.

The completed files for this exercise are in the Chapter 8 folder of the book's download files, and are named 8_2_col_padding.html and 8_2_col_padding.css.

Faking column backgrounds

A visual problem with CSS is that an element's background (both color and image) ceases with the end of the content and padding (both in height and width). Although this isn't problematic for all designs, you'll often want to have column backgrounds of equal height, even if they don't contain the same amount of content.

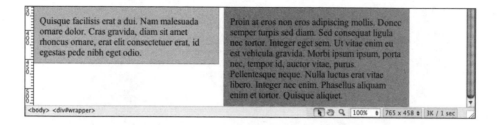

In many cases, the disparity in column heights won't be an issue, but some designs call for column backgrounds or borders that stretch the entire height of the design. There is a workaround in CSS, and although it's a bit of a hack, it involves only some basic editing of the CSS file (and, depending on your design, perhaps some small changes to the web page itself). The trick has already been touched upon elsewhere in this book: rather than adding the backgrounds to the columns, you create a background image and apply it to the page.

In the download files is an image named 8_column_background.gif. Copy this into the folder containing the files you completed in the previous exercise (or use 8_2_col_padding.html and 8_2_col_padding.css as a starting point). Double-click the #newsColumn and #infoColumn rules in the CSS Styles panel, and in each case, remove the Background color value. Then double-click the body rule and select the Background category. Use the Browse button to select 8_column_background.gif, and set Repeat to repeat-y, to tile it vertically. The column backgrounds are now effectively part of the background, so they both extend to the height of the tallest column.

The completed files for this version of the page are also available in the Chapter 8 folder of the download files—they're named 8_2_col_padding_background.html, 8_2_col_padding_background.css, and the aforementioned 8_column_background.gif.

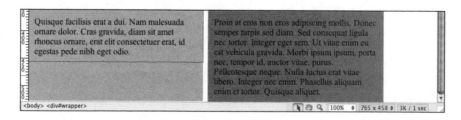

Working with liquid columns

The exercises so far have concentrated on fixed-width columns—those that have a defined width in pixels. However, some web layouts work better with columns that stretch as the browser window is enlarged. This type of design is commonly referred to as **liquid** design, and rather than use pixels for the width settings, you instead use percentages.

To rapidly create a liquid layout, take the completed files from the "Creating a two-column layout" exercise earlier in the chapter (8_2_col.html and 8_2_col.css) and in the Box category of the CSS Rule Definition dialog box, change the Width settings for both #newsColumn and #infoColumn to 50%. You'll end up with something like this:

When previewing this page in some web browsers, you may see a 1-pixel gap between the columns or to the right of the browser window. This happens when the window width is set to an odd number of pixels. Because we've set the column widths to 50 percent, some browsers cannot figure out what to do with the extra pixel, and place it between or to the right of the columns.

Also, some browsers very occasionally have problems with two-column designs where both columns are 50 percent wide and floated and have no margins or padding around them (nor are there margins and padding on the web page itself)—these browsers display one column under the other. (This is something you'll only find by thorough testing, and it's only happened to me a few times, despite the code for the pages being totally compliant.) In such cases, try reworking the page, or reducing one of the column widths to 49.999 percent.

As mentioned previously, padding is *added* to defined dimensions of boxes. Therefore, if you were now to add padding to either of these columns, their widths would be 50 percent of the browser window *plus* the defined padding. This has the result of "breaking" the layout, and one column then appears underneath the other. A common solution, when requiring padding in columns within a layout such as this, is to use nested divs. Within each of the columns is a nested div that houses the content for that column. This can be created by following the steps in the next exercise.

Adding padding to liquid columns

1. Open the liquid design created in the previous section (if you've not made this yourself, you can use the files 8_2_col_liquid_starting_point.html and 8_2_col_liquid_starting_point.css from the Chapter 8 folder of the book's download files). Select all of the content in the news column, and then click the Insert Div Tag button. For Insert, select Wrap around selection, and in the ID field, type newsColumnContent. Do the same with the information column, but type infoColumnContent in the ID field.

2. Create a new CSS rule for the advanced selector #newsColumnContent, #infoColumnContent. In the CSS Rule Definition dialog box, select the Box category, set Padding to 10 pixels, and click OK. The columns will appear to have padding, but the layout won't be broken.

The completed files for this version of the page are in the Chapter 8 folder of the book's download files, and are named 8_2_liquid.html and 8_2_liquid.css. These files have had the fix for Internet Explorer (mentioned in the previous focus point) applied, which is why the #infoColumn rule's width value is 49.999% rather than 50%.

Creating a three-column layout with fixed sidebars

Using the methods shown so far, it would be simple enough to create a three-column layout using three fixed-width columns or three liquid columns. However, a common layout is one with a liquid center column and two fixed-width sidebars. This is slightly trickier to create, and some explanation is required regarding the ordering of the elements.

As you've seen, we can create sidebars by floating divs. Because content flows around divs, we need to place the floated elements above static ones in the web page. Therefore, to create a page with a (floated) vertical navigation area, a (floated) sidebar, and a main content area, the two floated divs must be added to the web page before the main content.

1. Create a new web page and a new CSS document, link the latter to the former, and save them in a folder.

2. Click the Insert Div Tag button, and add a div with the ID value navigation. Click OK.

3. Click the Insert Div Tag button again, select After tag and <div id="navigation"> from the Insert menu, and type sidebar in the ID field. Click OK.

4. Click the Insert Div Tag button one last time, select After tag and <div id="sidebar"> from the Insert menu, type mainContent in the ID field, and click OK. Add a few paragraphs of text to the mainContent div.

5. Create a new advanced CSS rule for #navigation. In the CSS Rule Definition dialog box, set the following: in the Background category, set Background color to #bbbbbb; in the Box category, set Width to 100 pixels, set Float to left, and set Padding to 10 pixels. This floats the navigation div to the left and provides it with a set width, background color, and some padding around its contents.

6. Create an advanced CSS rule for #sidebar. In Background, set Background color to #999999; in Box, set Width to 200 pixels, Float to right and Padding to 10 pixels. This floats the sidebar div to the right and, like the navigation div, provides it with a set width, background color and some padding around its contents.

7. Finally, create an advanced CSS rule for #mainContent. In the CSS Rule Definition dialog box, select the Box category and deselect Same for all under Margin, set Top and Bottom to 0, and set Right to 230 pixels and Left to 130 pixels. The values for the Right and Left settings are the width of the floated div to that side of the content, plus the padding on those divs, and an extra ten pixels, so the main content area's content doesn't hug either of the floated elements.

This is another of those layouts that Dreamweaver's Design view still has minor problems with. It incorrectly moves the main content area downwards slightly; however, the CSS Layout Backgrounds visual aid makes it very easy to see the boundaries of each of the divs:

In a web browser, the page looks like this:

The completed files for this section are in the Chapter 8 folder of the book's download files—they are named 8_3_col.html and 8_3_col.css.

Adding a footer

If you've tried adding further content to the original two-column exercise in this chapter, you may have been frustrated, ending up with something like this:

Subsequent content appears to the right of the floated columns, because subsequent content wraps around floated elements (as you'll have seen when working on the boxout exercise earlier in this chapter). In order to create new content that sits underneath floated elements, you have to make use of the CSS property clear. This can be done in the following way:

1. Start off with the completed files from the "Creating a two-column layout" exercise (or use the files named 8_2_col.html and 8_2_col_css in the Chapter 8 folder of the book's download files). Open the HTML file and click the Insert Div Tag button. Select After Tag from the Insert menu and <div id="infoColumn"> from the second pop-up menu. (This is chosen because we want to create a new element after our final floated column.) In the ID field, type footer.

2. Now create a new advanced CSS rule, #footer. In the CSS Rule Definition dialog box, select the Box category, and set Clear to both (which ensures this element clears content that's floated *both* left and right). Click OK.

The content of this new div should then be displayed underneath the floated elements.

At present, the width of this footer is unrestricted, unlike the columns, but you can define a width measurement in the #footer rule, or create a new advanced rule for #wrapper and set a width value, in order to set a maximum width for the overall design.

The completed files for this section are in the Chapter 8 folder of the book's download files—see 8_2_col_footer.html and 8_2_col_footer.css.

> *For more on working with CSS layouts, check out Chapter 10, which combines elements from several chapters in this book to show you how to rapidly create several CSS-based web page layouts in Dreamweaver.*

Working with tables

Although web designers have historically used tables for web page layouts, I've shown that CSS-based layouts are a better choice. That doesn't mean tables are totally redundant, though—in fact, they still have a major role to play in web page design, because they enable you to lay out tabular data. Tabular data is data organized in a grid-like format, which enables you to cross-reference various elements (such as a playlist from iTunes):

Name		Time	Artist	Album	Play Count
☑	Summer Overture	2:35	Clint Mansell & Krono...	Requiem For A Dream	1
☑	99.9	7:42	Wire	Send	2
☑	Dirge #2	3:40	Death In Vegas	Dirge	7
☑	Mikki Maus	4:18	Ronnie And Clyde	Swim Team #1	1
☑	Unreal	5:10	Unkle	Psyence Fiction	1
☑	Emerge	4:48	Fischerspooner	Fischerspooner #1	8
☑	Obsidian	7:05	Banco de Gaia	Igizeh	3
☑	Jumbo	6:57	Underworld	Beaucoup Fish	2
☑	The Box, part 4	7:36	Orbital	The Box	3
☑	Untitled 1	3:48	Sigur Rós	( )	8
☑	No Man's Land	6:18	David Holmes	Pi (OST)	2
☑	Ghost Dancing	7:29	The Orb	Cydonia	4
☑	Templates	6:07	Silo	Instar	
☑	In My Heart	4:36	Moby	18	35
☑	Just Like You	4:23	Locust	Morning Light	1
☑	Blanket head	3:31	Veer Musikal Unit (V...	Also	1
☑	So Easy	4:09	Röyksopp	Melody A.M.	3
☑	Automagic	5:17	Worm Is Green	Automagic	5
☑	Cherry Blossom	5:25	Susumu Yokota	Grinning Cat	2
☑	Drink The Elixir	4:26	Salad	Drink Me	1

At its most basic, a table is made up of a number of rows, which are divided into data cells. The first row of website tables often replaces standard table cells with table header cells instead, which is a good idea from a logical structure standpoint (if someone sees a totally unstyled version of the page, it's still obvious what the headers are, due to default web browser styles), but this is also beneficial from the designer's point of view, because you can separately define styles for the header cells and data cells.

The Table dialog box

The Table button in the Common section of the Insert bar brings up the Table dialog box, providing you with a rapid way of creating a table for your web page. It contains the following fields:

- **Rows and Columns:** Enables you to specify how many rows and columns the table has.
- **Table width:** Sets the width of the table. The pop-up menu provides access to various units, including pixels and percentage.
- **Border thickness:** Sets the thickness in pixels of the table cell borders. A quick tip: anything over 1 looks like rubbish. Set this to 0 to remove the table cell borders entirely.
- **Cell padding:** Sets the amount of padding inside each table cell, in pixels.
- **Cell spacing:** Sets the distance between each cell in the table, in pixels. If you want this to be 0, some browsers demand that you explicitly set that value.
- **Header:** Determines where table header cells are positioned (if any are used). Note that if you were to create a table with three rows and choose the Top value for Header, the first row becomes the headers, and you have only two other rows to input content into.
- **Caption:** Provides a means of associating a table's title with the table itself. This is optional and rarely used, but useful nonetheless. It is particularly good for screen readers, to ensure a table's data isn't read out of context; generally, a screen reader will read the caption and then go on to read the table header cell contents.

- **Summary:** Enables you to provide a succinct overview of a table's data for screen readers. The summary is invisible in visual browsers.

After inputting whatever values you like, click the OK button, and you'll see something like the image below. "A lovely table" is the caption, which by default appears centered above the table. Table headers, by default, appear in bold and are centered. Note that all such styling can be overridden by using CSS.

By default, tables will evolve as you add content into them, trying to fit everything within the defined width as well as possible: the columns will shift and resize, and lines may wrap.

The green span lines and arrows under the columns and table are visual aids, accessed by activating the Table Widths option from the Visual Aids menu. These are not part of the design, but they provide you with a quick and easy way of accessing various elements of a table. For instance, click the menu triangle in the line that spans the table's entire width, and you have access to various options, enabling you to clear defined heights and widths for the entire table, make all widths the same, and simply select the table.

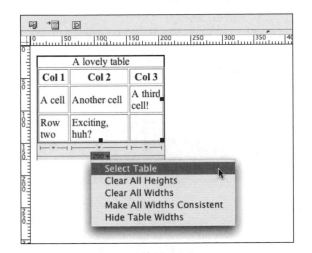

When the table is selected, the Properties panel changes to look like the following image. Here, you can edit a number of the settings mentioned at the start of this section, along with assigning the table a unique ID (in the Table ID field), or a class (via the Class menu). The lower section has a number of color and image options, but they only add deprecated code—if you want to add a background color or image to your table, do so using CSS. The two icon sets are a little more use: they enable you to clear column widths and row heights or convert existing defined measurements to pixels or percentages.

If you can't see the lower section of the Properties *panel, click the expand widget at the panel's bottom-right corner.*

Click the menu triangles under the individual columns to access options for inserting new columns in the table, or for selecting a column (thus allowing you to change various settings relating to just that column).

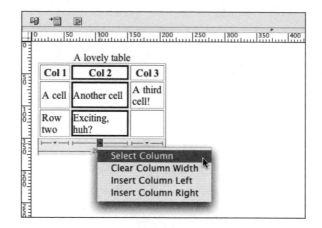

To use the Properties panel to edit options relating to a single cell, just click inside the cell to select it. In the following example, I've selected the No wrap option after clicking the second cell on the bottom row of the table. This disables the automatic line wrapping, making the entire text within the cell display on a single line. The Header option enables you to turn standard data cells into headers (and vice versa), which is handy if you forgot to create any headers when originally setting up the table.

Although most tables have a standard grid layout, you may sometimes need to merge or split data cells. Doing so is simple: Shift-click the cells you want to perform the action on, and then right-click or Ctrl-click and go to Table ➤ Merge Cells or Table ➤ Split Cell, depending on the action you want to perform. Alternatively, use the two icons towards the bottom left of the Properties panel, underneath Cell. (The one on the left is for merging cells; the one on the right is for splitting them.)

While you can set heights and widths for each cell, bear in mind that all cells within a row or column can only be reduced in size to the largest defined measurement. Generally, it's best to avoid setting heights or widths at all, because tables have the ability to resize automatically, depending on the content within them. One thing to note is that it's easy to accidentally set cell widths by dragging the cell borders in Design view. If you find you've done this, select Clear All Widths from the table's menu triangle.

Creating and styling a table in Dreamweaver

In this exercise, we're going to use Dreamweaver's built-in tools to create a table rather like the iTunes playlist shown earlier in the chapter. This design can be adapted for numerous data tables and will make use of CSS to style the table, overriding browser defaults.

215

1. Create a new web page and CSS document, and link the latter to the former. Select Insert ➤ Table to bring up the Table dialog box, and set Rows to 12, Columns to 5, Table width to 90 percent, Border thickness to 1, Cell padding to 2, and Cell spacing to 3. In Header, select Top, because our headers will be across the table. Add content to the Caption and Summary fields, as shown in the following image. Click OK.

Table	
Table size	
Rows: 12	Columns: 5
Table width: 90	percent
Border thickness: 1	pixels
Cell padding: 2	
Cell spacing: 0	
Header	
None Left Top Both	
Accessibility	
Caption: A playlist of great music	
Align caption: default	
Summary: Music selected by Craig Grannell, with details of song, playing time, artist, album and play count.	
Help Cancel OK	

2. Add some content to the table, as shown in the following image. You can move to the next cell by pressing the Tab key, and once cells have content, you can navigate between them using the arrow keys. (If you don't fancy adding all this information yourself, just open up 8_table.html from the Chapter 8 folder of the book's download files and go from there.)

A playlist of great music

Name	Time	Artist	Album	Play count
Summer Overture	2:35	Clint Mansell	Requiem for a Dream	7
99.9	7:42	Wire	Send	4
Dirge #2	3:40	Death in Vegas	Dirge	2
Mikki Maus	4:18	Ronnie and Clyde	Swim Team #1	3
Unreal	5:10	Unkle	Psyence Fiction	5
Emerge	4:48	Fischerspooner	Fischerspooner #1	5
Obsidian	7:05	Banco de Gaia	Igizeh	9
Jumbo	6:57	Underworld	Beacoup Fish	3
The Box, part 4	7:36	Orbital	The Box	3
Untitled 1	6:38	Sigur Rós	()	6
No Man's Land	6:18	David Holmes	Pi	9

90% (670)

`<body> <table> <tr> <th>`   100%   765 x 458   3K / 1 sec

At this point, we have a finished table. It does its job, but it doesn't look that great, so we'll use some CSS to improve its visual appearance.

3. We want to use CSS for the borders, because the default table border is a nasty bas-relief effort that looks terribly dated. Select the table (either by using the Visual Aids menu, or by clicking somewhere inside the table and then clicking the <table> tag in the status bar) and set Border to 0.

A playlist of great music

Name	Time	Artist	Album	Play count
Summer Overture	2:35	Clint Mansell	Requiem for a Dream	7
99.9	7:42	Wire	Send	4
Dirge #2	3:40	Death in Vegas	Dirge	2
Mikki Maus	4:18	Ronnie and Clyde	Swim Team #1	3
Unreal	5:10	Unkle	Psyence Fiction	5
Emerge	4:48	Fischerspooner	Fischerspooner #1	5
Obsidian	7:05	Banco de Gaia	Igizeh	9
Jumbo	6:57	Underworld	Beacoup Fish	3
The Box, part 4	7:36	Orbital	The Box	3
Untitled 1	6:38	Sigur Rós	()	6
No Man's Land	6:18	David Holmes	Pi	9

4. Create a new CSS rule. Use Tag as the Selector Type, and type table in the Tag field. In the CSS Rule Definition dialog box, access the Border category. Deselect all Same for all check boxes, and then set the Top and Left rows to solid, 1 pixels, and #c9c9c9. Click OK.

CSS Rule Definition for table in 8_table.css

Category
Type
Background
Block
Box
Border
List
Positioning
Extensions

Border

	Style	Width	Color
	☐ Same for all	☐ Same for all	☐ Same for all
Top:	solid	1 pix...	#c9c9c9
Right:		pix...	
Bottom:		pix...	
Left:	solid	1 pix...	#c9c9c9

Help   Apply   Cancel   OK

Note that when you click OK *to return to the web page, you may find it tricky to see this new border if the visual aids are still turned on. You can turn them off by selecting* Hide All Visual Aids *in the* Visual Aids *menu at the top of the document window.*

5. Create an advanced CSS rule for th,td. Again, in the CSS Rule Definition dialog box, access the Border category, but this time style only the Right and Bottom rows (using the same values as in the previous step).

The reason for dealing with borders like this is obvious if you try placing a border on every side of a table cell—doing so means that you end up with a double-thickness border where table cells meet. By only applying borders to the right and bottom edges of table cells, you effectively end up with a single-pixel border around every cell, except for across the left and top edges of the table—hence adding a top and left border to the table itself.

6. Create a new CSS style. This time, make it a tag selector for the caption tag. In the CSS Rule Definition dialog box, set the following: in the Type category, set Font to Arial, Helvetica, sans-serif, set Size to 120%, set Weight to bold, and set Case to uppercase; in the Box category, deselect Same for all under Padding, and set all the values to 0, apart from Bottom, which should be set to 10 pixels. These settings make the caption more prominent, and the padding setting separates it slightly from the table. Click OK, and you should see something like the following image.

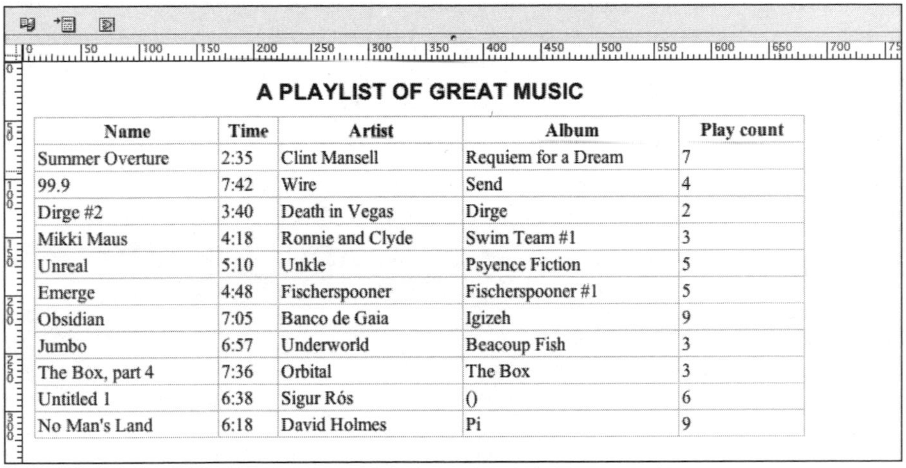

7. Create another CSS style using a tag selector—this time for th. In the CSS Rule Definition dialog box, set the following: in the Type category, set Weight to bold (this is the default for most browsers, but it's not for all, and it pays to ensure consistency wherever possible); in the Background category, set Background color to #bababa, Background image to 8_stripe.gif (from the Chapter 8 folder of the book's download files), and Repeat to repeat-x. This applies a "metallic" image horizontally across all table header cells. To center this vertically, set Horizontal position to 0 and Vertical position to 50%. In the Block category, set Text align to left to override the default centrally aligned text of table headers. Click OK.

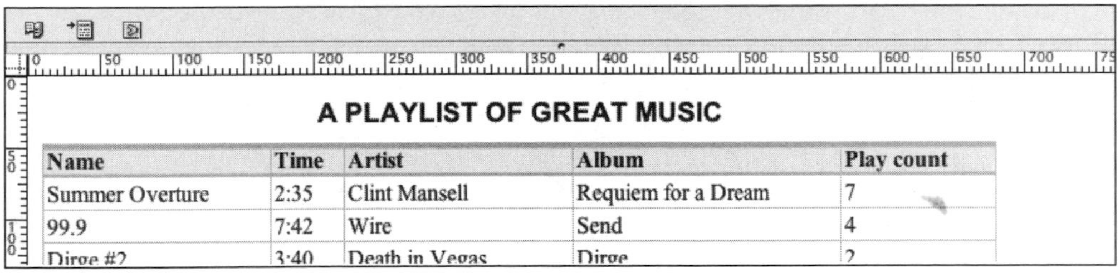

8. We now need to enhance the text used in the table cells, and the padding around this text. To do so, edit the th,td rule by double-clicking it in the CSS Styles panel. In the Type category, set Font to Verdana, Arial, Helvetica, sans-serif, and set Size to 80%; in the Box category, deselect Same for all under Padding, and set Top and Bottom to 2 pixels and Left and Right to 5 pixels. Click OK, and you'll see something like the following.

A PLAYLIST OF GREAT MUSIC

Name	Time	Artist	Album	Play count
Summer Overture	2:35	Clint Mansell	Requiem for a Dream	7
99.9	7:42	Wire	Send	4
Dirge #2	3:40	Death in Vegas	Dirge	2
Mikki Maus	4:18	Ronnie and Clyde	Swim Team #1	3
Unreal	5:10	Unkle	Psyence Fiction	5
Emerge	4:48	Fischerspooner	Fischerspooner #1	5
Obsidian	7:05	Banco de Gaia	Igizeh	9
Jumbo	6:57	Underworld	Beacoup Fish	3
The Box, part 4	7:36	Orbital	The Box	3
Untitled 1	6:38	Sigur Rós	()	6
No Man's Land	6:18	David Holmes	Pi	9

9. Although this is a perfectly good styled table, we can take things further, to make it more readable. The iTunes table has separator stripes (a background color in every other row of the table), and these could theoretically be added by manually adding a background color to alternate rows by applying a CSS class to them. However, if another row is added somewhere in the table, you'd then need to manually edit every subsequent row.

A better solution was found by David F. Miller (www.fivevoltlogic.com). Dubbed "Zebra tables," the technique uses JavaScript to automatically color alternate table row backgrounds. The script can be downloaded from the Zebra Tables article at www.alistapart.com/articles/zebratables. Once you've downloaded the script and saved it in the same folder as your HTML files (I saved it as separator_stripes.js), you need to link it to your web page. Do so by double-clicking the head content area above Design view, clicking the Script button in the Insert bar's HTML section, using the folder icon to browse to the script, and then clicking OK. If all goes to plan, you'll see the script element appear in the <head> section in Code view.

10. Next, select the table (for instance, by clicking inside it and then clicking the <table> tag in the status bar). In the Properties panel's Table Id field, type playlist.

11. Next, the body start tag (<body>) needs editing to run the JavaScript function as the web page is loaded. Right-click or Ctrl-click the <body> tag in the status bar, and select Quick Tag Editor. Change the <body> tag to read as follows:

```
<body onload="stripe('playlist','#ffffff','#dbe6fa');">
```

Take care not to leave out any characters, and don't add spaces anywhere inside the onload value. The first of the three values here is playlist. This makes the script run on the table with that ID value (which was defined in the previous step). The other two values are hex color values that the alternate stripes will be colored—in this case, white and light blue.

12. With colored background stripes, the bottom borders of the table cells are rather redundant. Therefore, open the th,td CSS rule via the CSS Styles panel, and delete the values in the Bottom row in the Border section. This will leave the table with no bottom border at all, so open the table rule and add the values solid, 1 pixel, and #c9c9c9 to the Bottom row of the Border category. Click OK.

You should now have a table that looks something like the following image when viewed in a web browser (note that Dreamweaver's Design view won't show the colored stripes):

A PLAYLIST OF GREAT MUSIC				
Name	**Time**	**Artist**	**Album**	**Play count**
Summer Overture	2:35	Clint Mansell	Requiem for a Dream	7
99.9	7:42	Wire	Send	4
Dirge #2	3:40	Death in Vegas	Dirge	2
Mikki Maus	4:18	Ronnie and Clyde	Swim Team #1	3
Unreal	5:10	Unkle	Psyence Fiction	5
Emerge	4:48	Fischerspooner	Fischerspooner #1	5
Obsidian	7:05	Banco de Gaia	Igizeh	9
Jumbo	6:57	Underworld	Beacoup Fish	3
The Box, part 4	7:36	Orbital	The Box	3
Untitled 1	6:38	Sigur Rós	()	6
No Man's Land	6:18	David Holmes	Pi	9

The completed table can be found in the Chapter 8 folder of the book's download files. The files are named 8_table.html and 8_table.css, and it also requires the image 8_stripe.gif and the JavaScript that you can get from www.alistapart.com/articles/zebratables, which is also available as part of the download files as separator_stripes.js.

You might think we went about this exercise in a rather roundabout way—after all, various appearance values that were set were later changed and replaced. My purpose was to show you how a table can evolve, and also to show you how to effectively create three different styles of table—just following this exercise, you learned how to create a basic HTML table, a table styled in CSS, and a table with automated separator stripes!

Adding scrollable areas

Sometimes, even in the best of designs, there's simply too much information to cram into a small space. In such cases, creating a scrollable area on a web page can be very useful. This is commonly seen in news pages, such as on Pixelsurgeon's website (www.pixelsurgeon.com)—the scrolling area enables the site to provide access to several days' worth of news; if a typical layout were used, the home page's length would be huge and the design compromised.

There are two ways you can add a scrolling area to a web page: one is to use CSS, and the other is to use an iframe.

Using CSS to create a scrolling area

1. Create a new web page and CSS document, and link the latter to the former. Use the Insert Div Tag button to add a div to your web page with an ID value of scrollable. Add a bunch of text to this div.

2. Create a new advanced CSS rule, #scrollable. In the CSS Rule Definition dialog box, select the Box category and set both Width and Height to 150 pixels. In the Positioning category, set Overflow to auto. Click OK. Dreamweaver's Design view will show the now-cropped div (below left). Preview the page in a browser, and you'll see that the area is now scrollable (below right).

3. In order to edit the text within the cropped div, either double-click it, or right-click or Ctrl-click it and choose Element View from the contextual menu, and then select Full; either choice temporarily increases the div's size, showing all its content, enabling you to make the edit. Once you're done, select Hidden from the same menu, which returns the div to a state resembling its display in a web browser. Note that the Reset All Element Views menu option does exactly what you'd expect, resetting all elements that can have hidden areas—handy if you've several on a page and want to rapidly return them all to their default states.

Note that divs such as this can be styled like any other, so you can add, for instance, a border in the usual manner. It's also worth noting that the auto value used in step 2 ensures that scroll bars only appear when the content is too big for its containing box. If you want scroll bars to always appear, use scroll as the value instead. Note, however, that this causes both scroll bars to appear, even if the content isn't too wide for its container.

The files for this brief exercise are in the Chapter 8 folder of the book's download files—see 8_internal_scrolling.html and 8_internal_scrolling.css.

Using an iframe to create a scrollable area

Although frames are rarely used these days, internal frames (sometimes referred to as floating frames, and often referred to by their HTML tag, <iframe>), are likely to stick around for some time after the last frames-based website has long passed. A distinct advantage of using iframes is that they allow for simple updates of text-based information without affecting the main page, since each iframe is a separate HTML document. This means that relatively unskilled people can update a portion of a site's information easily and without affecting the rest of the design. Of course, there are better strategies for such things—SSI (Server Side Includes), content management systems, and so on—but, if you're on a budget and have to enable someone to update some specific, simple content on a site, iframes might be the way to go. (Note, though, that if you just want to create a static scrollable area that won't be updated, the previous CSS example is the best method to use.)

Note that iframes can cause problems with regard to accessibility and search engine indexing, so they should be used in moderation and with caution. Also, iframe display varies across browsers, so thorough testing is required if you use them.

1. Create a new web page and add a few paragraphs of text to it. Save the page as 8_frame_content.html.

2. Create a second web page. This one will house the iframe. Because Dreamweaver doesn't have a simple way of adding an iframe, you have to do this via the Tag Chooser, which is accessed via Insert ➤ Tag. In the Tag Chooser, select HTML tags in the left column, and then scroll down to and select iframe in the right column.

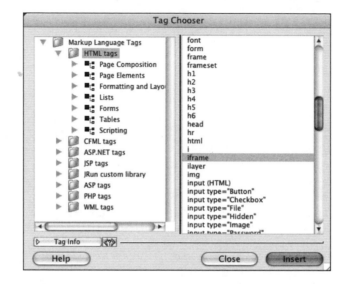

3. In the Tag Editor dialog box, use the Browse button to choose 8_frame_content.html, saved in step 1. Provide a Name for the frame, along with a Width and Height. Click OK and then Close to return to the web page.

Dreamweaver's Design view can't handle iframes, but a swift preview in a web browser shows the following result from the settings applied so far:

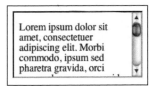

4. Unlike the CSS-based scrollable area, it's perfectly simple to swap out the content of the iframe for something else. Simply create a link elsewhere on the page with a Target value that's equivalent to the Name value applied in step 3 (the example in the download files uses scrollable).

The completed file from this example is in the Chapter 8 folder of the download files: 8_iframe.html.

There are a couple of issues with iframes, however. First, they're not accessible to all devices. Therefore, it's highly recommended that you include some alternate content, which can be added directly in Code view and placed between the iframe tags:

```
<iframe src="8_frame_content.html" ➡
name="scrollable" width="200" height="100"➡
 scrolling="auto">Your browser doesn't ➡
support iframes. Please <a href="➡
8_frame_content.html">click here to access➡
 the content</a>.</iframe>
```

The other issue is that Internet Explorer often spawns both horizontal and vertical scroll bars when content is larger than the declared width or height. This means that if your iframe is 200 pixels high, but your content is 400 pixels high, you'll end up with a vertical scroll bar *and* a horizontal one, even if your iframe content is narrower than the iframe dimensions. Other browsers don't make this mistake, creating only the relevant scroll bar.

A way around this is to add the following code to the <head> section of the iframe content web page:

```
<!--[if gte IE 5]>
<style type="text/css">
html, body {margin:0; width:180px;}
</style>
<![endif]-->
```

The width setting should be 20 pixels or so narrower than the width setting of the iframe itself.

Summary

This chapter is effectively the one that adds the final puzzle piece, enabling you to create full web page layouts. You can now combine your knowledge of how to work with CSS-based columns and page layouts with what you learned about working with text, images, and links over the past few chapters. In addition, you should now be comfortable creating and styling tables using Dreamweaver—but you should also be aware that tables should only be used for tabular data and not for web page layouts.

In Chapter 10, you'll see how to take various elements from the chapters in this book and combine them into effective web page layouts. First, however, Chapter 9 takes a look at getting user feedback by creating website forms that a user can fill in and submit to contact you.

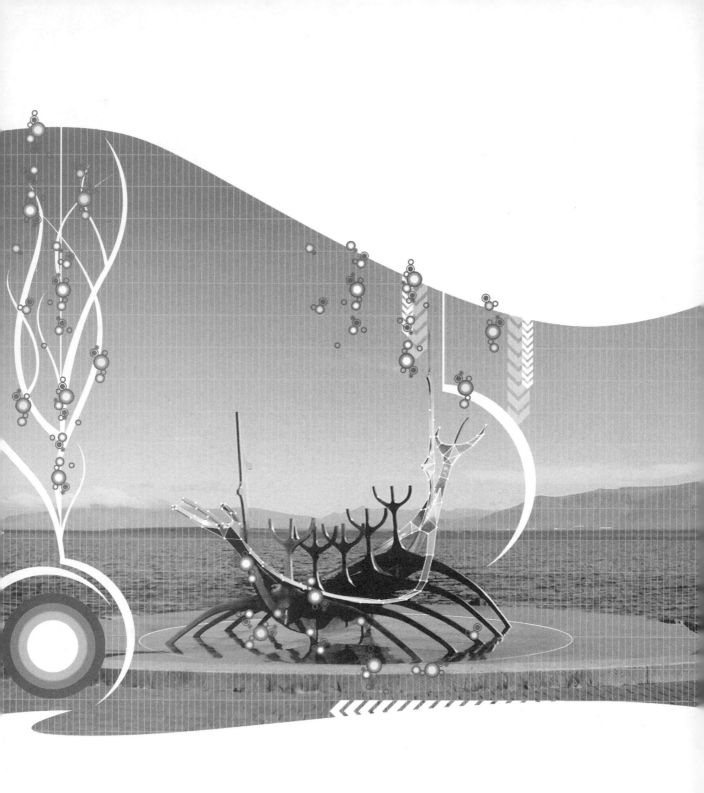

Chapter 9

GETTING USER FEEDBACK

In this chapter . . .

- Creating forms, and adding fields and controls
- Styling forms in CSS
- Configuring a FormMail CGI script
- Sending forms using PHP

One of the main reasons the Web has revolutionized working life and communications is its immediacy. Unlike printed media, websites can be continually updated at relatively minimal cost and also be available worldwide on a 24/7 basis. However, communication isn't one-way, and the Web makes it very easy to enable site users to offer feedback.

Using mailto: links

A common method of providing immediate user feedback is using `mailto:` URLs within links. Instead of the link's value being a filename or URL, it instead begins with `mailto:` and is immediately followed by the recipient's email address. This is added as usual, by selecting the text (or image) that you want to use for the link, and then typing the relevant value in the Properties panel's Link field.

It's possible to take this technique further. Multiple recipients can be defined using a comma-separated list; or by placing a question mark immediately after the final recipient address, you can add further parameters, such as a subject and recipients to carbon copy (cc) and blind carbon copy (bcc). If using more than one parameter, you must separate them with ampersands (&). A fairly complex example value may therefore look like this:

```
mailto:someone@your.domain,someoneelse@your.domain?subject=Contact ➥
from website&cc=theboss@your.domain
```

> *There should be no spaces in a* `mailto:` *value, with the exception of inside the* subject *string. Therefore, don't place spaces before or after colons, commas, or the ? or = symbols.*

There are, however, problems with `mailto:` links. First, email addresses online are often harvested by spambots. Second, a `mailto:` link relies on the user having a preconfigured email client ready to go—something that people working on college and library machines most likely won't have. Third, not all browsers support the range of `mailto:` options outlined earlier.

A way to combat the spambots is presented in the next section. To avoid the second problem (the `mailto:` link's reliance on a preconfigured mail client), I recommend using forms for any complex website feedback. For the third issue (the lack of support for the more advanced `mailto:` options in some browsers), I recommend keeping things simple. Place your email address online as a `mailto:` address, and enable the user to fill in any other details, such as the subject line.

Scrambling addresses

Having an email address online for just a few days is enough to start receiving regular spam. A workaround is to encrypt any email addresses you put online by using an almost bulletproof concoction of JavaScript. The Enkoder form from Automatic (formerly Hiveware) is perhaps the best example.

This online form at www.automaticlabs.com/products/ enkoderform/ enables you to create a mailto: link that's composed of complex JavaScript. You can then open Code view and copy and paste the Enkoder output code in place of your standard mailto: link.

Although in time spambots will likely break this code, as they have with simpler encoders, it's the best example I've seen, and the results I've had with it have been good. Beware, though, that any users with JavaScript disabled won't see the address, so ensure you cater for them by including some other means of contacting the site owner.

As an alternative to encrypting your email address, you could always just "spell out" your address (such as your-name AT yourdomain DOT COM) or add it as an image (although images won't print well, and they won't match text across platforms). Alternatively, use a form instead, which is less susceptible to spam.

> Enkoder is also available as an application for Mac OS X.

The Enkoder Form

Posting your email address on a website is a sure-fire way to get an Inbox full of unsolicited email advertisements. The Enkoder protects email addresses by converting them into encrypted JavaScript code, hiding them from email-harvesting robots while revealing them to real people.

This tool is only useful for protecting an email address on a web page you've designed in HTML. It cannot be used when sending email or when posting your address into a web form, or adding your comments to a forum.

If you would like to specify your own HTML for the link, scroll down to the Advanced Form, below.

And remember, the only way to be *completely safe* is to not publish your address at all.

Note: We do not support our free tools. Please do not email us regarding the Enkoder. As much as we wish we could provide support - even in the form of answers to simple questions - we cannot.

The Basic Form
Email Address:

The email address to be displayed

Link Text:

The text users will see and click

Link Title:

The "pop-up" text seen when your mouse is over the link

Subject (Optional):

An optional subject line for the email

(Enkode It »)

Working with forms

In this section, we'll work through how to create a form and add controls. We'll also look at how to improve form accessibility by using Dreamweaver to add accesskey and tabindex attributes, and label, fieldset, and legend elements.

A form is the best way of getting user feedback. Fields are configured by the designer, enabling the site owner to receive specific information. However, don't go overboard: provide users with a massive, sprawling online form, and they will most likely not bother filling it in and will go elsewhere.

> *Similarly, although you can use JavaScript to make certain form fields required, I'm not a fan of this technique, because it annoys users. For instance, I've been on several sites where providing an email address was mandatory, but what if the user doesn't have email and is accessing the form from a library? The user would have to either submit a fake email address, which helps no one, or give up, which certainly doesn't help you.*

So keep things simple and use the fewest fields possible. In the vast majority of cases, you should be able to simply create name, email address, and phone number fields, and include a text area that enables users to input their query.

Creating a form

The Insert bar's Forms section houses the majority of form elements, and you can use the icons to add them to your web pages.

To add a form to your web page, click the Form button (which is the leftmost one). At this point (and when the relevant <form> tag is selected via the status bar), the Properties panel will change to enable you to edit the form's parameters.

Don't worry about these options at the moment—we'll be coming back to them in the "Sending feedback" section of the chapter.

Adding controls

There are various types of controls that can be added to a web page form:

- Single-line text fields
- Hidden fields, used to parse information invisible to the web page viewer
- Textareas, which are essentially multiline text fields, often used for inputting comments
- Check boxes, for selecting multiple choices from a number of options
- Radio buttons, for selecting a single choice from a number of options
- Option lists, which are usually displayed as pop-up menus
- Buttons, typically used to reset or send the form

In the following exercise, we're going to build a simple form, which will utilize several of these control types.

Adding controls to a form

1. Create a new web page. If you've not already done so, use the Form button in the Forms section of the Insert bar to add a form to the web page. If the relevant visual aid is turned on (View ➤ Visual Aids ➤ Invisible Elements), the form's container will be outlined with a red dotted line.

2. Next, we'll add a standard text field, along with a visual identifier/label. Click the Text field button to start adding a text field to the form. Assuming your accessibility preferences are set as suggested in Chapter 2, you'll next see the Input Tag Accessibility Attributes dialog box. Here, you can add various values to assist screen readers (although, frankly, some of the values make everyone's life easier when using the forms). In the Label field, enter the label you want to be displayed next to the field—in this case, enter Name. The Style options specify how the label will be dealt with in code—Attach label tag using 'for' attribute is the best option. You can also use the Position options to set whether the label appears before or after the form item.

3. Still in the Input Tag Accessibility Attributes dialog box, there are two fields at the bottom: Access key and Tab index. Access key can be used to provide keyboard access to an element—the person viewing the web page simply presses the operating system's modifier key (usually Alt on Windows and Ctrl on Mac) and the (case-sensitive) key entered as the Access key to access the element. The Tab Index field is used to define the page's element tab order, and its value can be set as anything from 0 to 32,767.

Generally, Access key is more suited to navigation than form controls, but setting Tab Index is a must, because many browsers tab rather randomly among the various elements—controlling the tab order is therefore a good idea. However, because Tab Index values needn't be sequential, they can be set in increments of ten, enabling you to slot in others later, without changing every value on the page.

With that in mind, set the Tab Index value of this first field to 11. Assuming no lower Tab Index values have been assigned elsewhere on the page, this form field will be the first element highlighted when the Tab key is pressed. Click OK to add the field to the web page.

The reason I suggested starting with 11 rather than 1 was because if you ignore the last digit, the Tab Index *values become standard integers, starting with 1. In other words, remove the final digits from 11, 21, and 31, and you end up with 1, 2, and 3.*

4. While the field is still selected, use the Properties panel's Format menu to format the selection as a paragraph. Then click between the label and the form field, and press Shift+Enter to create a line break between the two. Select the label and use the Properties panel's bold button to embolden it.

5. Dreamweaver applies generic default IDs and sizes to all new form elements, so the one that's just been added needs amending. Select the text field, and the Properties panel will change, enabling you to define settings for the field. The leftmost field lets you to define the text field's ID, which should be set to realname (this ties in with the scripts used later in this chapter to send the form). Also, define a character width for the field by setting the Char width value to 30.

6. Because the text field's ID has been amended, we need to edit the associated label, too. Click the label, and you'll see (amongst other things) <p><label> appear in the status bar. Right-click or Ctrl-click <label> and choose Quick Tag Editor. Then change the value of the for attribute to realname, so it matches the ID value set in the previous step.

Note that browsers don't visually display the <label> *tag, although you can, if you wish, style the element in CSS. However, most browsers apply an important accessibility benefit: if a* <label> *element is used, as in this exercise, when you click the text it surrounds, the browser gives focus to the corresponding form control. In other words, click* Name, *which is surrounded by a* <label> *element with the* for *attribute of* realname, *and the form element with the* ID *attribute value of* realname *will be selected.*

7. Repeat steps 2 through 6 for two more fields, but using the following values: for the first field, use Email address for the Label value in the Input Tag Accessibility Attributes dialog box, 21 for the Tab Index value, and email for the field's ID (once it's added to the page) and the <label> tag's for attribute value; for the second field, use Telephone for the Label value in the Input Tag Accessibility Attributes dialog box, 31 for the Tab Index value, and phone for the field's ID (once it's added to the page) and the <label> tag's for attribute value.

> *Before adding a new field, deselect everything in Design view, use the cursor to move to the right of the previously entered form element, and then press Enter. This creates a new paragraph, ready for your form field.*

8. Now, we're going to add some radio buttons to the page, to enable the user to make a selection from a set list of options. Move the cursor to the right of the previously added field, and press Enter to create a new paragraph. Type Are you a Web designer?, press Shift+Enter to create a line break, and then select the text and make it bold. Use the arrow keys to move the cursor underneath the text again, and then click the Radio Group button (found in the Forms section of the Insert bar).

9. This brings up the Radio Group dialog box. In the Name field, add some details that represent the question, as this will be returned as the form element name by some scripts. Note, however, that you should avoid punctuation and spaces for best results—represent spaces by using underscores. Therefore, a good Name value for the radio group might be are_you_a_web_designer.

10. Using the Radio Buttons area, add the option labels and values for the choices the user is to be provided with. Note that if you want more than two options, you can use the plus-sign icon to add another radio button. The minus sign icon deletes the selected option radio button, and the up and down arrows move the currently selected item in the list. The Lay out using options provide two methods of display for the radio buttons. Adding a table for them is pretty pointless, so select Line breaks, because they're easier to edit afterwards. Click OK and the two radio buttons will appear on the web page, one underneath the other.

11. To compact the form's display slightly, move the cursor to directly after Yes, and add a space, a vertical bar, and another space. Then use the forward-delete key on your keyboard to move the second radio button onto the same line. After you've done that, move your cursor to after No and again use forward-delete to tidy up the end of the list.

12. Next, we're going to create a pop-up menu-based option list. Press Enter to create a new paragraph, and click the List/Menu button. The Input Tag Accessibility Attributes dialog box (shown in step 2) should appear. Type What platform do you favor? in the Label field, and 41 in the Tab Index field. Ensure Attach label tag using 'for' attribute is selected, and click OK.

13. Place your cursor between the two elements, and then press Shift+Enter to create a line break and separate them. Select the label and use the Properties panel to make it bold. Select the form list element, and the Properties panel will change, much like it did when working on the text fields earlier. In the leftmost field, type platform (which is to be the ID for this form element).

14. Click the List Values button to bring up the List Values dialog box. Enter the values you want in the list, and click OK. Back in Design view, you can select the menu and use the Initially selected field in the Properties panel to make one of the items the default for the list. (Alternatively, you can make your first item Choose an option, and select that in the Initially selected field.)

15. Because the ID of the menu was changed, its label also needs amending. Like before, click the menu, right-click or Ctrl-click <label> on the status bar, and select Quick Tag Editor. Change the for attribute value to the same as the menu's ID, as defined in step 13. (If you've forgotten, platform is the value.)

16. Move your cursor to the right of the menu, and press Enter to create a new paragraph. Click the Textarea button to bring up the now-familiar Input Tag Accessibility Attributes dialog box. Type Comments in the Label field, and 51 in the Tab Index field. Click OK and rearrange the label and form element as you did the menu and text fields. Select the textarea and change its ID to message, using the leftmost field in the Properties panel. Set Char width to 30 and Num Lines to 5 (the latter of those defines how many characters high the text area will be).

17. Because the textarea's ID has been changed, the label's for attribute needs updating, as with previous form elements and labels created in this exercise. Using the same process as in step 15 (and others), change the for attribute value of the label wrapped around Comments to message.

18. Move the cursor to the right of the textarea, and press Enter to create a paragraph to house the last of the form elements that will be added in this tutorial—the all-important "submit" button. Click the Button button in the Forms section of the Insert bar. There's no need to add a label to a submit button, so select No label tag from the Style options. In Tab Index, type 61. Click OK, and the submit button will be added to the page. The default options set by Dreamweaver—including titling the button Submit—are fine, so there's no need to change them. However, should you want the button to display something else, select it and then use the Properties panel's Button name field to amend this value.

And there we have it: a completed form, albeit one that doesn't yet work and that doesn't look that great. Both these issues will be dealt with later in this chapter. For now, you can check your work against the file 9_form_basic.html, found in the Chapter 9 folder of the download files.

Longtime web users may have noticed the omission of a Reset button in this example. This button used to be common online, enabling the user to reset a form to its default state. However, I've never really seen the point in having it there, hence its absence.

Adding a fieldset and legend

Before we get to the section on styling a form, there is another rarely used but useful accessibility element that can be added to a page: a fieldset (with accompanying legend). What the fieldset enables you to do is group a set of related controls on a form, and apply a label via the legend element.

However, because Dreamweaver's selection ability in Design view can be somewhat quirky, it's best to use Code view to select the elements that you want to enclose in the fieldset.

Starting with the page from the previous exercise, try using Code view to select the first three paragraphs, then click the Fieldset button. In the Fieldset dialog box, type Personal information in the Legend field, and click OK.

Preview the page in a browser. If everything's been done correctly, you should see the fieldset surrounding the three fields that were selected.

This form can be found in the Chapter 9 folder of the book's download files—the document's name is 9_form_unstyled.html.

> If you get a bunch of yellow HTML tags appearing in Design view after adding the fieldset, it means you didn't select entire elements—always ensure that you select the start and end tags of any elements you want to include in the fieldset, along with their contents.

Styling a form

Before we work through using CSS to style form elements, a word of warning: this is one area in web design where it's tricky to create a consistent look across browsers. At the time of writing, Apple's Safari browser ignores the majority of form element CSS styles entirely, preferring to base web page form elements on Mac OS X's Aqua user interface. And while other browsers accept things like borders and padding on forms, they each have their own idea about various things relating to spacing and alignment, so always go for a "good enough" approach and don't waste your time trying to get everything the same in all browsers, because you never will.

If you want to use the form from earlier in this chapter as a starting point for this section, but don't fancy working through that exercise, use the file 9_form_unstyled.html *from the* Chapter 9 *folder of the book's download files.*

One of the biggest differences between browsers is in how the fieldset and legend are displayed. However, by attaching a style sheet to the form document and creating a couple of rules using tag selectors, the fieldset and legend can be improved visually. Try creating the following:

1. For tag rule fieldset, select the Border category in the CSS Rule Definition dialog box, and set it to dashed, 1 pixel, and #555555.

2. For tag rule legend, set the following in the CSS Rule Definition dialog box: in the Type category, set Font to Verdana, Arial, Helvetica, sans-serif, set Size to 90%, set Case to uppercase, and set Color to #000000; in the Box category, deselect Same for all under Padding, and set Top and Bottom to 0 and Left and Right to 10 pixels; in the Background category, set Background color to #ffffff.

This results in an appearance like the following:

When styling form elements, be sure to rigorously test across browsers, because things are not consistent. For instance, omitting the Background color *setting for the* legend *rule makes the dashed line appear behind the legend in Internet Explorer, but this doesn't happen in most other browsers.*

Other form fields can also be styled, enabling you to get away from the clunky default look offered by most browsers. Although the default appearance isn't attractive, it does make it obvious which elements are form fields and which are buttons. Therefore, if you do style forms in CSS, ensure that the elements are still easy to make out from other page content, and to distinguish from one another.

To style text fields and text areas, create a class rule, .formField. In the CSS Rule Definition dialog box, select the Border category and set it to solid, 1 pixel, and #333333; in the Background category, set Background color to #dddddd. This rule can then be added to the relevant form elements by selecting them and choosing .formField from the Properties panel's Class menu.

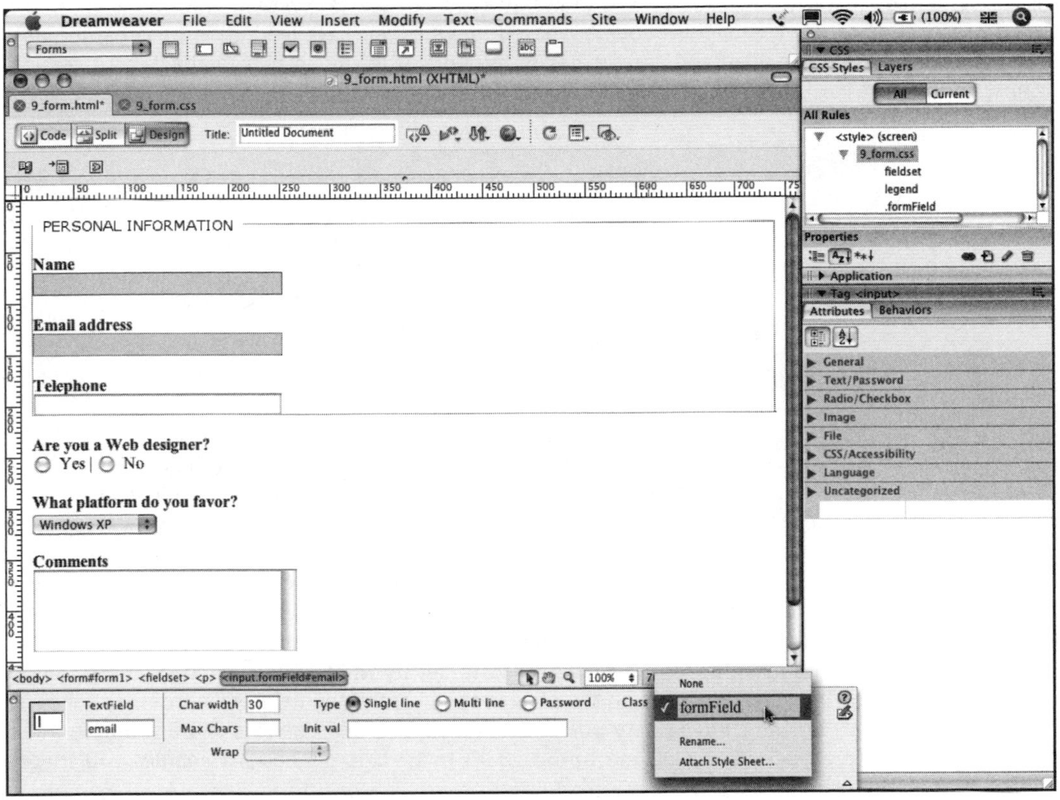

As you can see from the following screenshot, the style makes the text fields and textarea look more elegant, replacing the default 3-D border with a solid, dark gray border, and setting the background color as a light gray, thereby drawing attention to the form input fields.

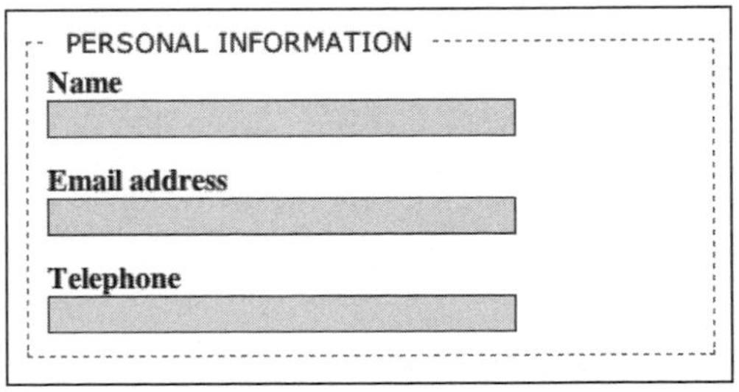

Although you can go further and add padding to these elements, Gecko and Internet Explorer apply the values as you'd expect, but Opera and Safari ignore them entirely. However, if you're trying to create a pixel-perfect design, it's perfectly feasible to set a width value for the .formField class.

The default Submit button style can be amended in a similar fashion. This is usually a good idea, because it makes the button stand out and draws attention to the text within. The following image shows one such style. Try creating this yourself, based on what you have learned in this chapter, and then take a look at 9_form.html and 9_form.css in the book's download files to check your version against mine.

Comments

SUBMIT

At the time of this writing, Safari ignores form styles, instead using the Mac OS X Aqua look and feel. Form functionality is not affected by this, but layouts could be, so ensure you test styled forms in that browser, even if they look fine in every other browser.

A final style point worth bearing in mind is that you can create a CSS style for the form itself (using the tag selector form). You might wonder why on earth you'd want to do that, but it can be useful to control the margins above and below the form, and also to set its width. The second of those points should be obvious if you've worked through the code in this chapter: the fieldset's border stretches to the entire window width, which looks very odd if the form labels and controls take up only a small area of the browser window. Reducing the form's width to specific dimensions enables you to get around this.

Sending feedback

In this section, we'll check out how to send form data using a CGI script and PHP. Although much of this section isn't strictly Dreamweaver territory, it's useful to know how to deal with form scripts when designing websites, hence its inclusion.

Once users submit information, it needs to go somewhere and it needs a method of getting there. Several techniques are available for parsing forms, but we're going to cover the most common: a server-side CGI script. Essentially, this script collects the information submitted, formats it, and delivers it to the addresses you configure within the script.

FormMail, available from Matt's Script Archive (www.scriptarchive.com), is probably the most common, and a number of web hosts preconfigure this script in their web space packages. However, FormMail does have flaws, and it hasn't kept up with current technology, as Matt acknowledges.

Therefore, I recommend using *nms* FormMail (available from http://nms-cgi.sourceforge.net/), a script that emulates the behavior of FormMail but takes a more modern and bug-free approach. Note, however, that if your web host supports PHP, you can skip the *nms* FormMail section and instead using PHP to send form data.

Configuring *nms* FormMail

The thought of editing and configuring scripts gives some designers the willies, but *nms* FormMail takes only a couple of minutes to get up and running.

First, you need to add two hidden input elements to the form on your web page. This is best done partly in Code view, in order to avoid errors. Position the cursor immediately after the form start tag (i.e. after `<form id="form1" name="form1" method="post" action="">`) and then click the Hidden Field button (in the Forms section of the Insert bar). This brings up the Tag Editor dialog box, enabling you to set values for the Name and Value attributes for the hidden input field.

Type subject for Name and Contact form from website (or whatever you want to see in the subject field when forms are sent to you) for Value. For the second field, use redirect for Name and for Value use the URL of a web page that you'd like the user to be redirected to once the form has been sent. This should be another page on your website, preferably with a message thanking the user for sending the form, and assuring them that their query will be responded to as soon as possible. For my own sites, I often just duplicate the page the form is on, and add the message above the form.

Now, the script itself needs to be edited. Because CGI scripts tend to break with slight errors, I highly recommend editing them in a text editor that doesn't affect document formatting, such as NoteTab for Windows (www.notetab.com) or BBEdit for Mac (www.barebones.com).

The first line of the script defines the location of Perl on your web host's server. Your hosting company can provide this information, and you can amend the path accordingly:

```
#!/usr/bin/perl -wT
```

Aside from this setting, you only need to edit some values in the user configuration section. The $mailprog value defines the location of the sendmail binary on your web host's server. You can get this from your web host's system admin:

```
$mailprog            = '/usr/lib/sendmail -oi -t';
```

The $postmaster value is the address that receives bounced messages when emails cannot be delivered. It should be a different address from that of the intended recipient:

```
$postmaster          = 'someone@your.domain';
```

The @referers value lists IP addresses or domain names that can access this script, thereby stopping just anyone from using your script and your server resources. For instance, the Snub Communications mail form has snubcommunications.com and the site's IP address for this value (as a space-delimited list):

```
@referers            = qw(dave.org.uk 209.207.222.64 localhost);
```

The @allow_mail_to value contains the addresses to which form results can be sent, again as a space-delimited list. If you include just a domain here, any address on that domain is valid as a recipient. If you're using only one address, set the $max_recipients value to 1, to increase security.

```
@allow_mail_to       = qw(you@your.domain some.one.else@your.domain localhost);
```

Multiple recipients

You can also use the script to email multiple recipients. To do so, an additional hidden input element is needed, with the value of recipient for Name and the value of emailgroup for Value.

```
<input type="hidden" name="recipient" value="emailgroup" />
```

In the script itself, two lines are changed. The @allow_mail_to value is removed, because it's catered for by the newly amended %recipient_alias. Both are shown here:

```
@allow_mail_to    = ();
%recipient_alias  = ('emailgroup =>
➥ 'your-name@your.domain,your-name@somewhere-else.domain',);
```

If a script is used for multiple groups of recipients, you need a unique value for each in the HTML, and you need to amend the %recipient_alias value accordingly:

```
%recipient_alias  = (
➥ 'emailgroup1' => 'your-name@your.domain,your-name@somewhere-else.domain',
➥ 'emailgroup2'  => 'foo@your.domain');
```

Script server permissions

Upload the script to your website's cgi-bin. The vast majority of hosts will have such a folder; if you're not sure where yours is, talk to your ISP or web hosting company. Once there, the script's permissions must be set. Exactly how this is achieved depends on what FTP client you're using. Some enable you to right-click and "get info," while others have a permissions or CHMOD command buried among their menus. Consult your documentation and find out which your client has.

If you can CHMOD the script file, set it to 755. If you have to manually set permissions, do so as in the screenshot to the right.

Finally, the location of the script needs to be set as your form's Action attribute value. To do this, select the form in Design view (click inside it and then click the <form> tag in the status bar) and type the full URL of the script in the Action field.

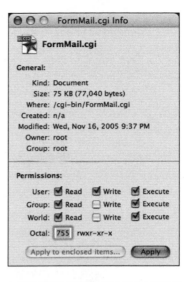

Sending form data by PHP

If your hosting company offers support for PHP, the most widely used server-side technology, there is no need to install a CGI script such as *nms* FormMail. Everything can be done with PHP's built-in mail() function. The function requires three pieces of information:

- The address the mail is being sent to
- The subject line
- The message itself

An optional fourth argument to mail() permits you to send additional information in the email headers, such as from, cc, and bcc addresses, and to specify a particular character encoding (if, for instance, you need to include accented characters or an Asian language in the email).

Although the PHP script can be put in a separate page, the most convenient method is to use a self-processing form. This displays the feedback page as normal when the user first visits the page, but it contains all the necessary PHP code to process the form, and simply displays an acknowledgment at the top of the form once the mail has been sent.

The code is straightforward. Even if you have no experience working with PHP, the following instructions should have you up and running very quickly.

1. Save the page containing the form with a PHP extension—for instance, feedback.php. Amend the opening <form> tag like this:

    ```
    <form action="<?php echo $_SERVER['PHP_SELF']; ?>" method="post">
    ```

2. At the top of the page, insert the following PHP code block above the DOCTYPE. Although you should never place any content above the DOCTYPE, it's perfectly safe to do so in this case, because the PHP code doesn't produce any HTML output.

    ```php
    <?php
    if ($_POST) {
      if (get_magic_quotes_gpc()) {
        foreach ($_POST as $key => $value) {
          $temp = stripslashes($value);
          $_POST[$key] = $temp;
          }
        }
      $to = 'email_address@your_domain.com';
      $subject = 'Feedback from website';
      // message goes here
      // headers go here
      $sent = mail($to, $subject, $message, $headers);
      }
    ?>
    ```

    The script begins by checking whether the POST array has been set. This happens only when a user clicks the form's Submit button, so this entire block of code will be ignored when the page first loads. It then makes sure the content from the form is in the right format to send by email. You will need to change the lines beginning with $to and $subject, and you will need to replace the lines indicating where the message and headers go with the actual message and headers. Don't panic, as this is all explained in the steps below.

3. Replace email_address@your_domain.com with the email address that the feedback is to be sent to. Make sure the address is in quotes, and that the line ends with a semicolon.

4. Replace the content inside the quotes in the following line with whatever you want the subject line to say.

5. Next, build the message. To do this, retrieve the value of each form field/element, and add any extra text you want. In the example from earlier in this chapter, there are the following form fields and elements: realname, email, phone, are_you_a_web_designer, platform, and message. PHP stores their values as $_POST['realname'], $_POST['email'], $_POST['message'], and so on. In other words, the field's name goes in quotes inside the square brackets of $_POST[].

    Surrounding text is put in quotes, and each part is joined together with a period. You insert new lines by typing \n inside double quotes. So, to build a message from the fields in the example form, you would use the following code:

```
$message = "From: " . $_POST['realname'] . "\n";
$message .= "Email: " . $_POST['email'] . "\n";
$message .= "Phone: " . $_POST['phone'] . "\n";
$message .= "Are you a web designer?: " . $_POST['are_you_a_web_designer'] .
"\n";
$message .= "What platform do you favor?: " . $_POST['platform'] . "\n";
$message .= "Message: " . $_POST['message'] . "\n";
```

Note that there is a period before the equal sign in all rows apart from the first one. This adds the value of the previous line to the message. This code should be placed after //message goes here, shown in step 2.

6. There are many additional headers you can add to an email. The following code shows how to add a from address, a reply-to address, a cc address, and UTF-8 encoding (for messages that require accents or Asian languages):

```
$headers = "From: " . $_POST['email'] . "\n";
$headers .= "Reply-To: " . $_POST['email'] . "\n";
$headers .= "Cc: copycat@example.com\n";
$headers .= "Content-type: text/plain; charset=UTF-8";
```

As with the message, the headers are built using the period to join text in quotes and the form's variables. Each of these headers (except the last one) must be followed by the PHP new line character (\n). Lines 1 and 3 don't contain any values from the form, so the \n simply goes before the closing double quote. On line 2, the \n follows a form value, so the two are joined by a period, and the new line character goes inside its own set of double quotes.

One nice little touch in this script is that the second line of the headers puts the user's email address in the Reply-to field of the email, so all you have to do is click Reply in your email program to send a message back to the right person.

If you want to use a special encoding, such as UTF-8, for your emails, make sure the web page containing the form uses the same encoding in its <meta> tag.

You don't need to use all these headers. Just remove the complete line for any that you don't want.

This code should be placed after //headers go here, shown in step 2.

7. The final line of code sends the email and sets a variable called $sent.

8. Immediately above the form in the main part of your page, insert the following code:

```
<?php
if (isset($sent)) {
  echo '<p><strong>Thank you for contacting us. Your message will be responded to
as soon as possible.</strong></p>';
  }
?>
```

This text will display only if the $sent variable has been set. Enter whatever message you like in place of the one shown here.

9. Save the page, upload it to your hosting company, and test it. In a few moments, you should receive the test message in your inbox. That's all there is to it!

A completed version of this form can be found in the Chapter 9 folder of the book's download files. It's named 9_form.php. Feel free to experiment with it for use in your own websites!

> *Although these instructions should be sufficient to help you get a PHP form working successfully, server-side coding can seem intimidating if you've never done it before. If you would like to learn more about working with PHP and Dreamweaver, along with learning how to protect your PHP forms from email injectors, which can use your form for spamming, check out Foundation PHP for Dreamweaver 8 by David Powers (friends of ED, ISBN: 1590595696). Also check the Apress online catalog at www.apress.com for non-Dreamweaver-specific books on PHP and other server-side technologies.*

Using email to send form data

In rare cases, it may not be possible to set up a form to send form data (although even most free web hosts tend to provide users with some kind of form functionality, even if it's a shared script). If you find yourself in this sticky situation, it's possible to use a mailto: URL for the form's Action attribute value. This causes browsers to email the form parameters and values to the specified address.

Select the form, as previously in this chapter, so you see its various attributes' fields in the Properties panel. In Action, type mailto: followed by the email address you want the form to be sent to; and in Enctype, type text/plain.

This might seem a simpler method than messing around with CGI scripts or PHP, but it has very major shortfalls:

- Some browsers don't support mailto: as a form action.
- The resulting data may arrive in a barely readable (or unreadable) format, and you have no control over this.
- This method isn't secure.
- The user won't be redirected and may therefore not realize data has been sent.

That last problem can be worked around by using Code view to add a JavaScript alert to the <form> start tag:

```
< form method="post" action="mailto:anemailaddress@somewhere.com"
enctype="text/plain" onsubmit="window.alert('This form is being sent by
➥ email. Thank you for contacting us.')">
```

Of course, this relies on JavaScript being active on the user's browser—but, then, this is a last resort method and should only be used if you have absolutely no other choice.

A version of this web page is in the Chapter 9 folder of the download files: `9_form_mailto.html`.

A layout for contact pages

Once you've completed a form, you need to integrate it into your site in a way that most benefits the site's visitors. I've always been of the opinion that it's a good idea to offer users multiple methods of contact on the *same page*. This makes it easy for them to contact you, as it requires fewer clicks than the fairly common method of display, which offers a form, and a link to other contact details on a separate page.

The following screenshot of the Snub Communications site shows what I consider a good layout.

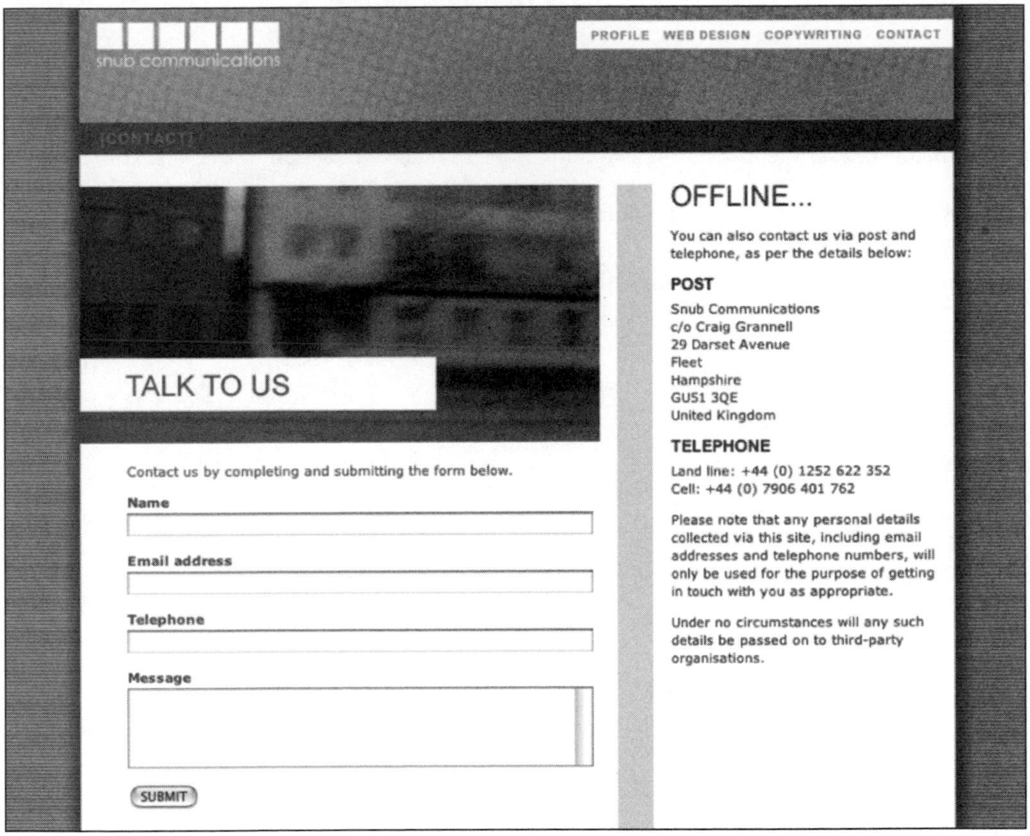

On the left is the form, with the fewest fields needed to be able to respond to someone effectively. On the right side of the page are other contact details, such as a mailing address and telephone numbers (along with a brief disclaimer confirming that Snub Communications uses personal details collected via the site only for the purpose of getting in touch with clients as appropriate, and that under no circumstances will any details be passed on to third-party organizations).

Here, everything is in one place, which makes sending feedback to or getting in contact with the organization convenient for the person viewing the web page. The Snub Communications site doesn't require a map of the local area, showing the company's location, but if it did, a link to it would appear on this page, too. The map page itself would likely resemble this one, but with the map in place of the form—after all, it's very frustrating to have a map to an organization's location, get lost, and then discover you don't have the organization's full address and telephone number. Make it easy on your website's users, and provide maps with other contact details on the same page.

We're not going to get into how to create this layout, because we've already covered the techniques earlier in the book. See the exercise on "Creating a sidebar" in Chapter 8.

Summary

We've covered plenty of ground here, and you should now be comfortable creating forms and setting one up to collect user feedback from a website. Now it's time to move on to the next chapter, which shows how to combine many of the elements of web design explored in this book to create cutting-edge web page layouts and templates in Dreamweaver.

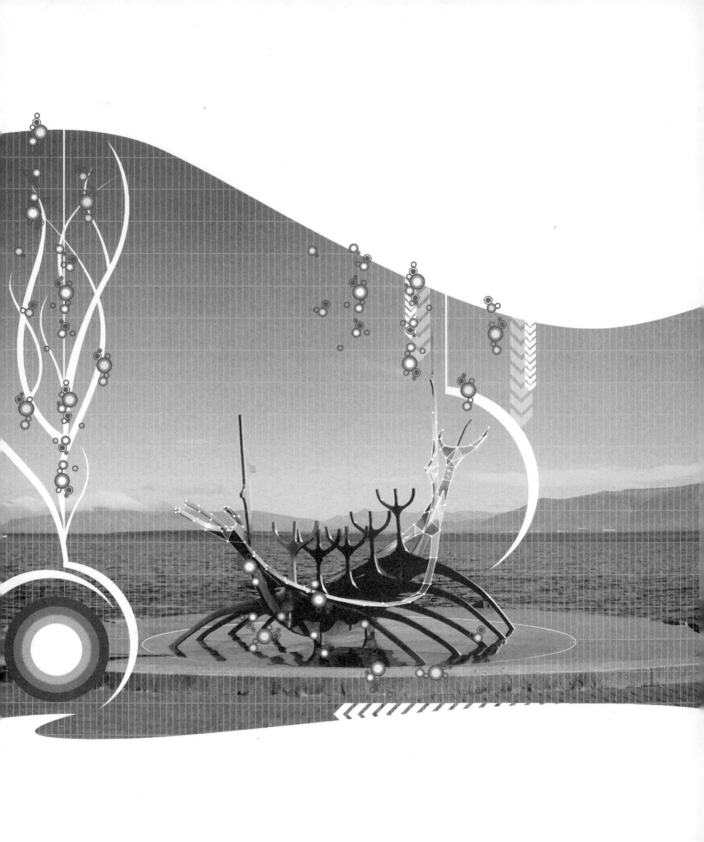

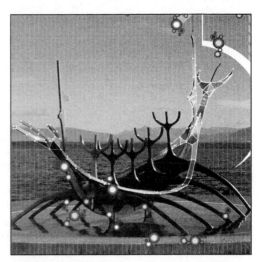

Chapter 10

PUTTING IT ALL INTO PRACTICE

In this chapter . . .

- Creating website layouts
- Creating and editing templates
- Working with editable regions
- Creating pages based on templates
- Working with embedded templates

This chapter will combine methods and techniques you've learned earlier in this book to create four distinct website layouts that you can then use as the basis for numerous websites. This should show how easy it is to take various elements, ideas, and approaches from these chapters and use them as the basis for your own designs.

Note, however, that this chapter is primarily intended to show how to deal with website layout, so I won't be including things like page titles and metatags—things that are essential to any public-facing web page. For more information on those, take another look at Chapter 4 and make use of the various elements discussed accordingly. Also, not every element will be styled in this chapter, but you can add to the exercises yourself by copying various rules from earlier chapters and amending them as appropriate.

It's also worth bearing in mind that, at this point, you should be more than capable of creating and nesting div elements in Design view, adding various content types, and creating CSS rules to style everything. Therefore, the exercises in this section are rather more succinct than in previous chapters, largely providing you with the relevant values, rather than hand holding at every step of the way.

Finally, bear in mind that we're creating standards-compliant documents here, which may not always display correctly in Internet Explorer 5.5 for Windows, due to that browser incorrectly placing padding within the defined dimensions of a CSS box. In cases where you wish to fully support this browser, you can make use of Tantek Çelik's box model hack (see `www.tantek.com/CSS/Examples/boxmodelhack.html`) to make sites appear as intended in older versions of Microsoft's web browser.

> *When you create and test the sites from this chapter, you may note that they are predominantly gray. This isn't because I have some sort of fixation with dreary colors, but because this ensures the examples look better in a black and white book. All presentation elements are driven by CSS, so it should be easy enough for you to swap out or edit various elements to add a dash of color to the designs!*

Creating website layouts

This section of the chapter will show you how to take the knowledge you've gained so far and use it to create four good-looking, standards-compliant website layouts. Because of the book's modular nature, you'll in some cases be able to copy and paste code and elements you've already created, just amending a few values here and there. For all four layout examples, both "before" and "after" files are provided as part of the download files for this book.

Creating a layout for an online diary or blog

This first layout is light and simple, and has just a few links at its top-right corner—perfect for a site that specializes in writing (such as a personal online diary or blog). Note the narrow width of the column, which restricts the width of the text column, thereby making the article easier to read.

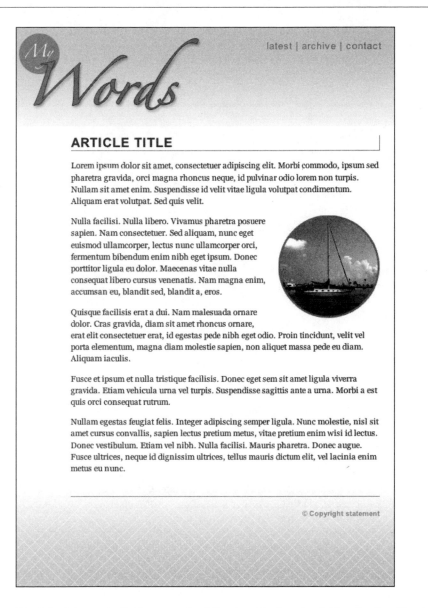

The files for this tutorial are available as part of the book's download files, in the Chapter 10/ layout_1_files folder. Copy the folder to your hard drive before working through the exercise.

Prior to working on any layout, you need to figure out its structure. Here, the design is a fixed width, so it will be contained in a "wrapper." Within that, at the top, is the masthead, within which is the navigation. Below the masthead is the content area, with an image that clearly needs to be floated right. And underneath the content area is a footer. Both the masthead and footer have background images, which are best added in CSS.

1. Create a new web page and CSS document, save both in the folder you copied to your hard drive, and link the CSS document to the web page. In the web page, add a div with an ID of wrapper. Inside that, add three divs, one after the other, with the ID values masthead, content, and footer.

See Chapter 7 for more on adding divs to a web page. Remember that to nest a div inside another, you need to set Insert *to* After start of tag *(in the* Insert Div Tag *dialog box) and then choose the relevant tag. To place a div underneath another, instead set* Insert *to* After tag *and choose the relevant tag after which to place the one you're adding.*

2. Select the default content for the masthead div, delete it, and then add a new div in its place with an ID value of navigation (and with Insert set to At insertion point). Replace the default content of this new div with three links (Latest, Archive, and Contact), separated by vertical bars.

```
11   </head>
12
13   <body>
14   <div id="wrapper">
15     <div id="masthead">
16       <div id="navigation"><a href="#">Latest</a> | <a href="#">Archive</a> | <a href="#">Contact</a> </div>
17     </div>
18     <div id="content">Content for  id "content" Goes Here</div>
19     <div id="footer">Content for  id "footer" Goes Here</div>
20   Content for  id "wrapper" Goes Here</div>
21   </body>
```

Latest | Archive | Contact
Content for id "content" Goes Here
Content for id "footer" Goes Here
Content for id "wrapper" Goes Here

`<body>`   100% ÷   766 x 309 ÷   1K / 1 sec

3. Replace the default content of the content div with a heading (level 1) and a few paragraphs of text. After the first paragraph, press Enter and add the boat.jpg image (which is in the assets folder). By default, Dreamweaver marks this up as an image inside a paragraph, which we don't want. Therefore, select the image, right-click or Ctrl-click the <p> tag in the status bar, and select Remove Tag to remove it.

Nulla facilisi. Nulla libero. Vivamus pharetra posuere sapien. Nam consectetuer. Sed aliquam, nunc eget euismod ullamcorper, lectus nunc ullamcorper orci, fermentum bibendum enim nibh eget ipsum. Donec porttitor ligula eu dolor. Maecenas vitae nulla consequat libero cursus venenatis. Nam magna enim, accumsan eu, blandit sed, blandit a, eros.

Quisque facilisis erat a dui. Nam malesuada ornare dolor. Cras gravida, diam sit amet rhoncus ornare, erat elit

`<body>` `<div#wrapper>` `<div#content>` `<p>`   100% ÷   766 x 309 ÷   3K / 1 sec

Remove Tag
Quick Tag Editor...
Set Class   ▶
Set ID   ▶

▼

259

See Chapters 5 and 6 for more information about working with text and images respectively.

4. Replace the default footer div content with a brief copyright statement, and format it as a paragraph. Then select the default wrapper div content and delete it. The web page itself is now complete, bar one tiny adjustment that will be made in step 15.

dolor. Maecenas vitae nulla consequat libero cursus venenatis. Nam magna enim, accumsan eu, blandit sed, blandit a, eros.

Quisque facilisis erat a dui. Nam malesuada ornare dolor. Cras gravida, diam sit amet rhoncus ornare, erat elit consectetuer erat, id egestas pede nibh eget odio. Proin tincidunt, velit vel porta elementum, magna diam molestie sapien, non aliquet massa pede eu diam. Aliquam iaculis.

Fusce et ipsum et nulla tristique facilisis. Donec eget sem sit amet ligula viverra gravida. Etiam vehicula urna vel turpis. Suspendisse sagittis ante a urna. Morbi a est quis orci consequat rutrum.

Nullam egestas feugiat felis. Integer adipiscing semper ligula. Nunc molestie, nisl sit amet cursus convallis, sapien lectus pretium metus, vitae pretium enim wisi id lectus. Donec vestibulum. Etiam vel nibh. Nulla facilisi. Mauris pharetra. Donec augue. Fusce ultrices, neque id dignissim ultrices, tellus mauris dictum elit, vel lacinia enim metus eu nunc.

© Copyright statement

`<body> <div#wrapper> <div#footer> <p>`   100% ÷   766 x 309 ÷   3K / 1 sec

5. From this point on, we're almost entirely working in CSS, adding rules. Create a Tag rule for the selector body. In the Type category, set Size to small and Color to #626262; in Box, set Padding and Margin to 0.

If you need a review of creating and working with CSS styles, see the "Working with CSS" section in Chapter 4.

6. Create an Advanced rule for the selector #wrapper. In Box, set Width to 600 pixels, the Left and Right settings of Margin to auto (to horizontally center the wrapper), the Top and Bottom settings of Margin to 0, and the Bottom setting of Padding to 20 pixels.

7. Create an Advanced rule for the selector #masthead. In Background, use the Browse button to select masthead.gif from the assets folder, and set Repeat to no-repeat. In Box, set Height to 155 pixels.

8. Create an Advanced rule for the selector #navigation. In Type, set Font to Arial, Helvetica, sans-serif, set Size to 120%, set Case to lowercase, and set Color to #b1b1b1; in Block, set Letter spacing to 1 pixels (to separate the letters slightly) and Text align to right; in Box, set the Top and Right values of Padding to 20 pixels and the other values to 0.

9. Create an Advanced rule for the selector #navigation a to style links within the navigation div. In Type, set Color to #b1b1b1 and Text decoration to none.

10. Create an Advanced rule for the selector #navigation a:hover to style the link hover state within the navigation div. In Type, set Color to #888888 and Text decoration to underline.

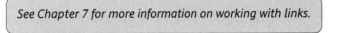

See Chapter 7 for more information on working with links.

11. Create an Advanced rule for the selector #content. In Box, set the Left value of Padding to 92 pixels and the Right value to 23 pixels.

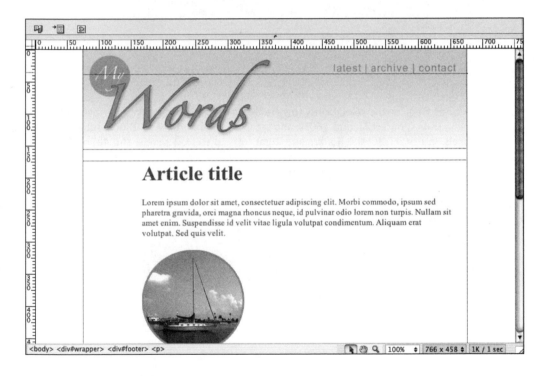

12. Create an Advanced rule for the selector #footer. In Background, use the Browse button to select footer.gif from the assets folder, and set Repeat to no-repeat. In Box, set Height to 168 pixels, and the Top, Right, and Left values of Padding to 10 pixels, 23 pixels, and 92 pixels respectively.

CSS Rule Definition for #footer in layout_1.css

Category: Box

Type
Background
Block
Box
Border
List
Positioning
Extensions

Width: [   ] [pix...]   Float: [   ]

Height: [168] [pix...]   Clear: [   ]

Padding

☐ Same for all

Top: [10] [pix...]

Right: [23] [pix...]

Bottom: [   ] [pix...]

Left: [92] [pix...]

Margin

☑ Same for all

Top: [   ] [pix...]

Right: [   ] [pix...]

Bottom: [   ] [pix...]

Left: [   ] [pix...]

(Help)   (Apply) (Cancel) (OK)

13. Create a Tag rule for the selector h1, to style the level-one heading. In Type, set Font to Arial, Helvetica, sans-serif, set Size to 160%, and set Case to uppercase. In Block, set Letter spacing to 1 pixels. In Border, set the Bottom and Right rows to solid, 1 pixels, and #b7b7b7.

CSS Rule Definition for h1 in layout_1.css

Category: Border

Type
Background
Block
Box
Border
List
Positioning
Extensions

Style _____   Width _____   Color _____

☐ Same for all   ☐ Same for all   ☐ Same for all

Top: [   ]   [   ] [pix...]   [ ] [   ]

Right: [solid]   [1] [pix...]   [ ] [#b7b7b7]

Bottom: [solid]   [1] [pix...]   [ ] [#b7b7b7]

Left: [   ]   [   ] [pix...]   [ ] [   ]

(Help)   (Apply) (Cancel) (OK)

14. Create a Tag rule for the selector p, to style the paragraphs. In Type, set Font to Georgia, Times New Roman, Times, serif, set Size to 100%, and set Line height to 1.4 ems.

15. To float the image right, create a Class rule for the selector .floatedImage. In Box, set Float to right, and set the Top, Right, Bottom, and Left values of Margin to 0, 0, 10 pixels, and 20 pixels respectively. Back in the web page, select the image and use the Properties panel's Class menu to apply the floatedImage class to the image. It should then move to the right of the design, allowing text to flow around it.

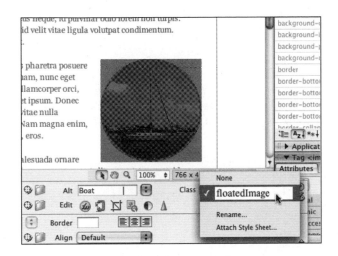

16. Create a Tag rule for the selector #footer p, to style paragraphs within the footer div. In Type, set Font to Arial, Helvetica, sans-serif, set Size to 85%, Weight to bold, and Color to #c4c4c4; in Block, set Text align to right; in Box, set the Top value of Padding to 20 pixels; and in Border, set the Top row only (not the others) to solid, 1 pixel, and #b7b7b7.

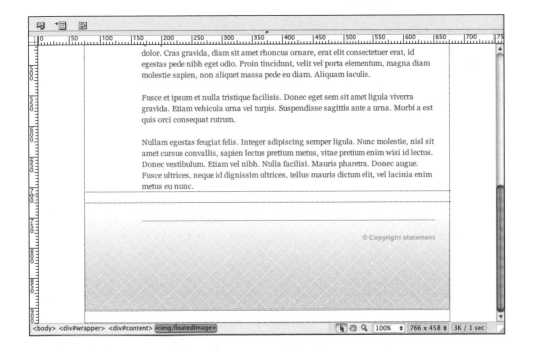

The completed website files can be found in the `layout_1_files_completed` folder, which is in the Chapter 10 folder of the book's download files.

Creating a fixed-width, businesslike layout

This second layout is also a fixed-width layout, but it has more of a businesslike appearance (and it would therefore be suitable for a small business site).

Its structure is simple: within the wrapper is a navigation div and a content div. Inside the content div is the main content, a two-column area (which is composed of two floated columns), and a footer (which is set to clear the floated elements). You may recognize the navigation bar from Chapter 7 (see "Creating and styling a vertically aligned navigation bar" and "Using JavaScript to create collapsible sections"), and we'll be using the completed files for that exercise in this tutorial—after all, there's no point in creating them from scratch again!

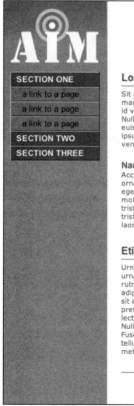

This JavaScript document, along with a number of images, are available in the book's download files, in the folder Chapter 10/layout_2_files. Copy this folder to your hard drive before working through the exercise.

1. Create a new web page and CSS document, save both in the folder you copied to your hard drive, and link the CSS document to the web page. Double-click the head content area above Design view to move the cursor inside the web page's <head> section. Then click the Script button in the HTML section of the Insert bar. Use the folder icon to link toggler.js to the web page.

2. Add a div with an ID of wrapper. Inside that, add two divs, one after the other, with ID values of navigation and content.

```
10   </style>
11   <script language="JavaScript" type="text/javascript" src="toggler.js"></script>
12   </head>
13
14   <body>
15   <div id="wrapper">
16     <div id="navigation">Content for  id "navigation" Goes Here</div>
17     <div id="content">Content for  id "content" Goes Here</div>
18   Content for  id "wrapper" Goes Here</div>
19   </body>
20   </html>
```

Content for id "navigation" Goes Here
Content for id "content" Goes Here
Content for id "wrapper" Goes Here

`<body> <div#wrapper> <div#content>`   100% ⬍   766 x 309 ⬍   1K / 1 sec

3. Open up 7_vertical_nav_bar_toggle.html from the download files. Carefully select the entire list, but not the containing navigation div (you can use Code view to more easily do this), and copy it. Select and delete the default content of the navigation div on your web page, and paste the copied information in its place. In Code view, remove style="display:none;" from the list with an id value of sectionOneLinks.

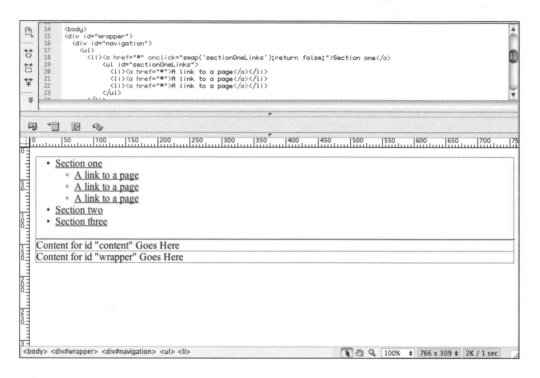

4. In the content div, add a level-one heading, a paragraph of text, a level-two heading, and then another paragraph of text. Click to the left of the top heading, and press Enter to add some space above it. Add the banner.gif image from the assets folder here, and then select it. Right-click or Ctrl-click the <h1> tag in the status bar, and select Remove Tag to remove formatting on this image.

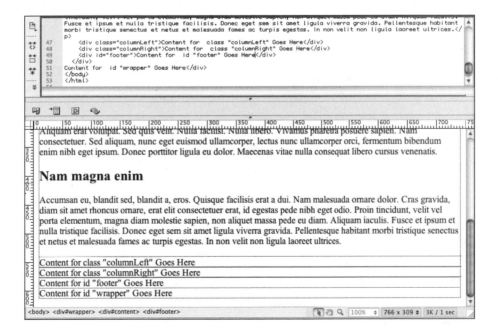

5. Position the cursor after the last paragraph in the content div, press Enter, and add three more divs, each under the previous, the first two with the Class values columnLeft and columnRight, and the third with an ID value of footer. Pressing Enter will have created an unwanted paragraph, which can be deleted by moving the cursor directly underneath the footer div and pressing Delete.

267

6. In the columnLeft and columnRight divs, add a level-one heading and a paragraph of text. In the footer div, add some content, but don't style it (ensure that the Format menu is set to None if you click inside the content once it's been added). Delete the default wrapper div content.

7. We're now working in CSS. Create a Tag rule for the selector body. In Type, set Font to Verdana, Arial, Helvetica, sans-serif, set Size to small, and set Color to #707070; in Background, use the Browse button to select page_background.gif from the assets folder, and set Repeat to repeat-y; in Box, set Padding and Margin to 0.

8. Create an Advanced rule for the selector #navigation. In Background, use the Browse button to select logo.gif from the assets folder, and set Repeat to no-repeat; in Box, set Width to 142 pixels, Float to left, and the Right setting of Margin to 22 pixels. Set the Top, Right, Bottom, and Left values of Padding to 110 pixels, 10 pixels, 0, and 10 pixels. The Top padding setting ensures navigation content starts underneath the logo (which was added as a background), while the Left and Right values mean content won't hug the navigation area background, which was added in the previous step (as part of the general page background).

9. To position the content div, create an Advanced rule for the selector #content. In Box, set Width to 534 pixels and Float to left.

10. To set padding above and below the two columns in the content div, create the Advanced rule .columnLeft,.columnRight, and in Box, set the Top and Bottom values of Padding to 15 pixels. In the same rule, set Float to Left and Width to 254 pixels, to make the columns sit side by side.

11. To add a gap between the two columns, create the Class rule .columnLeft, and set the Right value of Margin (in Box) to 25 pixels.

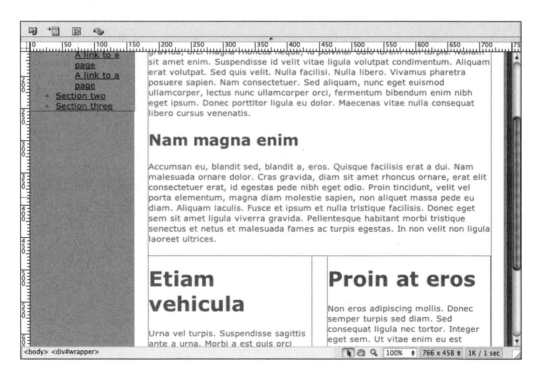

12. Create a Tag rule for the selector h1, to style the level-one headings. In Type, set Font to Arial, Helvetica, sans-serif, set Size to 125%, and set Weight to bold; in Box, set the Top value of Margin to 0 and the Bottom value to 5 pixels, and for Padding, set the Bottom value to 3 pixels; in Border, set the Bottom row only to solid, 1 pixels, and #888888.

13. Create a Tag rule for the selector h2, to style the level-two headings. In Type, set Font to Arial, Helvetica, sans-serif, set Size to 110%, and set Weight to bold; in Box, set the Top value of Margin to 1.3 ems and the Bottom value to 0.

14. Create a Tag rule for the selector p, to style paragraphs. In Type, set Font to Verdana, Arial, Helvetica, sans-serif, and set Size to 85%; in Box, set the Margin values to 0, apart from Bottom, which should be set to 1 ems.

15. To style the banner, create a Class rule with the selector .banner. In Box, set the Top, Bottom, and Left values of Margin to 20 pixels, 30 pixels, and 33 pixels respectively. Select the banner in Design view, and use the Properties panel's Class menu to apply the style.

16. Create an Advanced rule for the selector #footer. In Type, set Size to 77%; in Block, set Text align to right; in Box, set Clear to both, the Top and Bottom values of Padding to 20 pixels, and the Left and Right values of Padding to 0; in Border, set the Top row only to solid, 1 pixels, #888888.

17. To style the navigation bar, open up 7_vertical_nav_bar_toggle.css and copy all of the rules, except the body one, to the style sheet you created for this exercise.

Note that if the completed web page's navigation section doesn't display correctly in Internet Explorer for Windows, follow the procedure explained in the "Removing white space in Internet Explorer" section of Chapter 7.

The completed website files can be found in the layout_2_files_completed folder, which is in the Chapter 10 folder of the book's download files.

Creating a three-column, liquid website layout

This third design is somewhat different from the previous two, in that it's a liquid design that stretches to fill the entire browser window. It's also a three-column design, like the one explored in Chapter 8's "Creating a three-column layout with fixed sidebars" exercise; observant readers will also note that it includes the navigation bar created in Chapter 7's "Creating and styling a horizontal navigation bar" exercise. Although it is also suitable for a business site, this adaptable layout could be used for a wide range of purposes, such as a personal home page, a community website, and more.

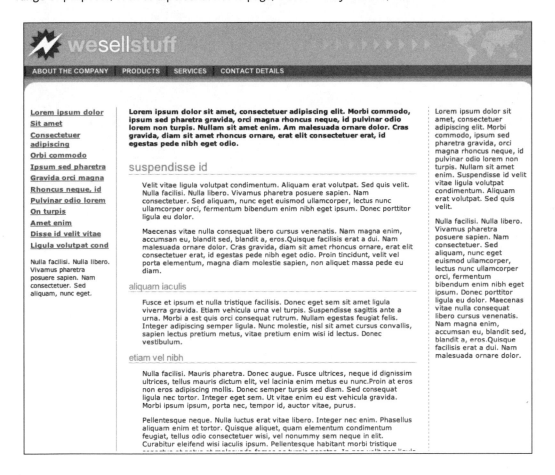

The files for this exercise are available as part of the book's download files, in the folder Chapter 10/layout_3_files. Copy the folder to your hard drive before working through the exercise.

1. Create a new web page and CSS document, save both in the folder you copied to your hard drive, and link the CSS document to the web page.

2. Add a number of divs to the page, each underneath the previous one. Give them the following ID values, in the following order: masthead, navigation, columnLeft, columnRight, content, and footer. Select the content of the content div and delete it, and then add a div with an ID value of contentArea in place of the deleted content.

```
12
13    <body>
14    <div id="masthead">Content for  id "masthead" Goes Here</div>
15    <div id="navigation">Content for  id "navigation" Goes Here</div>
16    <div id="columnLeft">Content for  id "columnLeft" Goes Here</div>
17    <div id="columnRight">Content for  id "columnRight" Goes Here</div>
18    <div id="content">
19        <div id="contentArea">Content for  id "contentArea" Goes Here</div>
20    </div>
21    <div id="footer">Content for  id "footer" Goes Here</div>
22    </body>
```

| 0 | 50 | 100 | 150 | 200 | 250 | 300 | 350 | 400 | 450 | 500 | 550 | 600 | 650 | 700 | 75 |

Content for id "masthead" Goes Here
Content for id "navigation" Goes Here
Content for id "columnLeft" Goes Here
Content for id "columnRight" Goes Here
Content for id "contentArea" Goes Here
Content for id "footer" Goes Here

`<body> <div#content> <div#contentArea>`   100% ♦ 766 x 309 ♦ 1K / 1 sec

3. In the masthead div, replace the default content with the image `logo.gif` from the assets folder.

4. Replace the default content of the navigation div with an unordered list that has a link in each list item (you can just copy and paste the one from `7_horizontal_nav_bar.html`).

5. In the columnLeft div, replace the default content with an unordered list containing a link in each list item. Underneath the list, add a short paragraph of text.

6. Replace the default content of the `columnRight` div with a couple of paragraphs of text.

7. Replace the default content of the `contentArea` div with a paragraph of text followed by a level-one heading, followed by another couple of paragraphs of text. Follow this with a level-two heading, another paragraph, another level-two heading, and a couple more paragraphs. Finally, add a paragraph of text to the footer.

8. Working in CSS now, create a Tag selector for the selector body. In Type, set Font to Verdana, Arial, Helvetica, sans-serif, set Size to small, and set Color to #555555; in Box, set Padding and Margin to 0.

9. Create an Advanced rule for the selector #masthead. In Background, set Color to #c2c2c2, use the Browse button to select `masthead_background.gif` from the assets folder, and set Horizontal position to right, Vertical position to top, and Repeat to repeat-y.

10. Create an Advanced rule for the selector #navigation. In Background, set Background color to #666666; in Border, set the Top row to solid, 1 pixels, #8d8d8d.

11. In Code view, copy across the rules from `7_horizontal_nav_bar.css` to the style sheet you created in this exercise. This should style the navigation bar.

12. To style the columnLeft div, create an Advanced rule #columnLeft. In Background, use the Browse button to select `left_column_background.gif` from the assets folder, set Horizontal position to left, Vertical position to top, and Repeat to no-repeat; in Box, set Width to 130 pixels, Float to left, the Top and Bottom values of Padding to 0, and the Left and Right values to 10 pixels.

13. To style the columnRight div, create an Advanced rule #columnRight. In Background, use the Browse button to select `right_column_background.gif` from the assets folder, set Horizontal position to right, Vertical position to top, and Repeat to no-repeat; in Box, set Width to 150 pixels, Float to right, the Top and Bottom values of Padding to 0, and the Left and Right values to 10 pixels.

14. To style the containing content div, create an Advanced rule #content. In Background, use the Browse button to select `content_background.gif` from the assets folder, set Horizontal position and Vertical position to 0, and Repeat to repeat-x; in Box, set the Bottom value of Padding to 40 pixels, and the Top, Right, Bottom, and Left values of Margin to 0, 170 pixels, 0, and 150 pixels respectively.

15. To style the contentArea div, create an Advanced rule #contentArea. In Box, set the Top and Bottom values of Padding to 20 pixels and the Left and Right values of Padding to 0. In Border, set the Right row to dashed, 1 pixels, #aaaaaa, and set the Left row to solid, 1 pixels, #aaaaaa.

16. The content of all three columns under the navigation bar need moving downwards, which can be achieved by creating and styling the Advanced rule #columnLeft,#columnRight,#content and setting the Top value of Padding (in Box) to 50 pixels.

17. Create an Advanced rule for the selector #footer. In Type, set Color to #ffffff, and in Background, set Background color to #c2c2c2. The footer needs to clear all floated content, so set Clear (in Box) to both; still in Box, set the Top and Bottom values of Padding to 20 pixels, and the Left and Right values to 30 pixels.

18. Style the paragraphs by creating a Tag rule for the selector p. In Type, set Size to 85%, and in Box, set the Top value of Margin to 0.

19. Next, set an indent on all paragraphs within the content area. Create the Advanced rule #content p, and set the Left value of Padding to 2 ems.

20. Create a new Advanced rule, #content p.intro, which will be used to embolden the introductory paragraph. In Type, set Weight to bold, and in Box, set the Left value of Padding to 0, and the Bottom value of Margin to 2 ems. Select the introductory paragraph in Design view, and use the Properties panel's Style menu to apply the intro style.

21. Create the Advanced rule #columnLeft ul to style the unordered list in the columnLeft div. In Type, set Size to 85% and Line height to 1.4 ems; in Box, set Padding to 0 and all Margin values to 0 apart from Bottom, which should be set to 1 ems; in List, set Type to none.

22. Create the Advanced rule #columnLeft li to style the unordered list items in the columnLeft div. In Box, set the Bottom value of Padding to 3 pixels. This places gaps between the list items, making them more visually distinct.

23. Create the Advanced rule #columnLeft p. In Type, set Size to 77% and Line height to 1.3 ems. This reduces the size of the text in the leftColumn div, making it visually distinct from text in the main content area.

24. Create the Advanced rule h1,h2, to set common property values to the two heading sizes that have been used in this design. In Type, set Font to Arial, Helvetica, sans-serif, set Weight to normal, set Case to lowercase, and set Color to #999999; in Box, set all Margin values to 0, except for Bottom, which should be set to 10 pixels; in Border, set the Bottom row only to dotted, 1 pixels, and #999999.

25. Create the Tag rule h1, and in Type, set Size to 150%. Create the Tag rule h2, and in Type, set Size to 120%. These last three rules make managing these elements much easier—all common property values can be managed by editing the h1,h2 rule, but specific values can be managed by editing either of the two rules created in this step.

26. Finally, to style links on the page, create the Tag rule a. In Type, set Weight to bold and Color to #666666.

The completed website files can be found in the layout_3_files_completed folder, which is in the Chapter 10 folder of the book's download files.

Creating an advanced website layout

Our final layout in this section is another fixed-width layout, this time taking advantage of Chapter 7's "Creating a horizontal navigation bar with rollover images" exercise and Chapter 8's "Creating a box-out" exercise (which, in both cases, are simply going to be copied verbatim). The design is quite stylish and contemporary, and because almost all of the graphical elements (masthead, navigation rollover, boxout, and page background) are applied using CSS, this layout can be used for almost any website you care to think of.

Structurally, this design is contained in a wrapper. There's a masthead, a navigation area, a content area, and a footer. Inside the content area is (unsurprisingly) some content, a floated boxout, and a section with three columns. Because of the many floated elements in this design, we'll occasionally have to make use of "separator" divs. These are effectively minor hacks, which enable you to clear subsequent content using a div with zero height.

The files for this tutorial are available as part of the book's download files, in the folder Chapter 10/
layout_4_files. Copy them to your hard drive before working through the exercise.

1. Create a new web page and CSS document, save both in the folder you copied to your hard
   drive, and link the CSS document to the web page. In the web page, add a div with an ID of
   wrapper. Delete the default content, replacing it with three divs, each under the previous one,
   with the following ID values: masthead, content, and footer. Inside the masthead div, add a div
   with the ID value of navigation.

2. Delete the default content of the masthead div. Replace the default content of the navigation
   div with an unordered list with four items (each one a link)—for this you can copy and paste
   the list from 7_rollovers.html.

3. The first separator (used to clear floated content) needs to go between the navigation div (which will contain floated elements once it's styled) and the content div. Therefore, add a new div with a Class value of separatorInvisible, positioning it correctly by setting Insert to After tag and <div id="masthead">.

4. In Code view, change this div's content to <!-- x -->.

5. In the content div, add a level-one heading, a level-two heading, and two level-three headings; in each case, add a paragraph of text after the heading.

6. Add a new div with an ID value of boxout. When in the Insert Div Tag dialog box, select After start of tag and <div id="content"> from the Insert menus. Inside the boxout div, delete the default content and add the image artwork.jpg (included in the assets folder) and then a short paragraph of text. Select the image, and if a paragraph tag (<p>) appears in the status bar, right-click or Ctrl-click it and select Remove Tag.

7. The next separator is actually a visible one—the thick line above the three columns. Therefore, we need a different class name from that in the previous step. Add a new div with a Class value of separator, and set Insert to Before end of tag and <div id="content">. Delete the default content when this div is added to the page, and use Code view to change this div's content to <!--x -->.

8. Add three divs under the separator div, each one with a Class value of column. (In each case, you can use Before end of tag and <div id="content"> for the Insert values, to position them correctly.) Once you've done this, add another div with a Class value of separatorInvisible—again you can use Before end of tag and <div id="content"> for the Insert values, to position this correctly. As with the earlier instance of this element, use Code view to change this div's content to <!--x -->.

9. In each of the three column divs, add a level-one heading and a paragraph of text. In the footer, replace the default content with a copyright statement, and format it as a paragraph.

10. Now working in CSS, create a Tag rule for body. In Type, set Font to Verdana, Arial, Helvetica, sans-serif, set Size to small, and set Color to #333333; in Background, set Background color to #ffffff, click Browse to select page_background.gif from the assets folder for the background image, set Horizontal position to 50% and Vertical position to 0; in Box, set Padding and Margin to 0.

11. Create an Advanced rule for #wrapper. In Box, set Width to 740 pixels, the Top and Bottom values for Margin to 0, and the Left and Right value to auto.

12. Create an Advanced rule for #masthead. In Background, use Browse to select masthead.jpg (from the assets folder) for the background image. In Box, set Height to 30 pixels and the Top value of Padding to 115 pixels.

13. Create an Advanced rule for #navigation. In Box, set Height to 30 pixels. Open up 7_rollovers.html and use Code view to copy across all of the rules to the style sheet you've been working with in this exercise. Change all instances of 7_rollover.gif in the code to assets/rollover.gif. (This change is required because the path to the rollover image—along with its filename—is different from that in the exercise from Chapter 7.)

14. Create an Advanced rule, #content. In Background, set Background color to #ffffff; in Box, set the Top and Bottom values of Padding to 20 pixels and the Left and Right values of Padding to 10 pixels.

15. Next, style the separators. For the invisible one, create a Class rule with the selector .separatorInvisible. In Box, set Clear to both and Height to 0. For the visible one, create a Class rule with the selector .separator. In Box, set Clear to both, Height to 5 pixels, and the Bottom value of Margin to 2 ems. In Background, set Background color to #a9a9a9.

16. Now, style the columns. Create a Class rule with the selector .column. In Box, set Width to 232 pixels, Float to left, and the Left value of Padding to 10 pixels (which creates a gap to the left of each column, so they don't touch each other). However, the leftmost column doesn't require any padding, so we need to create an inline style to override the one just created. Click inside the column, and then right-click or Ctrl-click the <div.column> tag in the status bar, and select Quick Tag Editor. Change the tag to read <div class="column" style="padding-left: 0;">. When you press Enter, all three columns should sit next to each other, as intended.

17. Create an Advanced rule, #footer. In Type, set Color to #dddddd; in Block, set Text align to right; in Box, set Clear to both, the Top and Bottom values of Padding to 20 pixels, and the Left and Right values to 10 pixels.

18. To style the boxout, you can mainly use the rules from 8_boxout.css. Copy everything from #boxout onwards to your style sheet. However, some of the rules need editing—to do so, double-click the relevant rule in the CSS Styles panel and make the necessary changes. For #boxout, access Background and change Background color to #a9a9a9, and click Browse and select boxout_corner.gif from the assets folder. For #boxout p, access Type and set Line height to 1.2 ems and Color to #333333; in Box, set Padding to 0.

19. The remaining rules all deal with styling fonts. Create the Advanced rule h1,h2, to set common property values for the top two levels of heading. In Type, set Font to Arial, Helvetica, sans-serif, set Weight to normal, set Case to lowercase, and set Color to #555555; in Box, set all Margin values to 0, apart from Bottom, which should be set to 10 pixels.

20. Create the Tag rule h1. In Type, set Size to 150%. Create the Tag rule h2. In Type, set Size to 120%.

21. Create the Tag rule h3. In Type, set Font to Arial, Helvetica, sans-serif, set Size to 90%, set Weight to bold, and set Color to #444444; in Box, set all Margin values to 0, apart from Bottom, which should be set to 5 pixels, and set the Left value of Padding to 1.35 ems.

22. Create the Tag rule p. In Type, set Size to 85% and Line height to 1.4 ems; in Box, set the Top value of Margin to 0 and the Bottom value to 1 ems, and then set the Left value of Padding to 1.4 ems.

23. Finally, a couple of overrides are required to make the column text look better. Create the Advanced rule .column h1, and then set Size (in Type) to 130%; then create the Advanced rule .column p and set Padding (in Box) to 0.

While Design view makes a good effort to show this design correctly, it makes a few mistakes, notably with the boxout. Test your page in a browser for best results.

Also note that Internet Explorer 5.5 for Windows does not correctly render the auto setting for margins. Therefore, if you want a site to center horizontally in that browser, you need to add two rules as a kind of hack. The first is a second body rule, where Text align is set to center; the second is a second #wrapper rule, where Text align is set to left.

Although you can use Dreamweaver's various dialogs for adding these rules, it's perhaps quicker to just add them directly to your CSS file in Code view:

```
body {
text-align: center;
}
#wrapper {
text-align: left;
}
```

The completed website files can be found in the layout_1_files_completed folder, which is in the Chapter 10 folder of the book's download files.

Introducing templates

Templates are one of Dreamweaver's best features. Instead of duplicating files and changing the content of the new page, common elements can be defined in a template and locked to ensure site-wide consistency. Dreamweaver notices when templates are updated and asks whether you want all associated pages based on the template to be updated—a process that typically takes mere seconds per page.

Of course, this kind of thing is fairly common in web design applications, but Dreamweaver takes things a step further, enabling you to create repeatable regions for repeated page elements that need to be consistent, optional regions for elements that aren't required for all pages, and embedded templates for a main template that only needs a few changes in certain sections of the site.

To close this chapter—and, indeed, the book—we're going to take the layout from the "Creating a fixed-width, businesslike layout" exercise earlier in the chapter, and use it as the basis for a template. You'll find out how to create a template, how to create pages based on the template, and how to take things further by creating embedded templates.

Creating a template

1. Copy the templates_tutorial folder from the Chapter 10 folder of the book's download files to your hard drive. Go to Site ➤ New Site. Click the Advanced tab of the Site Definition dialog box, and use the folder icon next to the Local root folder field to choose the templates_tutorial folder as the root folder for a new site. Use the Site name field to enter a name for the site, and then click OK.

```
                    Site Definition for Templates tutorials

                           [ Basic  Advanced ]

Category               Local Info

  Local Info
  Remote Info              Site name: [ Templates tutorials              ]
  Testing Server
  Cloaking          Local root folder: [ iBook HD:Users:craiggrannell:Sites:Foundation ] 📁
  Design Notes
  Site Map Layout                    ☑ Refresh local file list automatically
  File View Columns
  Contribute      Default images folder: [                              ] 📁


                  Links relative to: ● Document   ○ Site root

                     HTTP address: [ http://                            ]

                                   This address is used for site relative links, and
                                   for the Link Checker to detect HTTP links that
                                   refer to your own site.

                 Case-sensitive links: ☐ Use case-sensitive link checking

                            Cache: ☑ Enable cache
                                   The cache maintains file and asset information in
                                   the site.  This speeds up the Asset panel, link
                                   management, and Site Map features.




              (   Help   )                    (  Cancel  ) ( OK )
```

2. Open up default_page.html from the Files panel. The principle behind Dreamweaver templates is to define **editable regions**. In pages based on the template, these are the areas that will be editable (as their name suggests)—all other areas of the page will be locked. For a site such as the one we're working on in this example, only the main content area needs to be editable. Therefore, select all of the content within the main content area, as shown next, and right-click or Ctrl-click it and choose Templates ➤ New Editable Region (or go to Insert ➤ Editable Region).

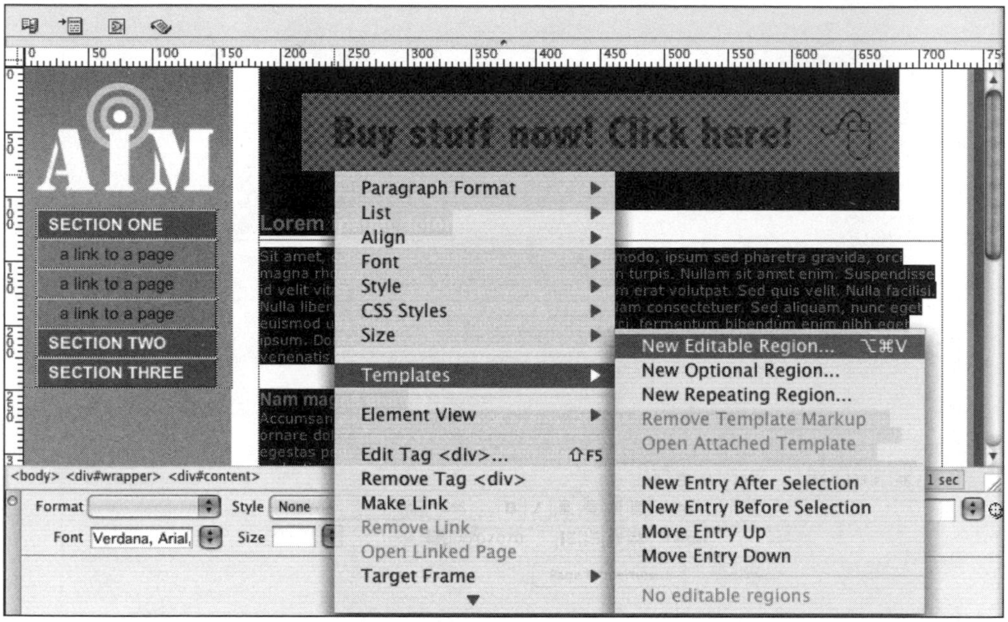

> *In step 2, the content of the div was selected rather than the div itself, because it's the content that's going to be made editable—not the entire div.*

3. Dreamweaver will then warn you that the document will be converted into a template. (You can turn this warning off in future by clicking the check box.) Click OK to continue.

4. In the Name field of the New Editable Region dialog box, type the name of your editable region, omitting spaces, underscores, and hyphens.

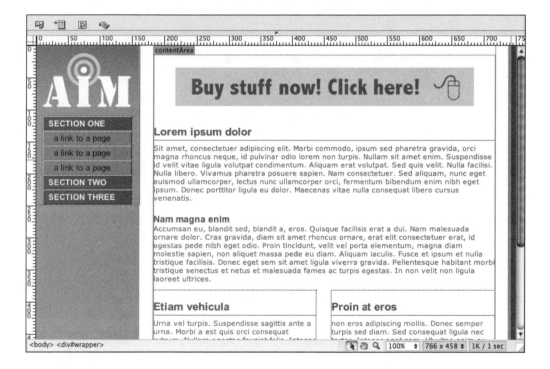

5. Click OK, and if you have invisible elements turned on in Design view (View ➤ Visual Aids ➤ Invisible Elements) you'll see the editable area clearly marked in Design view. The name provided in the previous step will be displayed on a tab surrounding the editable area, and a border with the same color will show the region's boundaries.

6. Go to File ➤ Save as Template to save your template, and give it a sensible, relevant, and memorable name, such as main. Click Save, and when the Update Links? dialog box appears, click Yes (otherwise external assets won't be linked to the template—see the next step for why).

7. Once you've saved the template, take a look in the Files panel. You'll see that Dreamweaver automatically saves the templates in a template folder inside the site's root folder. Templates have a file extension of .dwt (as you can see, main.dwt is in the Templates folder). If you don't initially see your template folder in the Files panel, refresh it using the refresh button or F5.

Do not move template files out of the Templates folder— they must remain there in order for them to work properly.

Creating a page based on a template

1. Go to File ➤ New, to access the New Document dialog box, and choose the Templates tab. Select the site you created in the previous exercise, and in the second column, you'll see the template you created. Select this template, and a visual preview will appear in the right-hand column. Ensure Update page when template changes is checked, and click Create to create a new document based on the template.

2. Moving over any of the locked areas changes the mouse pointer to a "no entry" pointer, signifying that you cannot change any content in these areas. Save this new document as first_page_from_template.html.

3. The area with the blue tab is the editable region. This is populated with whatever was in the template. Many designers remove all content from templates, but I think it can be useful to leave some there as a reminder, and you can often simply change bits of content, such as the title, as shown in the following image.

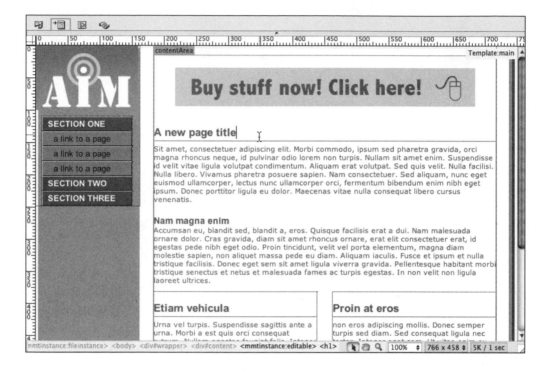

Note that templates themselves are the basic building block from which actual pages are made, and shouldn't be published on a live site. Furthermore, if anything needs changing in a locked area, you must change the template, or detach the relevant page from the template.

Editing the template

1. Close any open files, and open up `main.dwt` again. Change some of the locked content, such as the name of the first navigation link.

> *If you don't close template-based files prior to editing the template, Dreamweaver can't update those files as thoroughly.*

2. Save the template (just via the usual Ctrl+S or Cmd+S) and you'll see the Update Template Files dialog box.

3. Click Update and Dreamweaver will update all of the pages based on the template, providing a report when it's done so. (Check Show log to see a full report.)

> **Update Pages**
>
> Look in: [Files That Use... ⬍] main   (Done)
>
> Update: ☐ Library items   (Close)
>   ☑ Templates   (Help)
>
> ☑ Show log   Done
>
> ```
> Updating iBook HD:Users:craiggrannell:Sites:Foundation Dreamweaver
> 8:Chapter 10:templates_tutorial:
>
>  files examined: 1
>  files updated: 1
>  files which could not be updated: 0
> total time: (0:00:01)
> updated first_page_from_template.html
> ```

4. Open `first_page_from_template.html` and you'll see that the page you made based on your template has been updated with the new navigation link name. This isn't that exciting for a one-page site, but imagine if you had a 50-page site and needed to make such a change. Coupling CSS, for site-wide external layout control, with templates, for site-wide content control, can save huge amounts of time for any web designer.

> *Remember that when you update your pages, this is initially only done locally. For anyone on the Web to see the changes to your affected pages, they need to be uploaded again.*

Working with embedded templates

One of Dreamweaver's best features is the ability to create **embedded templates** (also referred to as **nested templates**)—that is, templates within templates. The great thing about embedded templates is that they "cascade" when you update them, providing you with massive flexibility for your site designs.

For instance, you may have a site based around a template (say, main.dwt), which contains a number of almost identical product pages. You could create an embedded template (say, products.dwt) for the product pages; updating this template would only update the product pages based on it. However, updating main.dwt would update all of the site's pages *and* the product template.

In some ways, this is a small variation on using one standard template, but as the following exercise shows, it's an important one. In this exercise, you'll create a nested template with a "pros and cons" table.

1. Create a new page based on the template created earlier in this chapter. Add a table below the main title in the editable region. (See Chapter 8 for how to add a table to a web page.) The table only needs to have two rows and two columns. The headers in the following image read Pros and Cons, and each cell below the headers has a three-item unordered list.

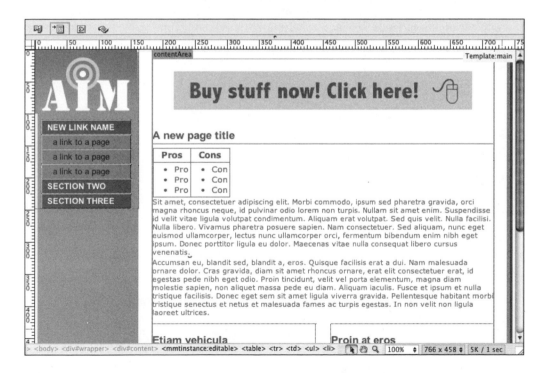

2. Add a new CSS rule, using Tag as the Selector Type and table as the selector name (in the Tag field). Ensure Define in is set to the CSS document and not This document only. In Box, set the Bottom value of Margin to 1 ems. This places some space underneath the table, so that it doesn't hug the paragraph of text that follows it.

3. Define two editable regions within the table, one of which surrounds the pros list and one of which surrounds the cons list.

4. Save the template via File ➤ Save as Template (I named my file proscons in the Save As Template dialog box). Once you do this, the original editable region's tab will turn yellow. This indicates that this region is now locked. Because the main content area, which was originally editable, is now locked, you need to unlock the title and body copy, so it can be edited in each page based on this new template. To do so, simply make some more editable regions (one for the title and one for the content underneath the table).

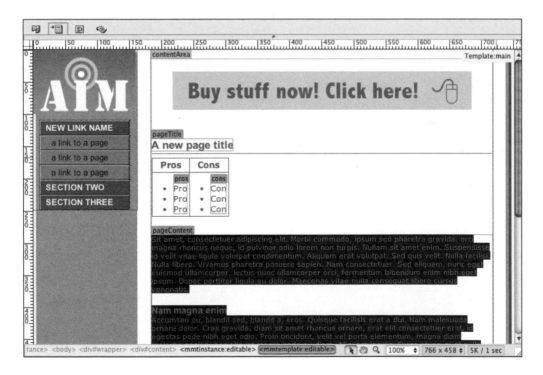

5. When you try to save the template, the following dialog box will appear. This indicates that an editable region was placed inside a block tag (the title); this means that only the content of the tag can be changed, but not the tag itself (in other words, you couldn't turn this heading into a level 2 heading when working on a page based on this template). This is exactly what's required for a template such as this, so just click OK.

6. When you now create a new page based on the proscons template, you have four editable regions in which to insert content.

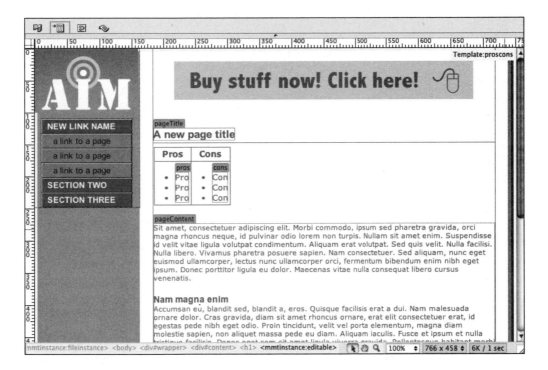

The completed templates from the exercises in this chapter can be found in the Chapter 10 folder of the book's download files, in the templates_tutorial_completed folder.

Editing template code

Although it's relatively unlikely that you'll ever need to edit template code, Dreamweaver does some-times add editable regions in areas where you weren't entirely intending them to go, notably when you're working with having editable regions within block elements. If you find that you want only the content of a block element to be editable, but that Dreamweaver has surrounded the entire element, you can edit the template code directly in Code view.

In such a case, you may see something like this in code view:

```
<!-- TemplateBeginEditable name="pageHeading" -->
<h1>Page heading</h1>
<!-- TemplateEndEditable -->
```

Note how the template code is placed in standard HTML comment tags, but also how it works rather like a typical HTML element in terms of how it's nested. To make just the heading content editable, you'd need to change the code to look like this:

```
<h1><!-- TemplateBeginEditable name="pageHeading" -->
Page heading
<!-- TemplateEndEditable --></h1>
```

As you can see, the entire template code is now nested inside the heading element. If this nesting is not done correctly, as in the *incorrect* example below, the page will break and not work properly. When such an error occurs, it's signified by an HTML tag with a yellow background inside of the editable region.

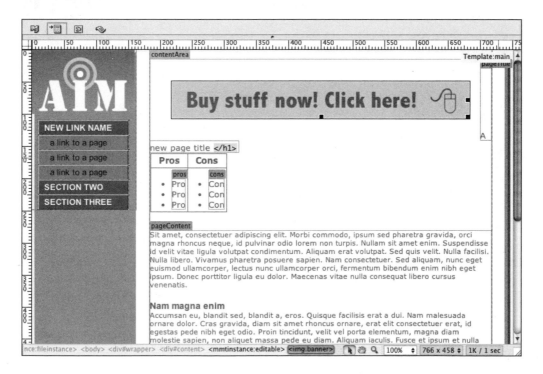

Outro

So, that's it: the book is at an end and my work here is done. I hope you've enjoyed working through the book, and that you now feel more comfortable working with Dreamweaver to create great-looking standards-compliant websites.

Don't forget that you can talk to designers and friends of ED authors via the friends of ED website (www.friendsofed.com) where you can also check out many other titles that will help you along the road to becoming an accomplished web designer.

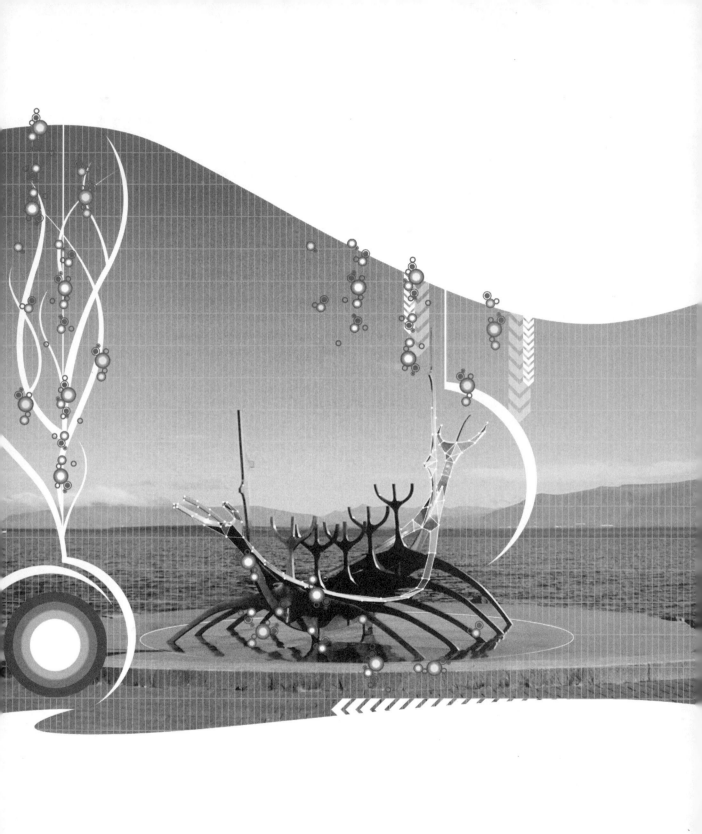

INDEX

Symbols

& ampersand, 232
\ backward slash, 160
../ characters, 159
: colon, 64\
{ } curly brackets, 64
/ forward slash, 160
. period, 68
? question mark, 232
; semicolon, 64
_ underscore, 10

Numbers

216/256 colors, 131

A

absolute links, 159
accessibility, 4, 34
accesskey attribute, 233
active state, 163
Advanced tab (Site Definition dialog box), 46
aligning text, 95
ampersand (&), multiple recipients and, 232
anti-aliasing, cross-platform issues and, 125
Application set, 22
Application Menu (Macintosh), panels and, 32
assets folder, 135
audiences, 7
automatic wrapping, 34
Automatic's Enkoder forms, 233

B

<b> tag, 94
backgrounds, 202
    adding to web pages, 75–84
    columns and, 204
    creating, 76–84
    sidebars and, 197
backups, 10
backward slash (\), in link paths, 160
BBEdit for Mac, 245
bcc (blind carbon copy), 232
Behaviors panel, 33
blind carbon copy (bcc), 232
Block category, 98
blogs, layout for, 256–264
BMPs, 132
body copy, graphics and, 133
<body> section, 56
bold text, 94
border thickness, of table cells, 211
borders, 188
    adding images to, 143
box model workaround, 125, 188, 256
boxouts, 190, 192–195
    creating, 192–195
breadcrumbs navigation, 59, 108, 179–181
    creating, 179–181
    styling, 180
brightness settings, 139
broken links, fixing, 52
Browser check menu, 30
browsers See web browsers
bullet-point lists, 102
bullets, 104

X

XML for Flash
1-59059-543-2 $39.99 [US]

Actionscript Animation
1-59059-518-1 $49.99 [US]

Flash 8
1-59059-542-4 $36.99 [US]

ASP.NET 2.0 for Flash
1-59059-517-3 $39.99 [US]

DOM Scripting
1-59059-533-5 $34.99 [US]

EXPERIENCE THE
DESIGNER TO DESIGNER™
DIFFERENCE

Fireworks MX 2004 ZERO TO HERO
1-59059-306-5 $34.99 [US]

Paint Shop Pro 8 ZERO TO HERO
1-59059-238-7 $24.99 [US]

Windows Movie Maker 2 ZERO TO HERO
1-59059-149-6 $24.99 [US]

Photoshop Most Wanted
1-59059-262-X $49.99 [US]

Flash MX Most Wanted
1-59059-224-7 $39.99 [US]

Flash 3D Cheats Most Wanted
1-59059-221-2 $39.99 [US]

Flash MX 2004 Games Most Wanted
1-59059-236-0 $39.99 [US]

Illustrator CS Most Wanted
1-59059-372-3 $39.99 [US]

Extending Flash MX 2004
1-59059-304-9 $49.99 [US]

Apache Essentials
1-59059-355-3 $39.99 [US]

Dreamweaver MX 2004 Design, Projects
1-59059-409-6 $39.99 [US]

New Masters of Flash
1-59059-314-6 $59.99 [US]

New Masters of Photoshop
1-59059-315-4 $59.99 [US]

Cascading Style Sheets
1-59059-231-X $39.99 [US]

Constructing Usable Shopping Carts
1-59059-408-8 $34.99 [US]

Extreme Photoshop CS
1-59059-428-2 $39.99 [US]

Web Standards Solutions
1-59059-381-2 $29.99 [US]

Podcast Solutions
1-59059-554-8 $xx.99 [US]